PRINCIPLES
and
PRACTICE
of
PREACHING

PRINCIPLES
and
PRACTICE of PREACHING

Ilion T. Jones

ABINGDON
Nashville

PRINCIPLES AND PRACTICE OF PREACHING

ISBN 0-687-34061-6

Library of Congress Catalog Card Number: 56-7761

MANUFACTURED BY THE PARTHENON PRESS AT
NASHVILLE, TENNESSEE, UNITED STATES OF AMERICA

PREFACE

In his Warrack Lectures James S. Stewart warned his hearers to beware of the person who announces a course on "How to Preach: by One Who Knows." He said that such a person deserves to be called an imposter, then added:

No man knows how to preach. You will have to reckon with this significant, disconcerting fact, that the greatest preachers who have ever lived have confessed themselves poor bunglers to the end, groping after an ideal which eluded them for ever. When you have been preaching for twenty years, you will be beginning to realize how incalculably much there is to learn. There will be days when the Socratic knowledge of your ignorance will desolate and overwhelm you. Even if Providence should spare you to this work for fifty years, your thought will be, as the gloaming closes in around you, "If only I could start all over again now!" [1]

Unquestionably he is right. Anyone who claims to know exactly how to preach or how to teach others to preach is overbold. And yet, as Stewart himself has done so expertly, one person may pass on to others what from observation and experience he knows should be done in order to preach well.

If there is any justification for adding another book to the expanding list of books on the subject, it is found in the postulates and purposes underlying this one. For years I have had two growing convictions: first, that a person learns to preach, insofar as anyone ever learns, by preaching continuously in a normal pastorate; and second, that the learning never ceases. Throughout the book, therefore, I have had in mind simultaneously the young man just beginning his ministry and the experienced preacher who feels the need of restudying his methods.

Generally speaking, theological students grasp few of the fun-

[1] *Heralds of God*, p. 104. Used by permission of Charles Scribner's Sons and Hodder & Stoughton, Ltd.

damental principles of homiletics while still in school. The significance of much that is said in the classes is missed because they have not had sufficient experience to judge its value and to realize the need of the principles and procedures enjoined upon them. Furthermore, the students do not speak to real congregations. A professor or two and a group of fellow students expected to sit in judgment upon sermons do not provide a natural preaching situation, or afford the proper motivations and stimuli for genuine preaching. Hence, within the first few years of their active ministry most preachers come to realize how little they learned in the seminary about preaching and wish they could go back to school for a refresher course in homiletics.

That is neither necessary nor advisable. When one finds himself in that mood he should secure a book that deals with the various phases of the subject and work his way through it, step by step, as he continues his weekly preaching. A person learns to preach by preaching regularly over a period of years while at the same time he is appraising and improving his techniques in the light of recognized principles. This book is designed as just such an "on-the-job" aid.

Technical proficiency is not attained once and for all. The time never comes when a person can boast, "Now I have served my apprenticeship and can call myself a master preacher." Goethe said, "The man who would be free must win his freedom afresh every day." Likewise, the preacher who would be skilled must win his skill afresh every week. Skill is the ability to use knowledge effectively. Knowledge is forever increasing and undergoing revision. Methods of utilizing it must, therefore, undergo modification from time to time.

Life never stands still. The minister and the society in which he lives are continuously in process of development and change. Preaching procedures must be adapted to the several stages of the minister's own growth and to the changing conditions of the people. Methods effectual in one period of life will not necessarily suffice for other periods. Even though the principles of effective preaching remain constant, the way in which they work out varies as situations change. Hence, homiletical methods need to be revised several times within a single lifetime. This book is planned to aid the experienced pastor who finds it advisable at intervals to evaluate and re-evaluate his techniques of sermonizing.

Like all other skills, preaching skill is achieved and retained by hard work, self-discipline, continuous practice, and regular revision of procedures. "I must be going downhill," said Thorvaldsen, the illustrious sculptor, "when I find my work equal to my aspirations." When a preacher becomes satisfied with his sermons he is on the downgrade, or, to use Walter Winchell's expression, "He's rusting on his laurels."

> From compromise and things half-done,
>   Keep me, with stern and stubborn pride.
> And when, at last the fight is won,
>   God, keep me still unsatisfied.[2]

So I offer this book, for what it may be worth, to the man, at whatever stage of his ministry, who wants to learn to preach more effectively and is willing to pay the price of the learning.

ILION T. JONES

---

[2] From Louis Untermeyer's "Prayer" in *Challenge*. Copyright 1914 by Harcourt, Brace and Co. Inc., and used by their permission.

CONTENTS

PART 1

BACKGROUND OF PREACHING

1. The Importance of Preaching

In a recent significant little book, *The Approach to Preaching*,[1] W. E. Sangster, a well-known British preacher, emphasized the importance for effective preaching of the habits, attitudes, convictions, and experiences the preacher brings to it. These constitute the background out of which his preaching springs. To a large degree they determine the importance he attaches to it, the purposes behind it, the energy and fervor he puts into it.

Before discussing technical skills essential for successful preaching, therefore, some consideration will be given to what the preacher brings to his sermonizing. First attention will be devoted to the part his conception of the importance of preaching plays in his preaching.

THE STEWARDSHIP OF WORDS

Basically the importance of preaching stems from the nature of man. Men communicate with one another through the medium of articulate speech. We are endowed by our Creator with mechanisms to produce words, to listen to them, and to react to them. Speech is the most unique of all human gifts, sets man apart from the rest of God's creatures, and constitutes his most solemn stewardship.

Words are one of the most powerful of all God's natural and elemental forces. If spoken, they are sound waves that strike eardrums and are carried quickly to brain centers. The human voice is capable of a wide range of tonal modulations and inflections as varied as those of musical instruments. In fact, musical instruments have been invented partly to reproduce artificially the tonal effects of the human voice. If written, words are light waves that strike the retina of the eye and are transmitted by way of the optic nerve to the brain cells.

[1] Philadelphia: Westminster Press, 1952.

Once in the brain these light and sound waves move through an intricate series of interlocking circuits in the complicated, delicately adjusted network of sensation, thought, emotion, imagination, and conviction, that make up what we call personality. Colored, twisted, augmented, modified by what goes on in the citadel of personality, other words emerge again to pursue their interminable, circuitous journey in ever widening circles through other ears, eyes, brains, vocal cords, hands, and bodily actions. That is why Fritz Kunkel called words "ignition devices." Mind affects mind by means of words. Soul moves soul by words. Words arouse emotions and stimulate action. The expression in Proverbs, "a word fitly spoken" (25:11), has been translated literally, "a word on wheels." Once released, words are on wheels all right, on wheels within wheels.

A word is dead
When it is said,
    Some say.
I say it just
Begins to live
    That day.[2]

Every public speaker uses the power of words to "manipulate the contents of the hearer's mind." He is "playing upon the contents of the hearer's mind as the pianist is playing on the strings." [3] Like all other forms of power this has its dangers. But it is a risk God took when he endowed us with speech and it goes on inevitably whenever one person communicates with others.

The same force may be used for desirable and for unworthy ends, for constructive and for destructive purposes. After hearing Demosthenes hurl his *Phillipics* against Philip of Macedonia, the people shouted, "Let us go and fight Philip." Adolph Hitler spoke and kept on speaking until the German people started a war that set the world on fire. The early Christian preachers conquered the Roman Empire for Christ. The Reformers revolutionized medieval Christianity and turned the course of history.

[2] *Poems by Emily Dickinson*, edited by Martha Dickinson Bianchi and Alfred Leete Hampson, Little, Brown & Company.

[3] John Edgar Park, *The Miracle of Preaching* (New York: The Macmillan Co., 1936), p. 30.

One man with a dream, at pleasure,
    Shall go forth and conquer a crown;
And three with a new song's measure
    Can trample an empire down.[4]

The difference between preaching and other forms of the spoken word lies in the purposes the preacher has in mind, the ends he hopes to attain. Christian preaching is the noblest use of the power of speech. But it *is* a power. Let no one overlook, deny, or minimize that fact. Until human beings are reconstructed on different principles there is no way to eliminate the necessity of using words to pass on the accumulated wisdom of the race, to convince men of the truth, to stimulate people to follow the highest ideals.

William Jennings Bryan returned about daybreak one morning from one of his political speaking tours, wakened his wife, and exclaimed: "Mary, I have had a strange experience. Last night I found that I had power over the audience. I could move them as I chose. I have more than the usual power as a speaker, I know it. God grant that I may use it wisely." [5] The consciousness of possessing speaking power is a heavy responsibility. The preacher's problem is to make sure he uses his power wisely, for Christian purposes, for God's great objectives.

USING WORDS TO PROCLAIM THE WORD

Preaching is required by the nature of the gospel. "Jesus came into Galilee, preaching the gospel of God." (Mark 1:14.) He called and trained his disciples, then sent them forth saying, "Go . . . . And preach as you go" (Matt. 10:5-7). Obeying his command they went out to make other disciples (Matt. 28:19), and to witness (Acts 1:8) by preaching. When they scattered because of persecution they "went about preaching the word" (Acts 8:4). Preaching is not the art of using words merely but the art of using words to proclaim the gospel, "the good news of Jesus" (Acts 8:35).

At a special time and place in history through a special person, Jesus the Christ, God on his own initiative acted to reveal him-

---

[4] From "Ode" by Arthur Wm. Edgar O'Shaughnessy.
[5] See Matthew Josephson, *The Politicos, 1865-1896* (New York: Harcourt, Brace and Co., 1938), p. 534.

self fully to men. The story of how God broke through into the stream of human history, unveiled his mind and character, unfolded his purposes and plans, proffered his love, offered his forgiveness, and promised his continuing presence and power until his children fulfill their divine destiny—this story *is* the gospel of Christ.

In the original Greek the word "gospel" (evangel) literally means "good news"—good news from God about God, about men, about life, about the world, about redemption. New Testament preaching was informing men of this good news. Several words were used to express this act of informing. These words meant to "tell," to "testify," to "publish," to "proclaim," to "evangelize." All of them mean essentially the same thing: to declare abroad the good news of redemption that came from God through Christ, as a herald announces the official proclamation received from his ruler.

Scholars call that good news the "kerygma," a Greek word in the New Testament for the message they preached. The New Testament documents were written to provide a record and interpretation of the historical events that revolved around Jesus. His birth, his ministry and teaching, his atoning death, his resurrection, his continuing presence in the person of the Holy Spirit, the establishment of the Church, his promise that he would come again to bring history to fulfillment and consummate God's plan for a new heaven and a new earth—these constituted the kerygma, the facts, they proclaimed.

In addition to the kerygma, the New Testament preachers proclaimed the "didache" or "the teaching." The kerygma was directed primarily to unbelievers, the didache to believers. "Teaching" meant to instruct, to explain, to instill doctrine, to expound. The good news of the gospel was proclaimed to win the unbeliever to Christ, the teaching to build up the believer in Christ, to show him how to live as a Christian, how to apply his beliefs to life, how to implement the gospel with individual and group living.

Another word used in the New Testament to describe preaching is a Greek word that means literally "calling to one's side" or "summoning" for the purpose of saying intimately something important. The word carries also the idea of "begging," "beseeching," "entreating," "exhorting," and at times "consoling."

This describes the mood in which they preached—with a yearning heart; and the purpose for which they preached—to persuade their hearers to accept the message, to act upon it, and to live by it. The persuasive aspect of preaching will be taken up in detail in the next chapter. But it needs to be mentioned here to complete the explanation of what is meant by Christian preaching as it is pictured in the New Testament.

In the New Testament sense of the term, then, to preach is to confront men with the "kerygma" and the "didache" of the gospel, to tell them what God did in the days of Jesus, to pass on to them the historical facts recorded in those ancient documents, and to try to persuade them to accept those facts and live by them. This good news from God can come to the attention of people only if they are told about it. Telling it is preaching. Preaching, then, is fundamental, indispensable for the proclamation of the gospel.

Preachers should use skill with words in the preaching of the gospel. But mere skill in the use of words is not preaching the gospel. One of the preacher's subtle temptations is to forget that, to substitute facility with words for preaching The Word. He is not a mere public speaker, entertaining audiences, talking pleasingly, glibly, and interestingly on all sorts of subjects. He is preaching the gospel. Gamaliel Bradford used the title Damaged Souls for a book in which he described that group of discredited figures in American history who used their tongues "with singular and passionate urgency, to forward their own purposes, to sway men and women, to achieve the conquest of the world." [6] The preacher who uses speech merely to gain a reputation for himself, to please and delight and sway people, to demonstrate cleverness with language, deserves to be put among Bradford's "damaged souls."

Speaking for God, Jeremiah said: "I am against the prophets . . . who use their tongues and say, 'Says the Lord' " (23:31). W. M. Macgregor remarks: "Their tongues, you see, for no deeper faculty in them is engaged: their preaching proceeds from the loquacious level of their nature." [7] In the preaching of the gospel as nowhere else in all uses of human speech, merely being fluent should be avoided. But fluency, facility of utterance, dex-

---

[6] Boston: Houghton, Mifflin Co., 1931, p. 13.
[7] The Making of a Preacher (Philadelphia: Westminster Press, 1946), p. 43.

terity in the use of words, for the purpose of preaching the gospel effectively, should be the aim of every preacher.

THE INSTRUMENT OF GOD'S REDEMPTION

The importance of preaching is still further emphasized when we realize that the very act of proclaiming the gospel becomes an instrument of God's saving word. Clearly this was the viewpoint of the New Testament writers. Paul told the Corinthians that he and his associates were "ambassadors for Christ, God making his appeal through us. We beseech you on behalf of Christ, be reconciled to God" (II Cor. 5:20). That is, God was actually doing the appealing through their sermons. Their preaching, therefore, was a continuation of the work of Christ. Paul said to the Thessalonians, "When you received the word of God which you heard from us, you accepted it not as the word of men but as what it really is, the word of God, which is at work in you believers" (I Thess. 2:13). The early preachers were not expressing their own ideas but publishing the word of God. Once accepted by the believer, that word became alive and active within them. Thus preaching was the means of starting God's redemptive work in the believer.

The rediscovery of this conception of preaching and the discussion revolving around it constitute one of the most significant trends in contemporary Christian thought, and promise to restore preaching to its primary place in Christianity. Every preacher of the gospel should face the implications of this interpretation of the function of preaching for his own preaching. P. T. Forsyth was one of the first in our century to stress this interpretation. He said:

The Gospel . . . is an eternal, perennial act of God in Christ, repeating itself within each declaration of it. . . . It is this act that is prolonged in the word of the preacher and not merely proclaimed. . . . The Gospel is an act of God . . . and it calls for an act, and inspires it. Its preaching must therefore be an act, a "function" of the great act. A true sermon is a real deed. It puts the preacher's personality into an act.[8]

[8] Positive Preaching and the Modern Mind (New York: A. C. Armstrong and Son, 1907), pp. 6, 22.

This viewpoint has been treated forcefully and at some length by two recent books: H. H. Farmer's *The Servant of the Word*, and Donald G. Miller's *Fire in Thy Mouth*. Farmer says:

The necessity of preaching resides in the fact that when God saves a man through Christ He insists on a living, personal encounter with him here and now.... [Preaching] is not merely *telling* me something. It is God actively probing me, challenging my will, calling on me for decision.[9]

Miller says: "To preach is not merely to say something, but to do something—it is to become the living arena in which Christ personally confronts men in judgment and redemption."[10]

Shortly before his death, Henry Sloane Coffin presented similar ideas in a series of lectures on preaching entitled *Communion Through Preaching*.[11] His main thesis is that preaching is the means of communion with God as certainly and as effectively as is the sacrament of the Lord's Supper. Sometimes preaching is spoken of as a "sacramental act." At other times it is actually called "The Sacrament of the Word." Protestants have never regarded it as a sacrament. But comparisons between it and the Supper are justifiable if the parallels are not drawn too closely. Christ "appointed twelve to be with him, and to be sent out to preach." (Mark 3:14.) His last command to them was to go, make disciples of all nations, and teach them his gospel. In connection with the command he promised. "I am with you always, to the close of the age" (Matt. 28:20). Jesus undoubtedly meant the preacher to act as an arbitrator or negotiator to bring men face to face with God, so that God's redeeming grace will have a chance to work within the hearts of all who yield themselves to his gracious influence. Hence preaching may properly be spoken of as communion with God.

Preaching may be, should be, and at its best will be, a redemptive deed. A sermon is not a lecture, an essay, a theological dissertation, a discussion of social, political, and world affairs, or instruction in morals, but God's "saving approach to the souls of men and women." This is not our human view of it, but God's

[9] P. 27. Used by permission of Charles Scribner's Sons and James Nisbet and Co., Ltd.

[10] New York and Nashville: Abingdon Press, 1954, p. 36.

[11] New York: Charles Scribner's Sons, 1952.

conception revealed through Christ and the early church. Preachers are partners with God in his continuing redemptive activity, sharers of God's responsibility for the salvation of the world.

Once one catches this vision of the divine possibilities and responsibilities in preaching he can never again think of it as insignificant or of secondary importance. Furthermore, he can never be content to do less than his best to develop competence in preaching. Here is the basic motivation for a diligent practice in the effective use of words. Jesus said, "I tell you, on the day of judgment men will render account for every careless word they utter; for by your words you will be justified, and by your words you will be condemned." (Matt. 12:36-37.) Could that statement mean that preachers will be called into judgment for the careless, hasty, slipshod manner in which they proclaim the gospel? If so, it is our challenge to rededicate all our powers to the task of improving our skill in the use of human language to proclaim the divine word of redemption.

> He that negotiates between God and man,
> As God's ambassador, the grand concerns
> Of judgment and of mercy, should beware
> Of lightness in his speech.[12]

DIVINE TRUTH THROUGH HUMAN PERSONALITY

In *The Public Worship of God*, J. R. P. Sclater gave a definition of a sermon that ought to be inscribed indelibly on the minds and hearts of every preacher. He said a sermon is "truth strained through a human personality." The gospel as recorded in New Testament documents is changeless. But it must be translated afresh into the language, the terminology, the mental concepts, and the experiences of every new generation. That translating is largely the responsibility of the Christian preacher. Biblical scholars perform an indispensable function in the matter, but the full results of their labors reach the common man through preachers. Those results are not transmitted in the form in which they are received from the scholars but only after being "strained" through the personality of the preacher. They must percolate through his mind, be assimilated into his thinking, translated

[12] From "The Task," by William Cowper.

into his experiences, before being handed on. By this means the people come to understand the gospel and to realize its relevance for their lives. Preaching bridges the gap between the ancient documents containing the gospel and the minds of modern men.

Paul speaks of this conception of Christian preaching in an arresting passage in I Corinthians. (Ch. 2.) He is talking about the wisdom of God unveiled in Christ, something never before dreamed of by the mind of man but kept hidden and secret. That wisdom, he says, can be understood only by those who have received the Spirit of God, for only the Spirit can comprehend the thoughts of God. But the Spirit who "searches everything, even the depths of God" has been given to Christians, making them spiritually minded and therefore capable of understanding the amazing things God has bestowed upon men in Christ. Then apparently speaking of those who proclaim the gospel, Paul says, "We impart this in words not taught by human wisdom but taught by the Spirit, interpreting spiritual truths to those who possess the Spirit" (vs. 13). Then he makes the bold claim, "We have the mind of Christ" (vs. 16). As startling as that may sound, it must be said that a main function of the sermon is to interpret to men the mind of God as it is revealed in the mind of Christ. A preacher is striving to bring about a meeting between the divine mind and human minds. No man can face that responsibility without shrinking and no man dares face it without reliance upon the workings of the Spirit in his soul.

Dan Crawford was one of the outstanding missionaries to Africa in the early part of this century. He stayed in Africa some twenty or more years learning to think like the people among whom he labored. When he finally took a furlough he wrote *Thinking Black.* In this book he tells how, as a European, he tried to think like the black man, to get inside the black man's mind, to understand him, and to interpret the gospel of Christ to him. All preachers have to do a similar thing in order to preach the gospel adequately. First they must understand the thoughts of God revealed in Christ, then assimilate them into their own thinking, then devise sermons that will explain those thoughts adequately to the minds of their listeners. Tennyson said of one of the knights of the Round Table, "He laid his mind on theirs

21

and they believed in his beliefs." A sermon lays the mind of the preacher on the minds of the hearers so they will believe in his beliefs.

This is sometimes mistakenly interpreted as imposing one's opinions upon others, trying to control their minds, dictating what they should think and do. A speaker at a minister's conference in the summer of 1955, referring to preaching, said that many men are not content "to sit passively and listen for half an hour while one man tells them what they should believe and how they should live." In the story of her father [13] Pearl Buck, the well-known author, said that her father and his six brothers went into the ministry because this gave them the chance they craved to exercise personal authority over other people's minds and lives. There may be some Protestant ministers who try to exercise authority over people's minds, or to stand on a pedestal and tell others what to do. But this is to be differentiated carefully from what we are talking about here: passing on to others truths that have first been assimilated into one's own thinking.

Most preachers do not presume to do the thinking for others. They try to prod people to think their own way into the mind of Christ, and to stimulate them to use their imaginations in formulating his truth in terms of their own living. Their message is the same as that of Paul: "Have this mind among yourselves, which you have in Christ Jesus" (Phil. 2:5). Emil Ludwig, noted for writing the biographies of famous men, once said that if an author hopes to make his subject live he must "live with him, think with him, eat with him." He went on to say, "Unless you have a certain mad, furious and passionate relationship to your subject, you can never make him live in the minds of others." [14] Preachers who hope to make Christ live for others must go through a similar experience. They must live with Christ, think with him, commune with him, until they come to understand him in terms of their own needs. Then they must have a "mad, furious, passionate" desire to help others understand him in terms of their thinking and living. When his purpose is achieved, a preacher becomes an essential factor in the transmission of the Christian faith.

[13] *Fighting Angel.*

[14] Quoted by Halford E. Luccock in *Christianity and the Individual,* p. 164.

CENTRAL IN PUBLIC WORSHIP

Preaching and public worship are sometimes set over against each other as if they were two separate things. Such is not the case. Worship *includes* preaching. Preaching is a component part of worship, not something added to it, not something taking place when the worship part of the service has been finished. Some people speak of the acts of worship previous to the sermon as "the preliminaries." Others are heard frequently to say that people go to church to worship God, not to hear a man speak. Both of these attitudes are unfortunate. All parts of the service, including the sermon, are constituent elements of the service as a whole. All are essential to a complete, well-rounded service of public worship. In short, worship is man's total experience of fellowship with God.

But the sermon occupies a central, strategic place in public worship. The higher elements of human personality are brought more fully into the sermon than in other parts of worship. Men are commanded to love God with all their hearts, souls, and minds: that is, with their whole personalities. How can the fullness of what God means to human beings be brought more clearly to a group of people than through another human being? A man with mind, conscience, moral judgment, and will; a man who can love, embody virtues in his character, be sensitive to moral values, and be moved with passion for social ideals; a man who can respond to truth, beauty, and goodness, whose personality is aglow with the Spirit of God—such a man is the highest symbol of God known. God is more like a human being than like any other "thing" in the universe. God can be conceived as a person nowhere else on this earth except in the mind of man. The truth of God brought to the people through the personality of the preacher keeps the worship of God on a high level of maturity.

The history of the Christian church shows that in the long run worship is kept spiritual and ethical largely through preaching. The higher powers of one human personality must be brought into play in order to stir the higher powers of other human personalities to their noblest expression. As stated earlier in this chapter, God endowed man, and man alone of all his creatures, with the gift of articulate speech, with mechanisms to produce

23

words, to listen to them and to respond to them. Mind affects mind, soul moves soul, conscience stirs conscience, ethical judgment and social passion stimulate those same things in others, primarily through the medium of spoken words. Preaching is the fundamental method whereby one person explains and demonstrates to others what God means to men, what God requires and expects of men. This is the main reason why preaching has been central in Christian worship from the start.

The sermon is also peculiarly fitted to become the climax of the whole worship service. It is capable of recapitulating the various moods and movements of the service, of drawing them together and focusing them upon the minds, the judgments, and the wills of the hearers. This not only is worship of the highest order but keeps the worship service from dissipating into mere emotions, or into mere formalities or empty words. The sermon presses for decisions, commitments, actions, deeds that prove a person means what he says and is changed by what he feels. It is the high point of public worship.

Basic to the Pastoral Ministry

The weekly sermon is a specialized form of pastoral counseling, a method of group spiritual therapy. If the excerpts from the preaching of the early Christians found in the book of Acts and the epistles of the apostles to the early churches are an indication of what they preached about, then we may be sure many of their sermons took the form of pastoral counseling—although it is certain they did not call it by that name. Their preaching was the instrument of God for preventing mental diseases, for treating what we call psychological ills, for restoring personalities to emotional health. Ever since then the sermon has played a prominent part in every minister's pastoral services.

As a minister goes about his pastoral work he shares with the people their various experiences. He is with them in times of sorrow and in times of joy. He sees them at their best and at their worst, when they are on their good behavior and when they are off guard. He visits the sick, conducts funerals, performs marriage cermonies, baptizes children, dedicates homes, engages in countless conversations, and mixes and mingles with all kinds of groups. As they come to believe in him, people of all ages unburden their hearts to him, confess their sins, describe their perplexities, and express their doubts about every item of our Christian faith. They seek his counsel about personal, family, and group problems. Through his varied associations with them he comes to realize how wonderfully and how fearfully human beings are made.

He comes to know the dissipated, the desperate, the emotionally disturbed, the heroic and the cowardly, the well-adjusted and the ill-adjusted, the driven, the hopeless, the bored, the confused, the lonely, the disillusioned, the despondent, the handicapped, the troubled and the tempted, the sinners and the outcasts. These people and their problems tug at his heart. Those who have lost and those who have never found their way, who do not know what life is for, who are living with mixed motives and are houses divided against themselves, who are trapped by their misdeeds and tricked by their conflicting desires, who are making a losing fight against great odds—all these and more look to him for help and guidance. Upon all of them he looks with pity, judgment, mercy, and love.

He does as much as he can for them, one by one. But there are so many, with so many problems, and he has so little time. Soon he realizes that he must counsel with them about their common problems from his pulpit. Ideas for sermons come trooping into his mind like a small army. Every problem he meets suggests a possible sermon. Twisted notions, gnarled emotions, complexes, fears, worries, antipathies, prejudices, hostilities, suspicions, jealousies, sins, and a host of other inner problems clamor for treatment weekly. A large proportion of the sermons of parish ministers always are—always have been—a form of group pastoral counseling.

No one who knows the history of Christian preaching at its best will doubt the validity of this type of counseling or question its value. There have been some in recent years who have discounted its worth and advised preachers to cease their unscientific methods of pulpit therapy and to devote themselves primarily to counseling individuals. Ministers should never cease to counsel individuals, using all the help modern psychology and psychiatry can offer. Let it also be said that preachers need to profit by what the experts are teaching about the best methods of handling emotional problems from the pulpit. But one method does not substitute for the other. Each has its own distinctive function to perform.

Interestingly enough, many professional psychiatrists, who have found the method of counseling with people one by one to be entirely too slow and too costly for themselves and their patients, are now using group therapy successfully. At one time some psychiatrists insisted that daily interviews of an hour's duration, for as long as three years, were necessary to get at the root of a patient's trouble. Dr. Edward A. Strecker, professor of psychiatry, School of Medicine, University of Pennsylvania, tells of one case that required 450 hours. Along with others he says this slow method has become too costly for most patients, has made too many demands on the time of the psychiatrists, and has restricted their services. Out of sheer necessity a shorter method had to be devised.

Some turned to the group method. For some fifteen years or so psychiatrists over the country have been successfully talking to groups of patients together about their emotional difficulties. The necessity of long, drawn-out conversations with patients is bypassed. Many patients are cured by listening to others instead of doing the talking themselves.

One psychiatrist has devised a method he calls "active psychotherapy," in which patients under certain conditions are given direct advice and emotional support. If necessary they are given a "psychological shock" that "catapults" them into solutions.[15]

This shift of emphasis on the part of psychiatrists is no surprise to most Christian preachers. For they do group counseling from the pulpit regularly. They know their sermons often produce divine "psychological shocks" that "catapult" people into decisions through which diseases of the soul are cured. One of the young men of his day said, "The effect of Newman's preaching on us young men was to turn our souls inside out." The English ambassador at the court of Scotland, describing what he observed of Knox's preaching, wrote, "I assure you the voice of one man is able in an hour to put more life in us than six hundred trumpets blustering in our ears." In our day, as a result of a sermon, one of the men responsible for the organization of

[15] See Bertrand S. Frohman, M.D., *Brief Psychotherapy* (Philadelphia: Lea & Febiger, 1948), pp. 157 ff.

Alcoholics Anonymous was cured of his alcoholism after all other methods of treatment had failed.

Unfortunately preachers too seldom are able to follow through on the effects of their sermons. But they are privileged to discover enough fruitage from their preaching to know that spiritual transformations and renewals take place consistently in people who listen to their sermons dealing with soul illnesses. Sermons are God's instrument for purging the hearts of people, straightening out their tangled emotions, relieving their guilts, fears, and worries, and making them new personalities in Christ. It was said in the days of John Chrysostom, "Better that Constantinople cease to be than John Chrysostom should cease to preach." Few preachers in our country are as influential in the life of a large city as was John Chrysostom. But if all the preachers were taken out of our cities, large and small, it would be fatal for the mental and spiritual health of each city and of the country as a whole. *The sermon is the most important single redemptive force of the week in every community where there are Christian churches.*

There is another, and perhaps more important, aspect of the situation: preaching is a powerful preventive spiritual force. Instead of shipping men home after serious trouble has developed, the army has recently devised a method of preventing emotional ills among occupation forces in Germany. They call it "preventive psychiatry." Briefly described, the method consists of giving men attention before their troubles get started and long before they would seek medical help on their own initiative. The army officers, including doctors and chaplains, believe the method is the hope of the future of civilian medicine also.[16]

Something comparable to that goes on in our churches regularly each week. Religion has always been as important for preventing serious inner problems as for curing them after they arise. Not all the people in churches are prepared to withstand outside pressure, to live by high ethical motives, and to achieve successful and wholesome living. But all available information indicates that among churchgoers there are fewer broken homes and marital failures, fewer mental breakdowns, less juvenile and grown-up delinquency, and fewer crimes than among nonchurch folk.

[16] See *Reader's Digest*, June, 1955, pp. 119-23.

Thousands of people in our churches learn how to keep in a healthy spiritual condition and thus prevent the breakdowns and moral disasters that beset so many other people. While they draw help from the other phases of the church's activities, much of their help comes from the weekly service of worship in which the sermon is a central factor. From sermons they learn how to keep sane attitudes toward life, how to develop the right motivations, how to handle ugly moods, how to cast out destructive and develop constructive emotions, how to adjust to people and situations—in brief, how to keep "whole," how to become "wholesome" personalities. Ralph W. Sockman says he believes that "Jesus' greatest healing work was not in the specific cases which he cured but in the cultivation of a healthy-mindedness which put the body in proper subordination to the spirit." [17] That healthy-mindedness is cultivated weekly in the spiritual health programs of our churches. An indispensable part of these programs is the weekly sermon. Those who are best able to appraise the total work of the church agree with John Watson that the sermon is "the most critical and influential event in the religious week."

If the above statements approximate a true evaluation of the importance of preaching, we should make sure preaching is given its rightful place in the work of the church. Yet, hardly a year goes by that someone does not suggest that preaching is becoming of less and less importance in the modern world. These suggestions usually fall into one of two groups. First, there are those who say that so many other specialized types of religious work are now being carried on by ministers, there is little time left for preaching. This was the conclusion drawn from an eighteen months' study of the lives of 1,600 clergymen of twenty Protestant denominations in forty-seven states, made by Samuel W. Blizzard, associate professor of sociology at Pennsylvania State University. As a result of that study he says that the traditional role of "preacher" in Protestantism is of "declining importance. It is being relegated to a less important position, and the roles of pastor, counselor, organizer, administrator, and promoter" are consuming the major portion of the minister's time.[18]

[17] See *Religion in Life,* Summer, 1955, p. 328.
[18] See *Presbyterian Life,* May 14, 1955, p. 25.

Second, there are those who say that preaching, in its traditional form, is becoming outmoded and of less and less importance in transmitting the Christian faith and in producing Christian character. "It is worse than futile," one writer says, "for the preacher to attempt to 'whip up' persons in behalf of righteousness on the basis of obligation and duty. No amount of scolding or fervid entreaty will avail anything." [19] No sensible preacher tries to "whip up" people's emotions or scolds them. But he does use "fervid entreaty" to move them to do something about righteousness, obligations, and duty. The question is: can the character-conduct-forming job of the church be done without such preaching?

A stockbroker sent his contribution to the church and attached a note to Fosdick saying he was not coming to church any more because the sermons created an inner tension between the ideals he heard on Sunday and the kind of world he lived in on Wall Street during the rest of the week. Is that sort of tension-creating work no longer of major importance? Good preaching is designed to create tensions inside the consciences of men between what they are and do and what they know they ought to be and do. In the past these tensions resulted not only in transformed lives but in transformed societies. The historian Green said that preaching during the Wesleyan revival in Britain resulted in reforming prisons, abolishing the slave trade, bringing clemency to penal laws, and giving the first impulse to popular education. Can preaching no longer achieve such results under modern conditions?

The effectiveness of preaching was discussed at the 1955 meeting in Chicago of the Association of Seminary Professors in the Practical Field. One group at the meeting insisted that "the actual effectiveness of preaching in changing people and in promoting their wholesome growth in the modern setting is greatly overrated." Those holding this position believe that the regular laws of learning do not operate when people are in church, and that the teaching method, in which both teacher and taught participate together, might be more effective in these respects than formal preaching. At the end of the discussion there was general agreement that teaching and preaching should be regarded as

[19] See E. Winston Jones, *Preaching and the Dramatic Arts* (New York: The Macmillan Co., 1948), pp. 49-52.

complementary forms of communication and integrated into the total program of the church.

In his address at the meeting Marshall L. Scott, director of the Presbyterian Institute of Industrial Relations in Chicago, who is engaged in the task of training young ministers to work among laboring men, questioned whether formal preaching can continue much longer to be effective in our modern society. He emphasized the fact that in labor-industry relations "one-way communication . . . is as outmoded as the Model T." Decisions in that area are now made through two-way communication, wrought out "across-the-table," not handed down from a high place. Traditional preaching is one-way communication. In his judgment such preaching will be less and less effective with men who are accustomed to two-way communication in other areas. He implied that preaching should be transformed into some form of two-way communication, though he did not indicate how this might be done. But he left no doubt that he thinks it is becoming outmoded and at least must be supplemented by other forms of communication, if the church is to do its job well.

Several times during the meeting, judgment was expressed that, for its maximum effectiveness, preaching needs to be done in the context of corporate worship. Also much was said, other than what has already been referred to, about the church's needing to supplement preaching with other means of communication.

Preaching methods need to be, and can be, improved to meet modern conditions. Corporate worship and preaching should supplement each other. Both of these positions are theses in this book. As our society becomes more complex and churches become more highly organized, specialists in the ministry are inevitable. The church long ago recognized this by setting up means for training these specialists. Other modern mediums of communication—radio, television, visual aids, drama—are being used by the church, though perhaps too slowly and too ineffectively. There seems no longer to be any serious difference of opinion in the churches about the wisdom of using these other mediums.

But whether this means that preaching itself is no longer of major importance is another matter. If modern conditions invalidate preaching or reduce its effectiveness in transmitting the

Christian faith and producing Christians, or if they require that it be relegated to a position of minor importance in the program of the church, then it is high time for Protestants to become vitally concerned about it. But if the general practitioner in the ministry—the preacher-pastor—is still of central importance in the total work of the Protestant church, then Protestant ministers and laymen had better join forces in seeing that preaching is given opportunity to perform its functions more effectually.

A revival of the preaching ministry is going on in the Roman Catholic Church. Roman Catholic ministers are primarily priests. The heart of their worship is the Mass, at which the priest pre- sides, and consists of fixed forms. Their people are expected to follow authoritarian truths handed down by the church from above. But even that church has found it necessary to put more emphasis on preaching in order to meet modern conditions. Just what effect the movement will have on that church is problemati- cal. Protestant ministers are primarily prophets. The heart of Protestant worship is the written and spoken word. Protestants are expected to think for themselves. Truth is believed to be self-validating. Protestant preachers are supposed to give the peo- ple time to make up their minds and to aid them in doing so. They cannot exercise dictatorial authority. They can only ex- plain, expound, and exhort, beseech and persuade. Protestantism cannot hope to survive in its historical, evangelical form without preaching. That plain, unadorned fact must be faced thoughtfully and prayerfully by the leaders of Protestantism.

At some time in his ministry every preacher grows discouraged and has misgivings about the worth-whileness of his preaching. He understands what Henry Ward Beecher meant when he said: "The churches of the land are sprinkled all over with bald-headed old sinners whose hair has been worn off by the friction of count- less sermons that have been aimed at them and have glanced off and hit the man in the pew behind." He knows what that preacher was talking about who said, "Forty years of preaching often look like forty years of beating the air." [20] He realizes that the effects of preaching often seem as uncertain as "discharging an eye

[20] See John Gossip, *Experience Worketh Hope* (New York: Charles Scribner's Sons, 1945), p. 109.

31

dropper out of a window into the street below in hope that the eye medicine will hit somebody in the right place." [21]

Also, every preacher at some time gets tired of talking, of "walking knee deep in words, words, words," as James A. Garfield expressed it during his candidacy for the presidency. He can quite understand why David Livingstone got tired of "public spouting for ever," and decided to serve God by his missionary travels; and why Albert Schweitzer[22] decided to be a doctor so he could put religion into practice instead of talking about it. At times, when the full import of the stewardship of words comes to mind, the preacher may also be haunted by these words of James:

Let not many of you become teachers, my brethren, for you know that we who teach shall be judged with greater strictness. For we all make many mistakes, and if any one makes no mistakes in what he says he is a perfect man, able to bridle the whole body also. (3:1-2.)

But in his more normal moods every true preacher also knows that there is no substitute for preaching, that it is essential for all true worship, necessary for the pastoral ministry, a prime requisite in the transmission of the Christian faith, and indispensable for the redemption of mankind. So he does not permit misgivings to divert him from his preaching ministry, while all the time he tries diligently to be a better preacher of the Word.

On the importance of the Sunday sermon, John Ruskin once made a statement that ought to be framed, given a prominent place in the study of every preacher, and read before he begins the preparation of each sermon:

That hour when men and women come in, breathless and weary with the week's labor, and a man "sent with a message," which is a matter of life and death, has but thirty minutes to get at the separate hearts of a thousand men, to convince them of all their weaknesses, to shame them for all their sins, to warn them of all their dangers, to try by this way and that to stir the hard fastening of those doors, where the Master Himself has stood and knocked, yet none opened, and to call at the opening of those dark streets, where wisdom herself has stretched forth her hands and no man hath regarded,—thirty

---

[21] See Harry Emerson Fosdick, *The Power to See It Through* (New York: Harper & Brothers, 1935), p. 60.

[22] *Out of My Life and Thought* (New York: Henry Holt & Co., Inc., 1933), pp. 114-15.

minutes to raise the dead in!—let us but once understand and feel this, and the pulpit shall become a throne, like unto a marble rock in the desert, about which the people gather to slake their thirst.[23]

Suggested Reading

Black, James M. *The Mystery of Preaching*. New York: Fleming H. Revell Co., 1924. Chapters I-III.

Brown, Charles R. *The Art of Preaching*. New York: The Macmillan Co., 1922.

Farmer, H. H. *The Servant of the Word*. New York: Charles Scribner's Sons, 1942.

Ferris, Theodore P. *Go Tell the People*. New York: Charles Scribner's Sons, 1951.

Miller, Donald G. *Fire in Thy Mouth*. New York and Nashville: Abingdon Press, 1954.

Schloerb, Rolland W. *The Preaching Ministry Today*. New York: Harper & Brothers, 1946.

Schroeder, Frederick W. *Preaching the Word with Authority*. Philadelphia: Westminster Press, 1954.

Weatherspoon, J. B. *Sent Forth to Preach*. New York: Harper & Brothers, 1954.

[23] Quoted by Newell Dwight Hillis in *Men of the New Era* (New York: Fleming H. Revell Co., 1922), pp. 212-13.

2. The Purposes of Preaching

Judging from their sermons some preachers seem to be preaching without any clear purpose or goal. They could appropriately sing the lines from the old song, "I don't know where I'm going, but I'm on my way." After many years of experience one minister confessed, "All too often we preachers aim at nothing and hit it." Lack of a clearly defined objective for sermons explains why many people remark as they are leaving the church, "What the preacher said was well said, but I didn't know what he was driving at." Techniques should never be permitted to get ahead of objectives. The purposes of preaching, its *raison d'être*, its justification for existence, should be well in mind before sermons are prepared. What, then, are the purposes of preaching?

To Make People God-conscious

Frederick C. Grant has said, "Religion is life controlled by the consciousness of God." The church is distinguished from all other institutions of society at precisely this point: it was established and is maintained for the express purpose of making people aware of God's existence, of his presence, of his claims, of his expectations, of his love and power. Essentially and primarily the work of a minister is not administrative, nor organizational, nor social, nor educational, but spiritual. His supreme function is to influence and aid people to live religiously. To live religiously is to live in the knowledge that life is a great trust, a solemn stewardship from God. The success of the church itself and of every other social institution depends upon whether the church can produce men who are God's men, men dominated and controlled by their allegiance to God, equipped by God with the inner resources necessary for their tasks.

Some physical scientists may pursue their labors without taking God actively into their thinking. For their immediate purpose they need only accept an orderly, systematic, mysterious universe as they find it, without inquiring whether there is "something" back of it. But the preacher must believe and try to persuade others to believe that the "something" back of the universe is "Somebody," a personal Being, who knows what he is doing and

34

why, who created and continues to sustain the universe for his purposes. Some psychologists may study the operations of the human mind and nervous system without feeling the need of considering whether a Divine Personality has or can have fellowship with human souls. But the preacher must believe and preach constantly that people need and can have communication with God, and that valid and essential psychological results flow from that meeting.

Some social scientists may explain the moving currents of human history solely as the result of the activities of men. But the preacher finds it necessary to ask people to believe that there is a "Power not ourselves making for righteousness." He will preach that men must harmonize with the physical laws of the universe or be broken by them; that they must conform to moral laws or bring disaster upon themselves and upon their societies and civilizations; that in the long run men cannot build a secure social order, or find the abiding values of life; unless they go along with, instead of fighting against, God.

Sunday is the day and the worship service the time and place where a concentrated, concerted effort is made to make the church family conscious of God. Actually, God is no closer in the house of worship than in homes or in places of business or in workshops. But the place of worship and the service of worship are such as to make it easier to become aware of God's nearness there than in other places. The service and its surroundings are intended to help people believe that God is, that they are accountable to him, that they should and may have fellowship with him, and to enable them both to understand and experience all that flows from those beliefs.

The whole program of the church focuses on a weekly worship service designed to lead men to experience—vitally and vividly experience—God. There God comes alive for them. There they become alive to God. The minister's responsibility is to plan the service so that it will achieve those ends. That is the main reason why conducting that service is the most important single thing he can do in any given week for his parishioners. That is the acme of the week's pastoral activities. What happens there gives direction and purpose to, sets the tone for, colors and vitally affects everything else in the life of the church, and in the daily life of the people.

The sermon, as an integral and central part of the service, should be designed to help people live their lives in the light of God. In every fiber of the preacher's being, motivating—yes, coloring—everything said, should be an enthusiasm for human living controlled by the consciousness of God.

To Translate the Gospel into Modern Thought Terms

As has already been said, preaching is proclaiming the gospel. That, of course, is its basic purpose. But there is a difference between proclaiming the gospel and actually communicating it. A minister of my acquaintance used the parable of the sower for the text of his farewell sermon in an unfruitful pastorate. The unfruitfulness was due in large part to dull, uninteresting sermons. In the course of his last sermon he stated with some feeling that there had been little wrong with the preaching of the Word but much wrong with its reception. Poor reception may be due to the closed, or preoccupied, or shallow minds of the hearers, as Jesus meant to say by his parable. An old New England shipbuilder said to his pastor at the close of a service, "I couldn't lay a single plank of my ship today." The man whose mind is engaged in building ships or in some other form of secular work while the preacher talks, is no more present at church than the man who is out playing golf.

But poor reception may also be due to the failure of the preacher to talk in the thought terms of the people. Reception is a two-way responsibility. A preacher cannot escape his responsibility by laying all the blame on the hearers. The purpose of the sermon is not merely to *announce* the gospel as a herald would publicly read a king's proclamation, but to *communicate* it. Can it be said that a sermon has been fully *preached* until it has been put in language which hearers can understand? Has the preacher's function been fulfilled until that is done?

After describing words of a speaker as "ignition devices," Fritz Künkel asked: "But what if the ignition does not ignite?" He answered his own question: "Some will watch the time, some yawn, and some begin to whisper about their next bridge parties. Oh, yes, they recognize that it is a wonderful speech, but they whisper nevertheless." [1] The act of preaching is completed only

[1] *In Search of Maturity* (New York: Charles Scribner's Sons, 1943), p. 107.

when the gospel has been proclaimed *in such manner* that the man who listens attentively understands its meaning in terms of his own thinking.

During one of Hilaire Belloc's political speeches someone from the rear of the room shouted, "Speak up!" Belloc, not disconcerted in the least, responded. "It's all right. I'm only talking to myself." More often than they realize, preachers talk to themselves. One minister described the following as the most disconcerting experience of his ministry. As he began his sermon an elderly woman, seated near the front, opened a little box, took out an elaborate hearing device, arranged its parts, screwed them together, and adjusted the receiver to her ear. After listening a few minutes she removed the receiver, took the device apart, repacked it in the box, and sat quietly in the pew during the remainder of the sermon. Many people, who need no hearing devices, have ways of shutting out the sermon as effectively as did that woman. When that happens because the preacher has failed to bring the gospel into vital contact with the minds of his listeners, the gospel may have been *proclaimed*, but it has not been *communicated*.

There is no certain way to prevent the minds of hearers from wandering outside the church. But translating the gospel into understandable language helps do this. That is one main purpose of preaching. Preachers easily forget that the Bible, containing the gospel and its antecedents, is an ancient book. In spite of the noble work of the translators it remains difficult for ordinary men. Its terminology, categories of thought, manners, and customs need to be still further translated into the experiences of his generation by the preacher. This job of translating consists of two steps. The preacher must regularly study the biblical truths until he understands what they meant to the people for whom they were first written. Then he must make the transition from ancient to modern times and show what the same truths can mean to his congregation. Preaching really takes place when the gulf between ancient and modern times has been successfully bridged. "Preaching may be described as the reproduction of the unique message of the Bible in the thought-forms of the modern world." [2]

The fundamental doctrines of our Christian faith were clothed

[2] Raymond Calkins. See *Contemporary Preaching*, ed. G. Bromley Oxnam, p. 47.

originally in terms far removed from the vocabulary of the ordinary man. Preachers often discuss these doctrines in language familiar to the theologians but unfamiliar to their hearers. Billy Sunday, the noted evangelist, had this in mind when he used to say to groups of pastors, "The trouble with some of you is that your people will go to hell while they are trying to figure out what you mean."

The director of his denomination's youth work kept a record of the experiences of more than a thousand young people in three successive summer conferences. Seventy per cent of them admitted they could not define such often-used pulpit terms as "grace," "redemption," "sanctification," and "justification." [3] Some young ministers selected a group of words, familiar and precious to them, and tried to write brief descriptions of them in language they thought would be understood by men in factories among whom they worked. These words were: forgiveness, redemption, salvation, God, grace, justice, sin, heaven, hell, death, and resurrection. They were never quite sure they had succeeded. "Communication is as effectively cut off by language failures as by deafness." [4]

Preachers deceive themselves when they announce a Christian doctrine, talk about it learnedly in theological language, and conclude that they have effectively preached it. Russell Henry Stafford tells of a meeting of college students in which

one young man spoke . . . on the philosophical subject under discussion for some twenty minutes, using the most extraordinary technical jargon any of us had ever heard; then he concluded with an apology for what he whimsically described as having gone on a vocabularistic jag. [5]

Preachers are well advised not to go on "vocabularistic jags" in the pulpit. Those preachers who blissfully keep up a steady flow of scholarly terminology while the people sit nervously in a state of mental opaqueness, deserve the biting words of W. S. Gilbert, "The meaning doesn't matter if it's only idle chatter of a transcendental kind."

---

[3] See *The Pulpit*, October, 1954, p. 20.
[4] Webb B. Garrison, *The Preacher and His Audience*, p. 90. Copyright 1954 by Fleming H. Revell Co. and used by their permission.
[5] *Effective Preaching*, ed. G. Bromley Oxnam, p. 184.

James Russell Lowell said, "We need the tongue of the people in the mouth of the scholar." That can truly be said of preachers. In his study the preacher should stint no toil to discover what scholarly minds are thinking concerning all aspects of the gospel. But when he gets into his pulpit he should translate the learned ideas of the scholars into the simple vernacular of the people. That should be one of the main objectives of his preaching. J. R. P. Sclater says the most incisive criticism he heard of pulpit work in Scotland in his day was that given by a woman who remarked, "It's nearly all a knotless thread." To qualify as real preaching, a sermon must present the gospel in such a way that it has a chance to fasten itself in the minds and souls of those who hear it.

That is the way Jesus preached, and it is recorded, "The great throng heard him gladly" (Mark 12:37).

> I seek divine simplicity in him
> Who handles divine things.[6]

When God decided to reveal himself to man he sent Jesus to live as a human being among other human beings so they could "see" the Word of God in human flesh (John 1:14). When Jesus preached, he clothed the deep things of the gospel in common, homey language familiar to the people. As God's messengers, chosen to bring heavenly truths to earthly people in Christ's stead, we should do our work with "divine simplicity."

To Show the Relevancy of the Gospel to Human Situations

Another function of preaching is to show how the gospel relates to life. One minister is quoted as saying: "My job is to set forth in my preaching the great principles of our faith. It is up to the parishioners to apply them." Preaching great principles is essential, but that is not the preacher's whole job. The relevancy of those principles must also be made plain. A "here-it-is, take-it-or-leave-it" attitude leaves the gospel dangling in the air: something to be admired perhaps, but nothing for the people to take hold of. A college student remarked that he was attending a certain

---

[6] From "The Task," by William Cowper.

church because "the preacher has such workable sermons." All sermons ought to be workable. They ought to have "handles of power," to use the title of a striking book by L. L. Dunnington. "Ordinary people," said W. R. Maltby, "if they want religion at all, want it to live by, not merely to look at."

Early in the ministry of Moncure D. Conway, American clergyman and writer, an elderly woman in his congregation said to him, "Brother Conway, you seem to be preaching to the moon." [7] If preaching is to be consequential it must be directed to earthly inhabitants in definite human situations, with specific needs. Fosdick says that true preaching should be "cooperative dialogue," not "dogmatic monologue." By that he means it ought to include people: what they are thinking, the questions they are asking, the problems they are facing. [8]

Preaching of that sort is known as life-situation preaching, and has been discussed pro and con for the last twenty-five or thirty years. The term "life-situation" has been so loosely used that it often conveys mistaken meanings. Sometimes it implies a particular form of sermon structure to be distinguished from traditional types such as textual or expository sermons. While some sermon forms are more suitable than others for discussing particular problems, no single type of sermon structure can be specified exclusively as a life-situation sermon. Any sermon, regardless of its form, can be such a sermon if directed to human situations.

Sometimes the term is used to mean sermons that begin, literally start out in the opening sentences of the introduction, with a life problem. Methods of beginning introductions, as we shall see later, should be varied. Sometimes introductions should begin with a life problem and sometimes in other ways. What determines whether or not a sermon is a life situation sermon is its general aim, not the way its introduction starts. "Beginning" a sermon with a life situation means planning, from its inception, that the sermon meet people at the point of their experience, in the situation where they are.

Life-situation preaching has also come to be identified with "topical" preaching. Many kinds of topics are discussed from pulpits. Some are live and interesting, and some are tame and

---

[7] See Luccock, *Christianity and the Individual*, p. 145.
[8] "What Is the Matter with Preaching?" *Harper's Magazine*, July, 1928.

dull. Any topic can be discussed without bringing the sermon to bear upon human need. Topical preaching can rightly be called life-situation preaching only when it deals helpfully with the practical problems and questions people face. Every preacher should certainly do some of this kind of preaching, if for no other reason than to give variety to his preaching. Discussion of live topics gives spark to preaching, catches the interest of people, keeps the preacher down to earth, "speaks to the condition" of the hearers.

In the minds of too many people life-situation preaching is identified with preaching on contemporary social problems. Sermons of this sort certainly deal with life situations. The number of such problems is limited, however. When the list has been exhausted a preacher is likely to find himself going around in circles, rehashing his pet social peeves, problems, and schemes. Any preacher is in a bad way when one member of his congregation says to another, "I can tell you ahead of time, that before our pastor finishes this morning's sermon, he will bring up at least one or more of these subjects: alcoholism, race prejudice, Communism, economic justice or international peace. Can't he find something else to talk about?"

A preacher who deals regularly with social problems as such is tempted to assume the role of a news analyst, lecturer, or social engineer. Every preacher worth his salt is sensitive to social problems and interested in seeing the gospel applied to their solution. But he should remind himself that he is a preacher, not a social technician. His concern is not with the details of social arrangement but with the people who operate social machinery and with the effect of social systems on people. His job is not to create a Christian society but to create its creators. Religion can never be a purely individualistic matter. One of the preacher's functions is to make the social implications and applications of Christianity so clear that none can escape them. He should seek to create Christian social consciousness and consciences. But he should "stick to his knitting."

When he turns social engineer, or social reformer, he forsakes his calling. What is worse, he leaves undone a distinctive work that no one else can or will do, and yet without which all other efforts at social improvement will ultimately fail. When a preacher goes into the business of drafting and enforcing laws, of doing the work of business executives and laborers, or of otherwise manipulating and operating social machinery, he has already failed. His primary job is to lead the church in producing Christian men and women of all walks of life who are equipped with the ideals, motivations, and resources to carry on the social experimentation necessary to build a social order in which people have a maximum chance to live like Christians. But the pulpit should never be turned into a lecture platform, a public forum, an academic classroom, a political meeting, or a medium for propagandizing social schemes.

A sermon should always be a sermon. And every sermon, however it starts, whatever its form, whether it is a topical sermon or some other kind of sermon, ought to get down to reality, to where people live. When it does that, it can properly be called life-situation preaching. To do that should be one guiding purpose of all preaching.

Getting down to reality is one sure cure for dullness in preaching. George A. Gordon, commenting on a sermon by a young man in his day, said, "He preached a polite little essay on Galatians which had no more relation to life than a quack of a duck in a milldam." A sermon that has nothing to do with life is certain to be uninteresting. Most preachers occasionally have the thrill of being told by a boy or girl of junior age: "I liked that sermon! I understood every word of it." That is equivalent to saying, "I was interested this morning because you got down into my world." When a youngster, or for that matter anybody else, says that about a sermon you can be sure the sermon did its appointed work. One of the interesting characters in George Eliot's *Felix Holt the Radical* is the Rev. Rufus Lyon whom she labels "A pious and painful preacher." One wonders how many painful sermons are preached by good, sincere men. Perhaps such preachers would wake up if some of their listeners told them frankly how they feel.

Emerson went to church one Sunday in Concord and heard a sermon that had little relation to the practical needs of the people. In a mood of righteous indignation he wrote in his journal:

At church today I felt how unequal is this match of words against things. Cease, O thou unauthorized talker to prate of consolation and resignation and spiritual joys in neat and balanced sentences, for I know these men who sit below.

Hush quickly, for care and calamity are *things* to them. There is . . . the shoemaker whose daughter has gone mad and he is looking up through his spectacles to hear what you can offer in his case. Here is my friend whose scholars are leaving him, and he knows not what to turn his mind to next.

Here is my wife who has come to church in hope of being soothed and strengthened after being wounded by the sharp tongue of a slattern in her house.

Here is the stage driver who has the jaundice and cannot get well. Here is B. who failed last week and he is looking up. O, speak *things* to them, or hold thy tongue.[9]

To Persuade Men to Believe the Gospel and Live by It

In the last chapter, reference was made to the word in the New Testament for preaching that means literally "calling to one's side" or "summoning" for the purpose of saying intimately something important. The word also carries the idea of "beseeching" or "entreating." With appealing eyes and tender words, with "the quality of a knock on the door," the early Christian preachers besought their hearers to accept the love of God and to be reconciled to him. The ultimate objective of all Christian preaching is to persuade listeners to believe in the gospel and to live by it. Always, always in every preacher's heart there should be the haunting, hurting desire to see people come to know Christ as "the way, the truth, and the life."

Over and over, educators tell us that professors in institutions of higher learning are supposed to be completely objective in their classrooms, that educational institutions do not take sides on questions discussed in their halls, that university students are not to be indoctrinated and propagandized. Those attitudes *may* be proper for university professors. But the preacher's purpose *is* to indoctrinate. He *is* propagandizing the truth of the gospel, openly and without apology.

In a boys' school a certain book was required reading. Each boy was supposed to state what moral lesson he derived from its reading. One of them wrote: "A moral principle I learned from this

[9] Quoted from Emerson's *Journal*, by Harold W. Ruopp, *The Christian Century Pulpit*, May, 1941, p. 117.

book was to love work. I can't do that, but it's a good moral principle anyhow." Another wrote: "I learned one valuable principle from this wretched book, and that is to lead one's children by good example. Although I have neither the inclination to lead children, nor any children to lead, I can see where the principle might help some parents." A preacher cannot commend the truths of the gospel in that manner, as abstractions held tenuously and tentatively, and expect hearers to believe them.

The gospel is not offered as hypothetical advice, as something about which the preacher has not made up his mind, or as something that has not yet been tested and experienced. He cannot be completely objective and unemotional. He is not neutral. He is a partisan, and unabashedly so. Life and death are in the issues on which he preaches. His avowed intention is to convince others, to persuade them to come to decisions and to make commitments. Austin Phelps rightly defined a sermon as "an oral address to the popular mind, upon religious truth, contained in the Scriptures, and elaborately treated *with a view to persuasion*." [10] The preacher uses his best skill to persuade his hearers to accept the gospel. Beethoven said of one of his compositions, "It came from the heart: may it go to the heart." What one preaches should come from the heart and he should desire with all his soul to see it go to the hearts of others.

In the delightful posthumous work *Pages from an Oxford Diary*, [11] where he bared his soul and admitted wistfully that he wished he could have been a preacher, Paul Elmer More wrote:

At times I am troubled by a longing, purer than ambition, for the gift of persuasion, for "that warning voice," clear and loud enough to rouse the world from its heavy slumber. If I could once before I leave speak out what I have known and felt of the sacred truth in such a manner that others should know and feel!

That is the deep-seated purpose behind preaching: the desire to persuade others to know and feel the gospel truth as one himself has known and felt it. To do that is the preacher's great opportunity and responsibility.

[10] Italics mine. From *The Theory of Preaching* (New York: Charles Scribner's Sons, 1881), p. 28.

[11] Princeton: Princeton University Press, 1937, p. 80.

To Offer Hope to Sinful Men

Phillips Brooks said that no man should choose the ministry unless he has a "quality that kindles at the sight of men." No person should undertake to preach the gospel unless he believes in men as potential sons of God, in the possibility of their redemption, and in the successful outcome of the human enterprise. Those beliefs are based, not on what men think about themselves, but on what God thinks of them. Paul said, "God shows his love for us in that while we were yet sinners Christ died for us." (Rom. 5:8.) That, I take it, is not only a cardinal doctrine of our Christian faith, but the only hope most of us have for ourselves and for our race. Faith in man, not because of what he is or has done, but because of what God hopes he can become under the power of His redeeming love—that is the taproot of all our human hopes.

Plenty of dark, ugly, disturbing facts can be mustered to cause us to distrust men. But the preacher with the right sort of heart must believe, and strive to make others believe, that man is indispensable to God. One of the distinctive teachings of our Judaeo-Christian faith is that man occupies a central place in the vast scheme of God. According to the Bible, man is not a result of the "accidental concourse of atoms" in a blind, mechanically operated universe. He was planned for by God from the beginning and has been nourished, cultivated, and loved all these millenniums by his Creator for certain great ends.

The preacher's duty is to think nobly about men and persuade them to think nobly about themselves; to remind every man and every woman that big issues hang on the fate of the human race and that everyone has a part in determining the outcome; to challenge each to become a hero or a heroine in God's redemptive undertaking. He should remind them of their divine calling in the words of Peter: "You are a chosen race, a royal priesthood, a holy nation, God's own people" (I Pet. 2:9); and appeal to them in the words of John: "See what love the Father has given us, that we should be called the children of God; and so we are" (I John 3:1).

He must also believe and persuade his hearers to believe that men are redeemable. Man's pathway is strewn with sordid sins and their consequences. Crushed beneath the burden of guilt and the wages of sins, men do not find it easy to believe they can be forgiven and begin life anew. The preacher's message from God must ever be that sin need not be final, that "if we confess our sins, he is faithful and just, and will forgive our sins and cleanse us from all unrighteousness" (I John 1:9). Many people will not have the courage to believe that, unless the preacher brings it to them repeatedly as the glad tidings direct from God himself; unless he beseeches them to hold tenaciously to it as the ladder by which to rise "from the lowly earth to the vaulted skies," till each at last stands by the grace of God "on the heights of his life with a glimpse of a height that is higher."

The gospel in all its phases, from the Incarnation through the Resurrection to the living presence of the Holy Spirit, is amazing, incredible to hosts of people. Paul found that the doctrine of the atonement was foolishness, a stumbling block, to both Jews and Greeks. (I Cor. 1:18 ff.) The Cross is still an obstacle to people. They find it difficult to believe God can or would suffer to forgive and redeem sinful men. They have to be persuaded that forgiveness, reconcilement, full redemption are credible, possible, true, real, and for every sinner.

The preacher also should create faith in the successful outcome of the human enterprise. Again and again the collapse and final failure of society have been predicted. The outlook for human civilization looms dark in our day, but probably no darker than it did in other days. In past generations when it appeared that hope would be extinguished in the earth, it was the preacher's supreme privilege to keep the spark of hope alive and fan it into flame. Tell the people of your generation, Mr. Preacher, that the dreams of the race were God's dreams before they were man's, that God initiated them, shares responsibility with us for their realization, even shares the consequences of our mistakes, failures, and sins, and agonizes with us and for us until at last we achieve that "one far-off divine event toward which all creation moves."

Whatever others may do, the ambassador of Christ cannot lose heart about people. If he does not nourish a belief in humanity nobody else likely will. The gospel is man's last best hope. Every sermon preached should issue from a tough, tenacious conviction of man's worth, a consummate faith in his possibilities, an inexhaustible patience with his weaknesses and sins, and an undying faith in the possibility of his redemption and in the final consummation of the kingdom of God upon the earth.

Make no mistake about it: this faith in people costs. Charles E. Jefferson characterized sermons as "drops of blood shed by the servants of the Lord for the redemption of the world." [12] Every preacher who believes in men as God believes in them, who yearns for their redemption with the passion and the compassion of Christ, comes to realize Jefferson was right. But nothing less than that should be the dominating purpose back of all preaching.

In Ibsen's play *The Pretenders* is a scene that describes the death of an infamous, intriguing bishop of Norway in the thirteenth century. His physician has informed him of his approaching death. He takes the physician to task for not being able to prolong human life, for not making man a perpetual motion machine. Then his eyes light up with a flash of insight:

> *Perpetuum mobile,*—I am not strong in Latin—but it means somewhat that has power to work eternally through the ages. If I myself, now, could but . . . ? That were a deed to end my life withal! That were to do my greatest deed in my latest hour! To set wheel and weight and lever at work in the King's soul and the Duke's; to set them a-going so that no power on earth can stop them; if I can but do that, then shall I live indeed, live in my work—and, when I think of it, mayhap 'tis that which is called immortality.[18]

That is not all that is meant by the Christian doctrine of immortality, not by a long shot. But the immortality of influence *is* vouchsafed to preachers. Their privilege is to be the instrument of God to start things moving in the souls of men and women so that no power on earth can stop them. A stirring begins in one life, communicates itself to another, leaps like fire from heart to heart and from generation to generation, until Christ's work is finished and God's redemption of his world is accomplished.

Suggested Reading

Bowie, Walter Russell. *Preaching.* New York and Nashville: Abingdon Press, 1954. Chapters III and VIII.

[12] *The Minister as Prophet* (New York: Thomas Y. Crowell, 1905), p. 60.
[18] From *The Collected Works of Henrik Ibsen,* II, 252 (New York: Charles Scribner's Sons, 1929).

Buttrick, George A. *Jesus Came Preaching*. New York: Charles Scribner's Sons, 1931. Chapters II-V, VIII.

Hoyt, A. S. *Vital Elements of Preaching*. New York: The Macmillan Co., 1914.

Kennedy, Gerald. *God's Good News*. New York: Harper & Brothers, 1955.

Luccock, Halford E. *In the Minister's Workshop*. New York and Nashville: Abingdon Press, 1944. Chapters VI-VIII, XXI-XXII.

Read, David H. C. *The Communication of the Gospel*. London: S. C. M. Press, Ltd., 1952.

Stewart, James S. *Heralds of God*. New York: Charles Scribner's Sons, 1946.

3. The Preacher's Part in His Preaching

Paul urged Timothy, his young assistant, "Do your best to present yourself to God . . . , a workman who has no need to be ashamed" (II Tim. 2:15). One's call to preach carries with it the obligation both to do good work and to be a good workman. Martin Luther once confessed, "I am more afraid of my own heart than of the Pope and all his cardinals." In our sober, thoughtful moments most of us would acknowledge we are our own worst enemies. Our failures are due more to our own weaknesses, inertia, procrastination, lack of self-discipline and of dedication, than to anything outside ourselves.

> The fault, dear Brutus, is not in our stars,
> But in ourselves, that we are underlings.[1]

Sermons cannot be detached from the person who preaches them. They are conditioned by what he is, what he does, what he thinks, and what he feels. So, let us now face squarely the part every preacher plays in the success of his preaching.

HIS WORK HABITS

The problem of finding time to prepare sermons is becoming increasingly difficult for the Protestant minister. The various responsibilities entrusted to him by his church are competing with each other so keenly for his time and energies that all leading denominations are perplexed to know what to do about it. Denominational leaders can do something by relieving part of the official pressures on ministers, deflating denominational programs, and attacking "conferenceitis," an ecclesiastical disease that has almost reached the epidemic stage. But for the most part every preacher must handle the problem for himself. He can do a great deal by forming the right sort of work habits.

A few explicit words of counsel about work habits can be offered with some confidence.

1. Accept and adjust to the fact that the ministry requires hard work. Samuel Johnson said, "No, sir, the ministry is not an easy calling and I do not envy the man who makes it easy." The per-

[1] Shakespeare's *Julius Caesar.* Act I, scene 2.

son who thinks it is easy simply does not know what he is talking about. The man who tries to make it easy is always distraught. All creative callings require hard work. Back of all great music, writing, and speaking are hours of grinding toil. Wilfred Funk, editor and publisher, recently said he had gathered definitions of genius by those who are called geniuses. Not a single genius spoke of talent, or inspiration. All spoke of work—hard, brutal work, drudgery—the capacity for taking infinite pains.

Thackeray said of Lord Macaulay, "He reads twenty books to write a sentence; he travels a hundred miles to make a line of description." Carlyle, said his brother, wrote with his heart's blood. In the British Museum in London may be seen seventy-five separate drafts of Thomas Gray's poem, "Elegy Written in a Country Churchyard." When Harry Emerson Fosdick said that preaching "is drenching a congregation with one's life blood," he was referring primarily to the hard work that goes into it. Accept hard work as one of the requirements of the job and be willing to "toil like a miner under a landslide."

2. Have regular hours for study. There are no rules about when to begin work or how long to remain at it. But one should have a fixed hour to reach his study and go there prepared in dress and determination to go to work in earnest. As for time killing, most of us can supply data from our experiences supporting the truth of what Sir Joshua Reynolds said, "There is no expedient to which a man will not resort to avoid the real labor of thinking." William James, of Harvard, confessed that after reaching his study he would potter around at all sorts of trifles to keep from settling down to business. Someone asked George A. Buttrick how, with everything else he does, he finds time to prepare sermons. He said, "When I finally reach my study I really work." Preachers punch no time clock. Nobody checks on them. They are their own boss and timekeeper. Each one has to learn how to supervise himself firmly.

Waiting for the right mood before starting to work is a delusion and a snare. In the presence of Samuel Johnson someone spoke of the happy moments of composition and how a man can write at one time and not at another. Johnson snorted, "A man can write at any time if he will set himself doggedly to it." That person spoke more seriously than perhaps it sounded who said, "The art of writing is the art of applying the seat of the pants to the seat of the chair." That goes also for the art of preaching. The Holy Spirit favors the prepared man. The man who comes into his study promptly, seats himself at his desk, and takes his pencil and paper in hand, at least opens the way for his mind to start functioning. Getting ready in this manner is a form of prayer that prepares one to take advantage of whatever inspiration comes from God. "Cursed is he who does the work of the Lord with slackness." (Jer. 48:10.)

3. Systematize your work. Samuel McComb, with some justification, says, "There is, perhaps, no body of men so guilty of frittering away their time in trivialities, in a fussy parade of being busy as ministers of religion." [2] James Black insisted that a man's laziness "often consists not in idleness, but in doing busily what he should be doing at some more appropriate time." [3] One way to avoid this is to prepare work schedules.

Work schedules reduce secondary things to habit and leave time and energy for the primary things. At least once a year a minister ought to render himself and his people the service of reading and heeding the famous chapter "Habit" in William James's *Psychology, Briefer Course*. James explains that the purpose of habits

is to make our nervous system our ally instead of our enemy. . . . For this we must make automatic and habitual, as early as possible, as many useful actions as we can. . . . The more of the details of our daily life we can hand over to the effortless custody of automatism, the more our higher powers of mind will be set for their own proper work.

Then he gives a number of basic rules and practical suggestions for the formation of habits.

All his general suggestions about habits apply specifically to work schedules. These schedules are an important type of habit. Once formed they make it unnecessary for one to expend energy trying to decide when and whether to perform the routine duties of life, thus leaving his precious energy for tackling the big tasks.

---

[2] *Preaching in Theory and Practice*, p. 39.
[3] *The Mystery of Preaching*, p. 83. Copyright 1924 by Fleming H. Revell Co. and used by their permission.

Work schedules ought to determine such things as: when to do pastoral visitation of different types, when to maintain office hours, when to answer correspondence, when to start on next Sunday's sermon and when to complete it, when to arrive at the study and how long to stay, when to plan the order of Sunday service, when to get material ready for the weekly bulletin, and so on through a long list of duties that must be performed regularly. Daily, weekly, monthly, and for some things quarterly and annual schedules may be made.

These schedules should be formed, first, for the sake of productiveness. Irregular, disorderly workers produce less than they could if they worked by schedules. Second, schedules should be formed for the sake of one's health. They are tracks for his energies. Irregular habits are hard on the nervous system. Were it not for habitual work patterns most of us would literally be in mental and emotional turmoil most of the time. Third, schedules should be followed for the sake of family peace and happiness. If each member of the household knows what the others' work schedules are, all can make plans for family duties and pleasures. The preacher has no right to demoralize home life and put everybody else's nerves on edge by forcing them to adjust to his irregular methods of working.

4. When a thing is scheduled to be done at a certain time, do it. Don't dawdle, procrastinate, temporize, or decide to do something else because it is easier. The schedule will be interrupted at times. Interruptions should be met cheerfully and without nervous irritation. A schedule should be a guide, not a master, and therefore should always be elastic.

5. Put laymen to work. One can find much time for preaching by delegating tasks to capable lay men and women. The growing lay movement in Protestantism is making this easier than it has been since the early centuries of the Christian church. Our century is now being widely spoken of as the century of the laity. The doctrines of the universal priesthood and of the universal pastorhood of all believers are being put into practical operation in the churches as never before. Churches are even turning over to laymen religious duties formerly considered the exclusive function of ordained ministers. A person's success in the pastorate will be measured as much by the number of people he trains and puts to work as by the work he does himself. Every job he can place in the hands of others means just that much time for the jobs he is technically trained to do—including preaching.

6. *Learn when and how to say "no."* "Mastery is acquired through resolved limitation." [4] Finding time for preaching is a problem consisting of a three-fold decision: what must be done, what may be delegated to others, and what needs to be left un-done. St. John Ervine once spoke of William Booth of the Salvation Army as "a man with a saint's concentration on essentials and indifference to mere irrelevances." All of us could stand a little of that type of sainthood.

Take preventive measure not to become so involved in other things that insufficient time is left for the primary things. Jesus refused to be diverted from his main task or to become so encumbered with other things that, within the time appointed him by God, he could not accomplish the redemptive work for which he came to earth. Preachers also are called of God to dedicate themselves to the primary jobs to which they are assigned in their parishes. To dissipate energies, scatter interests, and fritter away time on things on the periphery is to betray one's call.

We always pray for you, that our God may make you worthy of his call, and may fulfil every good resolve and work of faith by his power, so that the name of our Lord Jesus may be glorified in you, and you in him, according to the grace of our God and the Lord Jesus Christ. (II Thess. 1:11-12.)

HIS HEALTH AND MENTAL HABITS

Among the effects of James Russell Lowell after his death was found a miniature tombstone with the inscription:

> Here lies the part of J. R. L.,
> That hindered him from doing well.

The blame for the ineffectiveness of many ministers can be laid on their bodies—not on their bodies as such, but on the way they neglect, abuse, and misuse their bodies.

At the beginning of each week a preacher could well remind himself of these words of Paul: "Do you not know that your body

[4] Lord Acton.

is a temple of the Holy Spirit within you, which you have from God? You are not your own; you were bought with a price. So glorify God in your body." (I Cor. 6:19-20.) While we are in this world our bodies are our most precious possessions. They are the houses in which our spirits "live and move and have their being." Body and soul are so intimately interrelated that one cannot function properly without the other. In fact, we are body-soul organisms. The Holy Spirit cannot do some things in us and with us if our body-souls are out of order.

Dr. Alexis Carrel says that the facts discovered by scientists about the interdependence of mental activities and physiological functions do not uphold the old idea that the soul is found exclusively in the brain.

In fact, the entire body appears to be the substratum of mental and spiritual energies. Thought is the offspring of the endocrine glands as well as of the cerebral cortex. The integrity of the organism is indispensable to the manifestations of consciousness. Man thinks, invents, loves, suffers, admires, and prays with his brain and all his organs.[5]

If this is true, the whole body, every part of it, deserves to be treated as a sacred trust.

There are several reasons why a preacher should treat his body with the proper respect. The dedication of his body is included in his total dedication to God. Presumably he will want to live out his expectancy and function at his maximum efficiency to the end. He will be doing a great deal of preaching to others and counseling with them about the problems of their personalities, their personal adjustments, and their human relationships. If his ministry in these respects is to prove most helpful, he must have a measure of emotional stability, of spiritual maturity, of capacity for growth and understanding, and a wholesome family life.

But the reason for respecting the body to be most emphasized here is: preaching cannot be at its best unless the body-soul relationships are at their best. Bodily conditions, moods, and emotions are bound up in a bundle with preaching. These things unconsciously affect what one says and the way he says it. Con-

[5] *Man, the Unknown* (New York: Harper & Brothers, 1939), p. 144.

sequently, they determine the effect on the hearers of what is said.

As one reads the intimate biographies, diaries, and letters of men, he is impressed with the number of them who have been depressed by listening to sermons. Oliver Wendell Holmes once said, "I might have entered the ministry if certain clergymen I knew had not looked and acted so much like undertakers." So unusual was it to go to church and not be depressed that Robert Louis Stevenson once made this entry: "I have been to church today and am not depressed." Not only one's gloominess but his fatigue, his irritation, worry, and other ugly moods of the soul, due in part or in whole to an unhealthy body, color his sermon and control its effects. Healthy personalities and high quality preaching are inextricably bound together.

The facts pertaining to the functional interrelationship of mind and body discovered in the science of psychosomatics have been broadcast so often by so many mediums that they are common knowledge. Presumably by the time a candidate for the ministry has finished college, certainly by the time he has completed his theological course, he is well acquainted with these facts. And yet ministers are noted for ignoring them and failing to put them into practice.

The ministry is a difficult, many-sided work requiring a large measure of versatility. There are few callings, if any, that make as rigorous psychological demands, that exact such a heavy toll of nervous energy. First and last, a good many ministers fail to stand the strain. Some are unorganized personalities and some are disorganized. Some live on tensions, under pressures, with all sorts of gnarled and unhealthy emotions. Many are frustrated, morose, worried, harried, hurried, driven, irritable, difficult to get along with and to live with. Some develop stomach ulcers. Others have heart attacks. Still others have nervous breakdowns. A few commit suicide. These are ugly facts, but they should be faced by every minister at the beginning of his ministry.

If a minister needs to do so, he should seek wise psychiatric counsel about his emotional disturbances just as he consults a physician about his bodily ailments. He should feel no more embarrassment about doing the one than about doing the other. But there are many things he can do, and should do, from the very outset of his ministry, for his own mental health, especially by way of preventing serious emotional disturbances from developing.

Some of these things are a matter of exercising common sense and self-discipline. They simply amount to playing fair with one's body. One should form sane habits of eating and sleeping, learn to relax and give his nerves regular rest. We are told there are certain nerves whose function is to register fatigue, to warn us that we are tired. If those nerves become fatigued there is no way for our bodies to warn us that we are on the verge of a nervous breakdown. Learn to detect fatigue before it goes too far. Plan rest, recreation, and vacations as a sacred obligation to God.

Other things one can do for his mental health concern disciplines of his soul. A part of every preacher's reading time annually should be devoted to sensible books now available on mental and emotional hygiene. Each book should be read carefully, prayerfully, devotionally, applied to himself, and put into practice in his daily life. As stated previously, he will be doing a good deal of group counseling through his sermons. He should direct every such sermon first to himself.

Like everyone else a preacher needs regular times for self-examination and appraisal, self-wrestling, and honest confession before God. No minister can live up to the high demands of his calling in his own strength. Jesus himself could not do that; he fought for opportunity to have secret walks and talks with God. Over and over in the Gospel of Mark we are told that Jesus "strictly ordered" those he healed not to tell others about it, so he could get away from the strain of the daily work. (Cf. Mark 1:43; 3:12; 5:43; 7:36; 8:26.) He slipped into desert places, or across the Sea of Galilee, or beyond the Jordan, or into Tyre and Sidon, often hiding for a few days at a time or traveling incognito to get a chance to pray, rest, refresh his soul, and talk intimately with his disciples. (Cf. Mark 1:38; 3:7; 3:13; 4:35; 6:31; 6:45; 7:24; 9:30.) If Jesus could not live up to the demands of his ministry without taking the time to replenish his jaded spiritual powers, no human being should try to perform his ministry without doing likewise. Every person must discover for himself how and when to pray, to make therapeutic use of the Bible, to read devotional literature, in order to keep his soul healthy.

Everyone should also learn to entrust his life and labors to God. Bishop Quayle, the noted Methodist minister, used to delight to tell of sitting up once at midnight, worrying over the condition of the churches and pastors under his care, when he heard God say to him as clearly as though He were actually speaking, "Quayle, you go to bed; I'll sit up the rest of the night." One of the hardest things we ministers have to learn is to let God carry his share of the load. We find it difficult to believe, or at least to practice, the truth in the parable of Jesus in which he compared the kingdom of God to the growing and maturing crops:

The kingdom of God is as if a man should scatter seed upon the ground, and should sleep and rise night and day, and the seed should sprout and grow, *he knows not how.* The earth produces of *itself,* first the blade, then the ear, then the full grain in the ear. (Mark 4:26-28.)

All the efforts of the farmer cannot produce a crop if the natural forces resident in the soil fail to perform their life-giving functions. All the efforts of the minister cannot redeem human lives and build the Kingdom, if the Spirit of God does not work within the hearts of men. Most assuredly worrying and fretting about it can accomplish exactly nothing, while it saps one's precious energy. Every preacher should work on himself until he can believe, and act as though he believes, that he can do his work every day, sleep at night, and rise again another day, with confident assurance that all the while God is at work doing all He can, and what one himself cannot do, to bring his labors to fruition.

His Personal Life

After listing a number of virtues that should characterize the Christian's life, Peter exhorted, "Therefore, brethren, be the more zealous to confirm your call and election" (II Pet. 1:10.) One's call is validated by the Christian graces he exhibits. Joaquin Miller said to his fellow poets, "We must, in some sort, live what we write, if what we write is to live." One of the preacher's heavy responsibilities is the necessity of living to some degree what he preaches, if he expects what he preaches to live.

The people of the community look to him to set an example of godly living, to be a norm of conduct, to embody the morals he enjoins upon them. "More than any set of men on earth," said Charles R. Brown, "ministers are under bonds to live nobly." One of the solemn and sacred things about a preacher's ministry is what people expect of him.

Now and then we hear of a minister who tries to make himself popular by coming down to the level of the people and living by their standards. To prove he is a man's man, a hail fellow well met, he decides to participate in their worldly pleasures— in moderation, to be sure. Men and women of his community may not tell him so, but among themselves they express pity for him, disgust with him, even hold him in derision.

Sometime ago a general in the United States Army urged a group of students for the ministry to take seriously the high expectations laymen have of ministers. He said laymen do not want their pastor to come down to their level of morals, but to draw them up to his. He expressed for himself and others mild contempt for a minister who drinks, gambles, exchanges off-color jokes, and uses profanity, hoping thereby to attract people to himself and to the church. He said that folk do not expect a preacher to be an angel and they like to discover he has his share of human weaknesses, but they look to him to set a standard of conduct which down in their hearts they long to attain.

Strangely enough, a few ministers seem to pity themselves for not being privileged to engage in worldly pleasures. They regard giving these up as a great sacrifice and let it be known they are making the sacrifice grudgingly. This is a distorted, unworthy view of their calling. Jesus said, "For their sake I consecrate myself, that they also may be consecrated in truth." (John 17: 19.) Like the Master, one should voluntarily, and gladly, dedicate himself to noble living in order to inspire others to live nobly. One can do this without giving the impression of being self-righteous, goody-goody, and otherworldly, of trying to be a perfectionist, of "wearing piety on the sleeve." And he will be respected for being genuine, for living consistently by high ideals, for making attractive to his parishioners a better way of life. A man in England dedicated a book to his friend, J. Y. Simpson, "Who makes the best seem easily credible." The people of his parish expect the preacher to make the best moral life seem not only credible but possible.

George Wharton Pepper, one of the few laymen to deliver the Yale Lectures on preaching, gave his lectures the appropriate title A Voice from the Crowd. Speaking for all ordinary laymen making up that crowd he said to preachers:

My own experience supplemented by extended inquiry satisfies me that it is impossible to exaggerate the weight which the man in the pew attaches to the integrity of the preacher. . . . Speaking generally, let the hearer even suspect that all is not well with the man who is exhorting him, and the message, however true, will have lost its penetrating power.[6]

That attitude is almost universal among laymen and ought to be taken seriously by ministers. Willard L. Sperry said, "Preaching can survive countless honest errors; it cannot stand insincerity." [7] The people will overlook their preacher's limitations, his faults, his personal eccentricities; but they will not overlook his unethical dealings and his immoral behavior.

Charles Spurgeon once told of a man who preached so well and lived so badly, that when he was in the pulpit everybody said he ought never to come out again, and when he was out of it they declared he never ought to enter it again. On all the days of the week he nullified everything he said on Sunday. A preacher may think he does all his preaching from the pulpit, but in the eyes of the people he is preaching everywhere he goes by everything he says and does. The sermons one preaches by his life will either annul or help make fruitful the sermons he preaches from the pulpit. "Unless you preach everywhere you go," said St. Francis, "there is no use to go anywhere to preach."

George Herbert said to the ministers of his day, "You are in God's stead in your parish." Instead of shying off from that as a heavy responsibility preachers should welcome it as one of their choice privileges. "There is no greater benefit that a man can confer on his fellows than his own achievement of some measure of personal holiness, some experience of the discipline, organization and intensification of his own inner life." [8] The

---

[6] New Haven: Yale University Press, 1915, pp. 23-24.
[7] We Prophesy in Part (New York: Harper & Brothers, 1938), p. 126.
[8] Park, The Miracle of Preaching, p. 42

moral laxness of our age makes it imperative for ministers to hold themselves rigidly to high Christian standards of morals. If the church of our day becomes corrupted, it will be, as in other days, primarily because the ministry becomes worldly.

No man can hope to live up to these expectations of the people in his own strength. He must be "strong in the Lord and in the strength of his might," and put on "the whole armor of God," that he may be able to stand. (Eph. 6:10-11.) Only thus can he succeed in setting "the believers an example in speech and conduct, in love, in faith, in purity" (I Tim. 4:12).

His Christian Experience

Preaching will be most impressive when the congregation knows the preacher has experienced what he talks about. The French have a saying, "It must come out of one's self." That is true of a sermon. In his letters Paul spoke many times of "the" gospel. But occasionally he used the expression "my" gospel. (Cf. Rom. 2:16; 16:25; II Tim. 2:8.) By this he usually meant not what he had heard from others but what he had received from Christ directly and experienced for himself. He closed his letter to the Romans with a benediction beginning, "Now to him who is able to strengthen you according to my gospel and the preaching of Jesus Christ . . ." (16:25). He committed them to One whose strength he had felt. That was not hearsay but something he knew from the inside. One cannot preach "the" gospel effectively until, by right of his own experience, he can call it "my" gospel.

When asked his opinion regarding the kind of man needed as the pastor of a vacant parish, Carlyle replied, "What this parish needs is a man who knows God otherwise than by hearsay." Every parish needs such a pastor. A firsthand experiential knowledge of God is a basic requisite for preaching. Charles Kingsley used to fold his arms, lean upon his pulpit, look his people in the eyes and say, "Here we are again to talk about what is really going on in your soul and in mine." When the people know a preacher is talking about what is going on in his soul, as well as about their souls, they will listen more eagerly to what he says.

After all, whether we like it or not, truth is something caught as well as taught. Plato said he would never write a treatise on philosophy because philosophy is something that must be acquired by conversation, "the flame leaping from speaker to speaker until the soul itself catches fire." The gospel must leap like a flame from preacher to people. The early Christians were taught to consider their Christianity defective until they had received the Holy Spirit. By this they meant, among other things, their religion was not genuine until what they believed took fire within, until it rushed into their souls burning for expression. So Paul said to the Thessalonians, "Our gospel came to you not only in word, but also in power and in the Holy Spirit and with full conviction." (I Thess. 1:5.) And so John Bunyan used to say, "I preached what I did feel—what I smartingly did feel." Unless the preacher feels keenly the truth of what he says, it is almost certain to leave others unmoved.

In *Hypatia* Charles Kingsley pictures a Jew on board a ship observing with deep interest and envy a group of Christian travelers. They had pitched their tent on the deck. He observed them for a number of days; then, frankly longing for a faith like theirs, he said:

I am sick of syllogisms, and probabilities, and pros and contras. I want a faith past arguments. . . . I don't want to possess a faith. I want a faith which will possess me. And if I ever arrived at such one, believe me, it would be by some practical demonstration as this very tent has given me.

The people want the kind of faith they can tell has taken hold of the preacher, has worked in his life. If humanity is ever saved, so someone has said, it will be by goodness propagating itself.

Much will be said later about the language in which sermons should be preached. Let it first be said that the language of action, of deeds, of experience is the real genius of the Christian religion. While preparing their sermons preachers ought to imagine a chorus of voices coming from the pews saying to them what Nietzsche, the German philosopher, said to the Christians of his day: "You must show me you are redeemed before I will believe in your redeemer."

HIS CALL AND HIS COMMITMENT

Most denominations are concerned about the number of ordained ministers who forsake the ministry for other types of work, or who are restless, dissatisfied, unhappy, and ineffective. Ministerial miseries and failures cannot be attributed to any single cause. But a large share of them are traceable to the lack of commitment to the ministry as a divine calling for life.

The more one learns of the inner problems of ministers, the more one is disturbed by the fact that so many seem not to have experienced anything that resembles a "call" from God. Some suffer from what Bishop Stephen C. Neill, formerly of India, described as "vocation externally induced." They permit themselves to be unduly influenced by well-meaning parents, pastors, and counselors of youth to make a hasty and premature public choice of the ministry. As time passes they begin to doubt the wisdom of their decision but do not know how to admit their mistake without embarrassment. So they go on for years— occasionally for a lifetime—preparing for and engaging in a work about which they have serious misgivings. One should seek the judgment and counsel of others while he is considering the ministry. But the final decision should be his—his own, personal, independent—decision.

Some appear to have chosen the ministry largely for prudential reasons. With the assistance of vocational and aptitude tests and the help of vocational counselors they analyze themselves and the ministry with a view to discovering whether it is the work for which they are best fitted and which offers the most promising opportunities and rewards. Convinced by the analysis that the work offers opportunities, and that they are fitted for it, they choose it as they would any other promising vocation. This type of analysis is now a standard requirement for candidates for the ministry in some denominations, and wisely so. But if one stops there he leaves out the decisive factor in his choice, namely: What is God's will for my life?

Some men who are actuated by the noblest humanitarian motives in choosing the ministry leave God out of their decision. They love their fellow men. They are sensitive to human need. They are eager to serve unselfishly. They have a passion to build a brotherly social order on Christian principles. They believe in the primacy of spiritual values. But they seem not to know what is meant by God's call to the ministry. What more is required, they ask, than to be aware of human needs and to be willing to serve them? All these motives are worthy, Christian, vital to the ministry. But one thing more is needed and that is to discover the will of God. All the while one is analyzing himself and the work, seeking the judgment of others, and studying the needs of people and how to meet them, he should be asking God to make clear His purpose for his life. As the time for decision approaches, no human being can or should try to be of any further help. One should expectantly await the moment when God says clearly, "This is (or this is not) the work to which I am calling you." When God speaks—then, and only then, should he choose.

This call is one of the blessed mysteries of the ministry. No one can explain it adequately to another. He lacks terms in which to do so, for as Goethe said, "The highest cannot be spoken." Ordinarily there is nothing spectacular or supernatural about it. The heavens do not open. No audible voice is heard. No angelic form appears. There is a mystical, indefinable but certain and satisfying feeling that God has made his will known.

The call follows no set pattern. To some it comes at a particular moment to which they can always refer back, as did Paul to his experience on the road to Damascus, as the exact hour when God chose them for the ministry. To others it comes at the end of a process. There is a slow awakening to human needs, an increasing realization of their ability to meet those needs, a deepening conviction that God is opening a door, then a certainty that they have chosen his way. A few answer it immediately, as Peter, James, and John left their nets immediately to follow Jesus. Many heed it doubtfully, hesitatingly, or even rebelliously at first, only to move ahead with mounting enthusiasm as some future event confirms their judgment that God is leading them. A few receive it in a moment of crisis, in a violent, all-but-overwhelming spiritual upheaval. But most men receive it quietly as a "still, small voice" that tips the scales in a certain direction while they are striving sincerely, calmly, and prayerfully to weigh all the factors. In whatever form it comes, it must somehow validate itself to each individual as coming from God.

Those who enter the ministry, stay in it to the end, and perform their labors with joy, speak not of having chosen the ministry, but of having been chosen for it. Paul began his salutation to the Romans, "Paul, a servant of Jesus Christ, called to be an apostle, set apart for the gospel of God . . ." (1:1). To the

63

Corinthians he said, "Woe to me if I do not preach the gospel! For if I do this of my own will, I have a reward; but if not of my own will, I am entrusted with a commission." (I Cor. 9: 16-17.) That feeling of being "conscripted" by God to preach the gospel is a prerequisite to a happy, fruitful, and satisfying ministry.

Once a person is sure of God's commission and of his own acceptance, he should commit himself to it for life with no thought of turning back. When Charles Kingsley finally decided to go into the ministry he wrote in his diary: "I have devoted myself to God; a vow never, if He gives me the faith I pray for, to be recalled." The acceptance of the call should be a point of no return. There should be no mental reservations. When the call is accepted, one should burn his bridges behind him and launch out with the willingness to abide by all the conditions, to take all the consequences, to pay all the costs, and to be content with all the compensations. Above all else, he should have faith that God will see him through to a triumphant end.

One cannot put his heart into the ministry if in the back of his mind he secretly entertains the desire for, or the possibility of seeking, another calling. If for long one supposes he could do better at some other work, envies those engaged in other professions, wishes he were doing something else, seriously contemplates engaging in some other form of work, he should sit down and quietly review his call. What John Dos Passos said about writing is doubly true of the ministry: "No durable piece of work . . . has ever been accomplished by a double-minded man. To attain the invention of any sound thing, no matter how trivial, demands the integrated efforts of somebody's whole heart and whole intelligence." [9] A minister should be "a single-minded person born to a great task."

A preacher cannot keep up his morale unless he is sustained by the conviction that he is engaged in God's work. A minister shares many of the temptations and perils common to men. But he has some peculiarly his own. His work makes severe demands upon all the powers and resources of the soul. The results from his labors are largely intangible: "One sows and another reaps" (John 4:37). Paul said, "I planted, Apollos watered, but God

[9] Quoted by Gerald Kennedy, *With Singleness of Heart* (New York: Harper & Brothers, 1951), p. 15.

gave the growth." (I Cor. 3:6.) But most of the growth often comes after both the minister who sowed and the one who watered have passed on. No person can sustain his efforts easily when he knows there is little chance of gathering the fruits of those efforts.

From the very beginning a minister realizes he must live on a relatively modest salary determined largely by the ability and willingness of churches to pay, and only to a small degree by diligent efforts to merit more remuneration. He is an idealist in a starkly realistic world that is often hostile and indifferent, and always resistant and unpliable. He deals with undependable human beings who seem at times incapable of being permanently Christianized or of holding their moral gains. "With the Lord one day is as a thousand years, and a thousand years as one day" (II Pet. 3:8) and God can afford to wait. But the preacher is incapable of viewing the world with God's awful patience. For all these reasons he is especially susceptible to impatience, discouragement, frustration, and disillusionment.

To avoid growing weary in well doing and giving up in despair or disgust, he needs all the inner resources he can command or muster. There is no human reservoir on which to draw either in himself or others. Nothing suffices except the undergirding, the reinforcement, that can come only from God. Nothing can better give needed daily sustenance than the feeling one is doing the work to which God has called him, has answered the call, has committed himself to it for life, that it is God's work, and therefore he cannot fail. Daily he needs the reassuring word from God: "Be steadfast, immovable, always abounding in the work of the Lord, knowing that in the Lord your labor is not in vain" (I Cor. 15:58).

Professor Bliss Perry once said that Harvard University was paying him for doing what he would gladly pay for the privilege of doing if only he could afford it. Ministers who are sure of God's call feel that way about their work. Samuel A. Moffett, for twenty-nine years a missionary in Korea, used to say to his five sons, all of whom ultimately went into the ministry, "Don't become a minister if you can possibly help it." Fortunately most ministers could not help going into the ministry. They do not want to be doing anything else. They would choose the ministry

65

again if they were once more young and faced with the necessity of choosing a life's work.

Such is the significance of the preacher's call. Without that call, the faith back of it, and a full acceptance of all implied in it, he cannot hope to preach at his best, move others to believe the gospel to which he has dedicated his life, perform his work to its maximum efficiency, and keep going to the full extent of his potentialities to the end.

His Joy and Satisfaction in His Work

One more thing is needed. After a person has heard the call to preach, committed himself to it for life, and entrusted the outcome to God, he ought to enjoy preaching. Much is being said now about laymen making their vocations Christian. Preachers also need to do some serious thinking about how to engage in their vocations in a Christian manner. A person can engage in a work as distinctly Christian as that of the ministry in an unchristian spirit. Every preacher ought to ask himself: Can a person really be fully Christian in the practice of his vocation unless he finds genuine satisfaction in it?

Jesus was the most joyful person who ever lived, even when he knew he was going to the cross. Within a few hours of his crucifixion he said to his disciples, "These things I have spoken to you, that my joy may be in you, and that your joy may be full" (John 15:11). New Testament Christians literally radiated joy in their work, even rejoiced "that they were counted worthy to suffer dishonor for the name" (Acts 5:41). Can a preacher perform his work in the spirit of Christ and of the early Christians unless he also radiates joy?

> Work done grudgingly is servitude.
> Work done willingly is service.
> Work done lovingly is a sacrament.[10]

A preacher's work should be not only his way of serving both God and man, but his way of finding satisfaction in living. In it he should find his full share of the abundant life promised by Christ. His highest reward is not what he does for God through his work but what God does for him through it. Did not Paul say, "I do it all for the sake of the gospel, that I may *share in its*

[10] From *Today*, September, 1933.

blessings"? (I Cor. 9:23.) The joy one gets out of his daily work is one strong proof that he is engaged in a divinely appointed calling. James Barrie used to insist, "Nothing is really work unless you would rather be doing something else." If a preacher had rather be doing something else, if his work produces only boredom, it is time for him to question the validity of his call.

Many people in all walks of life have learned that the delight they take in their work is a sign it is what they are best fitted for, *their* vocation. Louis Agassiz, the naturalist, glowed with enthusiasm, beamed with joy, when he was lecturing on his favorite subjects. Joseph Jefferson, the noted actor, claimed he received back in full measure from his audiences all he gave them in inspiration and artistic effort. Even though the particular play was one he had been acting in for thirty or more years, he always came off the stage refreshed instead of exhausted. Someone asked a locomotive engineer if, after several decades, he still liked his job. He replied: "I could never be happy at any other kind of work. I confess that it has almost as much fascination for me now as it had when I was a lad playing hooky and begging engineers to let me ride with them." When a metalsmith was thanked for his work on some beautiful wrought-iron gates, he responded: "My work is a satisfying destiny. I take great delight in shaping metal into pleasing forms like poetry." Speaking of his own profession, J. B. Priestly, the British writer, said writers must be fascinated by the art itself, "engrossed," "spellbound." Surely preachers should be able to say: "I know from the joy I experience in it that it is God's work for me, my Christian vocation."

Most of us have to fight to achieve an enthusiastic attitude toward our work. Paul said, "I have *learned*, in whatever state I am, to be content." (Phil. 4:11.) He had to learn it: it was not a natural endowment nor was it achieved overnight. A few verses previously in this same letter he admitted he had not "already obtained" or already become "perfect," and that he was still pressing "on toward the goal." (3:12-14.) That was written near the end of his life. Not a great while before that he urged the Ephesians to "put on the whole armor of God" to equip themselves for the fight that goes on within the soul. (6:10 ff.) We may be certain he was referring as much to his own inner struggles as to the struggles of others. If a preacher must wrestle with himself to achieve Paul's state of mind concerning his work, let him enter the fray with enthusiasm. The fight will be worth it to him and to his total ministry. If he wins, his parishioners will detect it in his manner of preaching and reflect it in their favorable response to his sermons.

SUGGESTED READING

Baxter, B. B. *The Heart of the Yale Lectures.* New York: The Macmillan Co., 1947. Introd. and Part I.

Davison, F. E. *I Would Do It Again.* St. Louis: The Bethany Press, 1948.

Gresham, Perry E. *Disciplines of the High Calling.* St. Louis: The Bethany Press, 1954.

Guffin, Gilbert L. *Called of God.* New York: Fleming H. Revell Co., 1951.

Kennedy, Gerald. *With Singleness of Heart.* New York: Harper & Brothers, 1951.

Macgregor, W. M. *The Making of a Preacher.* Philadelphia. Westminster Press, 1946.

Neill, Stephen C. *Fulfill Thy Ministry.* New York: Harper & Brothers, 1952.

Sangster, W. E. *The Approach to Preaching.* Philadelphia: Westminster Press, 1952.

Spann, J. Richard, ed. *The Ministry.* New York and Nashville: Abingdon Press, 1949. Parts I and III.

PART II

PLANNING THE SERMON

4. Taking the Initial Steps

When one faces the necessity of actually producing a sermon, where does he begin? What are the first steps?

THE IDEA

The first thing he needs, of course, is an idea. The exact point where a sermon originates is where the idea first occurs. Harold Blake Walker tells of asking Bertita Harding how she went about writing a book. "Well," she replied, "it is like the old man's description of his recipe for rabbit pie: 'You makes your dough, mixes the makin's, cooks it in the oven till it's brown, but not too brown—but first you catches your rabbit.'"[1] Before one begins the preparation of a sermon he must catch the idea it is supposed to develop. Sermon ideas are often spoken of as "seed thoughts" or "germ sermons." Throughout his preaching ministry one needs a continuous supply of these ideas coming along like the conveyer belt of a factory assembly line.

For the most part these ideas come while they are not being sought, a process known as serendipity. Webster's dictionary defines serendipity as, "The gift of finding valuable or agreeable things not sought for; . . . coined by Walpole, in allusion to a tale, *The Three Princes of Serendip*, who in their travels were always discovering, by chance or sagacity, things they did not seek." If, as they journey through life, preachers are as alert as the princes, they will find most of their ideas for sermons while they are engaged in things other than sermonizing. James Russell Lowell once said:

> I wait for subjects that hunt me,
> By day or night won't let me be.[2]

[1] Monday Morning, Oct. 9, 1944.
[2] From "A Familiar Epistle to a Friend."

Many of the best sermon ideas are not sought after: they search out the preacher.

Where do they come from? From here, there, and everywhere. A large share of them come while one is reading. Many appear suddenly when one is moving about, mixing and mingling with people. Some flash into the mind as one is looking up the derivation of words. Now and then the line of a poem or the title of a book suggests a subject. Occasionally a letter or conversation revealing someone's personal problem provokes the seed thought for a sermon. If you wish to see the varied ways in which ideas for sermons come to others, check rapidly through several volumes of sermons by different preachers and read the introductions only. Introductions frequently reveal how sermons were first suggested.

Someone is reported to have wished for a "homiletical self-starter." The preacher's only self-starter is his alertness at finding ideas from his daily activities. Whittier said that in his early youth, through reading volumes of Burns's poems, he found out that

the things out of which poems come were not, as I had always imagined, somewhere away off in a world and life lying outside the edge of our own New Hampshire sky—they were right here about my feet and among the people I knew. The common things of our common life I found were full of poetry.[3]

Wise and fortunate is the preacher who early in his ministry learns that sermons come from the common things of ordinary life about him.

> The poem hangs on the berry bush
> When comes the poet's eye;
> The street begins to masquerade
> When Shakespeare passes by.[4]

All preaching may properly be called "idea preaching," since every sermon must contain an idea or truth. But sometimes the term "idea preaching" is used to describe the use of clever, catchy topics for sermons. This sort of preaching has its advantages.

---

[3] Quoted by John A. Kern, in *The Ministry to the Congregation*, p. 219.
[4] From "We See as We Are" by William Channing Gannett. Used by permission.

One should always be on the alert for fresh and interesting ideas or topics for sermons. Willard L. Sperry used to say that preaching in a college chapel where attendance is compulsory is a modern form of being thrown to the lions. Preaching regularly to the same congregation can be almost as hazardous because regular listeners become more or less sermon hardened. Utilizing arresting ideas for sermons prevents monotony both to preacher and people, surprises the hearers with new approaches to old truths, even "stabs their spirits broad awake" with unusual thoughts.

But continuous preaching on novel ideas has its dangers. Anyone who does too much of it runs the risk of becoming fascinated with the search for clever ideas and of overlooking solid Christian thinking. As exciting pleasures call for still more novel methods to provide the excitement, so ingenious ideas call for still more and more ingenious ideas to sustain interest in the search. The pursuer of such ideas may find himself sitting in an easy chair dreaming up fantastic ideas far removed from real life. Congregations tire of sermons that are too clever. A careful check of volumes of sermons by leading preachers of our times reveals that they use relatively few sermons of this type. This is not because these men are dull, old fashioned, unwilling to learn up-to-date and more interesting methods, but because they realize this method of sermonizing all too quickly reaches a point of diminishing returns.

One can avoid these dangers to a large extent by taking three steps shortly after the idea strikes him.

1. **Decide on the exact truth the idea contains.** No matter how brilliant the idea, it needs to be brought down to earth in the form of a specific truth that can be related closely to life.

2. **State clearly in a brief sentence, and in terms of definite human needs, the purpose of the sermon intended to embody the idea.** Henry Sloane Coffin for years wrote at the top of the first page of every sermon under preparation, "I wish and am required in this sermon to. . . ." One is not likely to get too far from reality if he writes out a brief statement of the precise purpose to be achieved by a sermon before he plans it in detail.

3. **Find a suitable passage from the Bible on which to base the sermon.** A Scottish professor of homiletics used to say to his

classes, "Every sermon should begin in Jerusalem and end in Aberdeen, or begin in Aberdeen and end in Jerusalem." He meant by this that if a sermon begins with a Bible text, it should come quickly to the needs of the people in the parish; and if it begins with a human situation in the community, it should go quickly to a truth of the Bible.

The ability to think of fitting texts develops from a careful, lifelong study of the Bible. By a hasty, frantic, last-moment search through the Bible with the help of a concordance, one cannot expect often to find an appropriate biblical basis for a sermon. R. W. Dale relates an amusing and pathetic story of a minister in England preparing a sermon on some words he supposed to be in the book of Proverbs. At the last minute before leaving for the church on Sunday morning, he decided he should be sure of the exact source of his text. He searched hurriedly through Proverbs but could not find it. He turned to his concordance but still could not locate it. When he began his sermon he said, somewhat nonchalantly, "You will remember, my friends, the words of the wisest of kings," and proceeded with the sermon. Later he discovered, somewhat to his dismay, that the words came from one of the prayers in the Anglical *Book of Common Prayer*.[5] The only way to avoid some such farce as this is so to saturate mind and memory with the contents of the Bible that texts to fit ideas will leap out upon call whenever an idea for a sermon strikes.

A few examples will make clear the procedures suggested. A preacher read in the *Reader's Digest* that a mother said of her daughter, "She is a good girl, but she is constantly majoring in minors." Reflecting a moment or two upon the expression "majoring in minors," he thought of what Jesus said to the scribes and Pharisees, "You blind guides, straining out a gnat and swallowing a camel" (Matt. 23:24). In due time he developed a sermon on "Majoring in Minors," an appeal to give one's major attention to the primary rather than to the secondary things in life.

One preacher came across the expression "the advantage of disadvantages" in the autobiography of Booker T. Washington, *Up From Slavery*. He immediately recalled what Paul wrote to

[5] *Nine Lectures on Preaching,* p. 125.

the church at Corinth: "I will stay in Ephesus until Pentecost, for a wide door for effective work has opened to me, and there are many adversaries" (I Cor. 16:8-9). A sermon on "Opportunity and Opposition" was soon on its way.

A preacher heard the president of a large state university give the members of a graduating class the statistics showing what each of them had cost the state, and then ask, "Are you going to be worth what you cost?" The minister wrote on his program a possible sermon subject, "Are you worth what you cost?" with a possible text: "You are not your own; you were bought with a price" (I Cor. 6:19-20). This was the beginning of a future sermon. Another minister heard the refrain of a song coming over the radio:

> Ac-cent-tchu ate the positive.
> Eliminate the negative.
> Latch on to the affirmative.[6]

He recalled two famous chapters in Carlyle's *Sartor Resartus*, "The Everlasting No" and "The Everlasting Yea"; at the same time he remembered Paul's words: "For the Son of God, Jesus Christ, whom we preached among you . . . was not Yes and No; but in him it is always Yes" (II Cor. 1:19). Out of this emerged a sermon on "Affirmative Living."

Looking up the derivation of the word "hypocrite" so frequently on the lips of Jesus, a preacher discovered it originated in the Greek theater. In classical Greek it meant "actor." Since most actors in those days wore masks, it meant literally "a mask-wearer." Taken over into the common language, it was applied to a pretender, someone acting a part. Applied to religion it means one who keeps up the appearances of religion on the outside while his heart is far from God. This ultimately led to a sermon on "Staging Religion."

The Text

The custom of using texts for sermons is as old as Christianity. Jesus used passages from the Jewish scriptures as the basis of his sermons, as did Paul and other New Testament preachers. Dur-

---

[6] Used by permission of the copyright owner, Edwin H. Morris & Company, Inc.

ing the early and middle medieval times, when preaching was in decline, the use of texts fell into disfavor. But preceding the Reformation the custom of using texts was revived and has continued unabated now for some six or seven hundred years. In 1945, Hugh T. Kerr, Jr., made a survey of more than 1,500 sermons that appeared in *The Pulpit* during the previous ten years and found slightly more than 200 without texts. This would seem to indicate that the use of texts is still highly favored by most contemporary Protestant preachers.

The word "text" has come to mean a single verse of scripture announced at the outset of a sermon. This gives the word a somewhat narrow meaning. In the broader and more correct sense it means the biblical passage on which the sermon is based. In that sense a sermon can be based on scripture—saturated with it, in fact—without having an announced text. Some sermons have two or more texts from widely separated portions of the Bible. Some are based on all the facts about a biblical character, or on a whole book of the Bible, or on a long passage of the Bible. So perhaps the word should be thought of in its wider meaning of "biblical basis."

The primary reasons for using texts are not, as some say, to give the preacher a right to speak, or merely to lend biblical respectability to what he says. The reasons lie much deeper and are as follows.

The Bible is the original source of our knowledge of the gospel. Our Christian faith and practice and the Christian church are based upon the original witness in the changeless historical documents of the New Testament. Those documents are forever the standard for what the gospel is and therefore the primary source of sermons intended to proclaim it.

The gospel cannot be understood apart from its antecedents. Christ emerged at the end of a series of historical events extending over some fifteen hundred years. Those events prepared the way for his coming. So Paul could say, "When the time had fully come, God sent forth his Son." (Gal. 4:4.) The New Testament cannot be understood except as the fulfillment of the Old. Christ began his public ministry with the announcement, "The time is fulfilled, and the kingdom of God is at hand" (Mark 1:15). Christ believed he was bringing to completion God's redemptive acts in the history of his people, that his teach-

74

ing was an interpretation of the meaning of the Jewish scriptures, that his ministry was a fulfillment of both the Law and the Prophets and his death the fulfillment of the ancient sacrificial system. Over and over in the New Testament it is said that things were happening that the scriptures "might be fulfilled." The Apostolic church preached this, not only to the Jews but to the Gentiles. No one in any age or place can grasp the true meaning of the gospel without coming to it through the Old Testament. Simply because the Old Testament prepared the way for the gospel, it became an integral part of that gospel. Both testaments are, therefore, indispensable for Christian preaching.

The Bible contains the truth and the experiential processes by which the truth became known. Christian preachers need to have an empirical background for what they preach. The historical processes by which the truth is arrived at are essential for its understanding. Those processes and the truth are both found in the Bible. Texts of scripture, therefore, provide the preacher with a long perspective of human experience as the basis for sermons, with an empirical background for what he has to say.

The Bible offers a wide range of moral, religious, and social truths. The Bible contains every type of human sin, of human problem, and of human situation, as well as every kind of virtue and of resource essential for handling them. There are no new sins and no new virtues. There are only new ways of committing old sins and of practicing old virtues. There are no new social problems, but only new social situations in which the same age-old problems arise in different forms. There are no new moral and spiritual needs. People the world over, generation after generation, require the same inner resources.

Anne Morrow Lindbergh, speaking of certain Bible stories, said: "They are so simple that they are like empty cups for people to fill with their own experiences and drink for their own need over and over again through the years." The fact that biblical stories can be filled with the experiences of people in every new generation makes the Bible a perennial book. The preacher can be sure that material taken from it as the basis of sermons will always be fresh, will never grow old.

The Bible may also be thought of as a mirror which the preacher holds before each person so that each may see in the men and women who come and go across its pages, the weaknesses and the strengths, the virtues and the vices, the sins and the shortcomings, the various moods and tricky emotions, of which he also is capable. The social, political, economic, and religious problems which the Jews faced from century to century are mirrors in which the people of our generation may see their own social struggles and conflicts, their corporate blunders and injustices, their risings and fallings, their successes and failures, the messing up of their lives and the lives of their children unto many generations.

So, the Bible is not only the authoritative source of Christianity itself but the authoritative source of all Christian instruction and preaching. By basing a sermon on scripture the preacher is in effect saying, "What I have to say is not my opinion but the revealed truth of God."

The Bible provides a variety and an inexhaustible supply of interesting ideas for sermons. By using them a minister can keep from making the common mistake of undertaking too much in any one sermon and can avoid unnecessary anxiety over what to preach about. James Black tells how, in the early part of his ministry, he tried to treat every subject exhaustively. At the end of a few months he had not only exhausted all he knew but had exhausted himself in the process. Then he discovered he had an unlimited supply of varied and fresh ideas if he were only content to preach from single passages of scripture. He added: "In attempting to crush a whole subject into one sermon, I was only attempting the impossible, spoiling the subject by unnatural compression . . . and ruining my own peace of nerves." [7]

When analyzed, the objections to the use of texts usually turn out to be objections to the abuses of the method rather than to the method itself. The preacher's primary problem, then, is to learn how to use the method properly and to avoid its abuses. To assist in doing this a list of principles for using texts will now be given.

1. Make sure the text is a genuine passage of scripture and properly translated. Quite a few sermons have been preached on texts that do not belong in the Bible, or that do not mean what preachers thought they meant. The recent Revised Standard Version of the Bible is making it necessary for some preachers

[7] Op. cit., pp. 152-53.

to discard some old sermons, or else find different texts for them. For example, the old version translates Prov. 29:18, "Where there is no vision, the people perish" (or "cast off restraint," A.S.V.). Many sermons emphasizing the necessity of having great purposes, ideals, and social dreams, have been preached on this text. The Revised Standard Version translates it, "Where there is no *prophecy* the people cast off restraint." Prov. 23:7a, translated in the American Standard Version, "For as he thinketh within himself, so is he," reads in the Revised Standard Version, "For he is like one who is inwardly reckoning." Another text will have to be sought for sermons on the importance of what takes place in the mind. One minister of my acquaintance tells of having preached a sermon several times at different places on I Cor. 6:9, "The . . . *effeminate* . . . shall not inherit the kingdom of God." He used the word "effeminate" in its general meaning of the soft, the pliable, those who take the easy road. To his amazement and chagrin he discovered upon reading the text in the R.S.V. that "effeminate" is translated "homosexuals." Before a text is used, recent versions of the Bible, the commentaries, and, if possible, the original language ought to be checked to be sure of its proper translation.

2. *Make the truth of the text the theme of the sermon.* Willard L. Sperry once declared that the use of a Bible passage as a point of departure is "one of the most deadening devices handed down from the past." [8] A careful distinction needs to be made here between using the text as a *point of departure* and using it as a *point of development.* In one sense the text is used as a point of departure in all topical sermons. That is, the text is given and its truth identified and explained, after which it is more or less laid aside, although it may be referred to now and then as the sermon progresses. Even so, the points of the sermon, though the preacher's own, are definitely based on the truth in the text. This could accurately be called using the text as a point of development.

Using the text as a point of departure is attaching it loosely to the sermon, perhaps after the sermon is finished, so that neither it nor its precise truth plays an important part in the unfolding of the sermon. This is what Spurgeon once spoke of as preachers

* *Op. cit.,* p. 115.

"touching their hats, as it were, to that part of scripture," and passing on—using the text as a courteous gesture to scripture. A modern professor of homiletics refers to it as "jacking up topical sermons and running texts in under them." [9] Donald Miller calls it using the text as a self-starter for one's own thoughts, which, like the starter on a car, "immediately drops out of the picture the moment the motor begins to run." [10]

The connection between the theme and the text should be clear and unmistakable. The text should be chosen before the sermon is prepared, and the sermon should be built around the truth in the text. If the truth of the text and the theme of the sermon do not harmonize, another text with the appropriate truth should be found, or another sermon on the truth contained in the text should be prepared.

3. Use the text in its original, natural meaning. Unfortunately the Bible has been grievously misinterpreted and misused by some Christian preachers in every generation. The ways by which this is done may be roughly grouped together under the heading "accommodating scripture." The scripture is adjusted to the meaning of the sermon instead of the sermon being adjusted to the meaning of the scripture. There are so many ways of doing this and so many degrees of accommodation, it is not easy to classify them. But some of the more glaring ways of doing it will be listed so they may serve as a warning and possibly as a deterrent.

a) *Lifting a few words completely out of a sentence and building a sermon on them without any reference to their original meaning.* Spurgeon once took as a text Isa. 43:6, "I will say to the north, Give up; and to the south, Keep not back" (A.V.). This was the simple promise of God to bring his people back from captivity in countries both to the north and to the south. Spurgeon lifted the words "give up" and "keep not back" out of the sentence and used them to make two points: (1) the things people ought to give up; and (2) the corresponding things they should not keep back. T. DeWitt Talmage lifted the word "needle," mentioned by Jesus in Matt. 19:24, completely out of

---

[9] John C. Irwin, "Some Thoughts on Biblical Preaching," *The Pulpit*, September, 1952.

[10] *Fire in Thy Mouth*, pp. 37-38.

the sentence and used it for a sermon on "Martyrs of the Needle," the half-starved women in the sweatshops of New York who made their meager living by using their needles. A preacher needing a text for a sermon in honor of the tailors in the congregation finally found it: "A remnant shall be saved" (Rom. 9:27 A.V.).

A modern preacher took as his text the first four words of the sentence spoken by Jesus: "Look at the birds of the air: they neither sow nor reap nor gather into barns, and yet your heavenly Father feeds them. Are you not of more value than they?" (Matt. 6:26.) Ignoring the reason why Jesus referred to the birds, he invited his congregation to think with him in general about birds. First he asked, "What is it about birds that endears them to the human heart?" He answered, "Why, because they sing, of course." Then he asked, "But why do they sing?" His answer to that question gave him his subject, "Why Birds Sing," and the points of his sermon. They sing, he said, because they know a fourfold secret: (1) They are created to sing; (2) They are in love with life; (3) They are in love with one another; (4) They have wings. All of this was duly applied to human beings.[11] This is very lovely and quite true. But note: he detached words from a sentence and gave them a meaning foreign to what Jesus had in mind when he used them.

The mere existence of a word in the Bible does not justify its extraction from a sentence and its use for any and every purpose desired by the preacher, irrespective of what it meant in the original sentence. No one would think of using the words and phrases of any other book in this fashion. This way of misusing the Bible was one thing that provoked Vinet to say, "No human book has . . . been so tortured and sported with as Holy Scripture."

b) Using a text merely to start the imagination off on a tangent. T. DeWitt Talmage read in Exod. 38:8 that a part of the furnishings for the tabernacle were made "from the mirrors of the ministering women." The word "mirror" stimulated his imagination to think of how a mirror reflects the features of those who use it. Then he began to think of how the gospel might be

---

[11] Hobart D. McKeehan, *Life's Golden Hours* (New York: Fleming H. Revell Co., 1946), p. 79 ff.

compared to a mirror. Finally he came out with a sermon on "How the Gospel Reflects the Moral Features of Man." A modern preacher got a clever sermon out of "Show me a coin" (Luke 20:24), the words of Jesus to those who were trying to get him to commit himself on the controversial subject of whether it was lawful to pay taxes to Rome. As soon as the idea of the coin's being placed in Jesus' hand occurred to him, the preacher began to meditate upon the *touch* of Jesus. He then imagined that someone found an old coin that proved to be the coin Jesus *touched* that day. The preacher said to himself: How many people would seek to touch it, or kiss it, merely because Jesus had touched it! The value of that coin would be raised manyfold because of the divine touch of Jesus! So he arrived at his subject "Raised Values," which he developed by five ways in which Jesus raises the value of what he touches in our lives.[12] Exercising "a moderate amount of exegetical sleight of hand," or "a little perverse ingenuity," [13] in this way enables anyone to make any passage yield any meaning he chooses.

c) *Using "eisegesis" instead of "exegesis" to interpret a passage.* "Eisegesis" is reading one's own ideas *into* (eis) a passage, whereas "exegesis" is bringing *out* (ex) the real meaning of the passage. Herrick Johnson tells of a minister who drew from Jacob's crossing his arms over two of Joseph's children when he blessed them (Gen. 48:13-14) the subject "There Is No Blessing but Under the Cross." [14] Many of the doctrines of Christianity have been read into Old Testament passages by the simple process of interpreting them metaphorically. Howard Chandler Robbins tells of a clergyman who was able, from whatever text he preached, to educe the five points of Calvinism. One Sunday morning he took for his text II Sam. 9:13, "So Mephibosheth dwelt in Jerusalem; for he did eat continually at the king's table. And he was lame in both his feet" (A.S.V.). These were his five points: (1) The lameness of Mephibosheth indicated *natural human depravity;* (2) That he was lame in both feet signified *total depravity;* (3) His dwelling at Jerusalem meant *justification;* (4) His eating at the king's table meant *adoption;* (5) His eating there continually indicated the *final perseverance of the saints.*

[12] *Ibid.,* p. 49 ff.

[13] John A. Kern's expressions.

[14] *The Ideal Ministry* (New York: Fleming H. Revell Co., 1908), p. 49.

Robbins added, "It is written that 'the king spared Mephibosheth'; one wishes that preachers would do the same." [15] R. W. Dale said when he watched preachers developing doctrines and interesting speculations from texts by this process he was always reminded of the tricks of a conjurer.

d) *Breaking texts into fragments.* Bishop Wilberforce, visiting a parish, asked the curate, "What have you been preaching on?" The curate answered, "Hear the church." The Bishop thought a moment and said, "But there is no such text in the Bible." The curate replied, "Surely, my Lord: If any man will not hear the church." Whereupon the Bishop remarked, "Well, I will give you another for next Sunday: Hang all the Law and the Prophets." A preacher addressing an audience of newspaper reporters used as his text, what was said of Zacchaeus, "He sought to see Jesus who he was; and could not for the press" (Luke 19:3 A.V.).

In a half humorous but deadly serious article in *Harper's Magazine*, May, 1929, entitled "How to Preach a Sermon," Frederick Lewis Allen said:

Let us begin with the text. Not that the text really matters. Any competent parson can arrive at any conclusion from any text. . . . In fact, I have known ministers so expert in finding their way from point to point that when they announced their texts groups of worshippers, who at once laid modest bets among themselves on the probable topic of the forthcoming sermon, would all be so completely wrong that the cash in the pool would have to be assigned to either the Church's Work at Home or to Missionary Endeavor.

Handling the sentences of the Bible as though they could be stopped at any point and made to yield any meaning has made sermonizing ridiculous in the eyes of many thoughtful people.

e) *Allegorizing texts.* This is the "art" of bringing out hidden spiritual meanings in what at first look like ordinary statements. Hence it is sometimes spoken of as "spiritualizing" scripture. Many preachers become fascinated with it and seem to think that interpreting the Scriptures means searching for veiled meanings hidden from ordinary readers. One man preached a sermon, entitled "Youth's Goliath and Five Smooth Stones," based upon the

---

[15] *Preaching the Gospel* (New York: Harper & Brothers, 1939), p. 14.

five smooth stones David picked up out of the brook, put in his bag, and later used in his sling to kill the giant" (I Sam. 17: 40). He suggested that modern youth store away in their lives the following five stones: (1) quiet self-confidence, (2) acceptance of self, (3) ability to earn the confidence of others, (4) unselfish devotion to something beyond oneself, (5) faith in God.[16] A preacher used Acts 27:27 (A.S.V.), "The sailors surmised that they were drawing near to some country," as the text for an Easter sermon on "The Undiscovered Country." [17] He accomplished this by treating the unknown country they were approaching as a symbol of the heavenly country.

One common type of allegorizing is that of overworking, or straining and forcing, the interpretation of a simile or metaphor. John A. Kern reports a sermon on Isa. 64:6, "We all fade like a leaf." Asking how leaves fade, the preacher arrived at a five-point outline. Leaves fade (1) gradually, (2) silently, (3) differently, (4) characteristically, (5) preparedly.[18] Allegories perform useful functions but are better suited for children's stories than for sermons for adults. Only an experienced minister can do them well, and wise ministers use them seldom. If used too often they open the door to unnatural, mechanical, and fanciful comparisons.

Samuel Butler spoke of the "irritating habit of theologians and preachers telling little lies in the interest of a great truth." To twist a text to make it fit a sermon, or to break it into fragments, or to read into it unnaturally something that is not there, or otherwise to accommodate the scripture to the message, no matter how true the message, impresses lay folk as being unethical and an unworthy use of the Book that is the source of our Christian faith. There is little justification for mishandling texts in these ways, since there are literally hundreds of texts that need no accommodating to make them yield their truths.

4. Use "textual" sermons sparingly. As here used "textual" is a technical word to describe a particular form of sermon structure. In a textual sermon the points of the discussion are found

[16] See *The Pulpit*, June, 1947.

[17] See G. G. Atkins, *The Undiscovered Country* (New York: Fleming H. Revell Co., 1922), p. 13.

[18] *Op. cit.*, p. 287.

in the text itself. In a topical sermon a text is used, but the points are devised by the minister after due reflection. Mic. 6:8, "He has showed you, O man, what is good; and what does the Lord require of you but to do justice, and to love kindness, and to walk humbly with your God?" is an example of a text that lends itself naturally to the "textual" treatment. It states clearly three things that may become the three points of the outline. Isa. 40:31 is another example of a suitable text for a "textual" sermon. William P. Merrill once used it for a sermon on "The Practical Value of Religion." He had three points as follows: (1) "They shall mount up with wings like eagles"—strength for keeping up ideals; (2) "They shall run and not be weary"—strength for meeting crisis; (3) "They shall walk and not faint"—strength for the daily routine.[19] Someone has estimated that it would be difficult, however, to find in the whole Bible a hundred texts suitable for textual treatment.

Handling most texts in this manner readily becomes more or less artificial and tends to develop into what James S. Stewart called a form of "textual vivisection." An illustration of this is Spurgeon's sermon on Mark 10:45 (A.V.) which he divided as follows: (1) "The Son of Man"—humanity; (2) "Came"—antecedent existence; (3) "Not to be ministered unto"—vicarious life; (4) "But to minister, and to give his life a ransom"—vicarious death; (5) "For many"—amplitude.[20] Vinet used to say that ministers are supposed to "develop rather than to decompose the text." Much so-called textual preaching consists of taking passages apart rather than expounding them.

Mechanically carving up a sentence of the Bible and expatiating on the meaning of each separate word or phrase in this manner is one thing that provokes public caricatures of preachers every few years. Some years ago "Chic" Sale, a noted vaudeville actor, used to convulse his audiences with laughter and provoke extended applause by his sermon on "Old Mother Hubbard." He overemphasized the significance of the separate words and phrases of the nursery rhyme in precisely the way some ministers treat their texts, and he also mimicked their delivery. Among the

[19] See C. W. Ferguson, *The Great Themes of the Christian Faith* (New York: R. R. Smith, 1930), pp. 107 ff.

[20] See A. W. Blackwood, *The Preparation of Sermons* (New York and Nashville: Abingdon Press, 1948), pp. 60-61.

phonographic records, a similar thing is done in a current best seller entitled "It's in the Book," the use of "Little Bo Peep" as the text of a sermon that makes sport of the unnatural way in which preachers treat their texts. Such imitations come regularly enough and attract attention enough to be taken seriously by preachers. We are engaged in the solemn business of "rightly handling the word of truth" so as not to be ashamed of our workmanship (II Tim. 2:15). We should be ashamed of proclaiming the gospel of Christ in a way that causes us to be laughed out of court by even a handful of our congregations.

THE SUBJECT

After the idea and the text for the sermon get together it is time to begin thinking of a subject.

The purposes of a subject mainly are three: (1) to define and limit the discussion for the preacher, (2) to focus the attention of the hearer, (3) to keep both the preacher and the hearer on the track. By some the subject is spoken of as a "magnet" to keep one on the track, and by others as the "focus," the "axis," or the "orbit" of the sermon.

Some writers call the heading of a sermon the subject, while others call it the topic, or the title. There are technical distinctions which apply to these three terms. "Subject" is the word for the broad, general field to be discussed. "Topic" indicates more specifically the particular phase to be discussed. "Title" is a label intended primarily to arouse curiosity and attract attention. All of these are to be distinguished from the "theme" or "thesis" or "proposition," as it is variously called by different writers. The theme is the gist of the sermon in one sentence.

Two examples will make clear the distinction among these four terms. Here is one for college students given by Roy C. McCall: (1) Subject—"Fraternities"; (2) Topic—"The Abolition of Fraternities"; (3) Thesis—"Fraternities should be abolished"; (4) Title—"Out with the Greeks." [21] Here is an example specifically for preachers: (1) Subject—"Scapegoats"; (2) Topic—"The Modern Practice of Using Scapegoats"; (3) Thesis—"You cannot get rid of your sins by making someone or something else a scapegoat for them"; (4) Title—"Passing the Buck."

[21] *The Fundamentals of Speech*, p. 25. Copyright 1949 by The Macmillan Co. and used by their permission.

The ideal way to state a subject is to make it the actual theme or thesis of the sermon and to make it coextensive with the text. This ideal is difficult to attain without making the subject too long and involved, because the theme should be a complete sentence. But a theme properly stated does set forth adequately the specific truth in the text that the sermon proposes to discuss. Whether or not the theme is used as the actual subject of the sermon, it should be clearly formulated before the preparation of the sermon begins, should appear for the hearers in some form in the introduction, and should guide the structural development of the sermon.

Ordinarily a "subject" is too broad and needs definitely to be limited for purposes of discussion. "Titles" are usually the most arresting and intriguing to the listener. But many titles give not the slightest hint of what the preacher is going to talk about and to that extent are confusing. They also can easily become sensational. Probably most sermon subjects are and should be "topics." A topic can assume a variety of lengths and forms and at the same time can be striking without being sensational. Whatever its form, the heading should suggest what the preacher is going to talk about. To announce a subject and not talk about it or to announce one subject and treat another, both are misleading. If either is done deliberately it is obviously unethical. If done unintentionally it indicates a carelessness that can only be called "slob" work. Such workmanship is unworthy of the minister's high calling.

In form the statement of the subject should be as striking concise, comprehensive, and simple as possible. All verbiage should be discarded. The briefer it is the better. There are two basic rules to be kept constantly in mind while drafting a subject. First, vary the types of subjects. Do this deliberately as a matter of policy to keep out of a rut. Second, before settling definitely upon the form, experiment with drafting the subject in several different ways. Express the same idea, first as a question, and then as a declaration, either positive or negative. Put it down in the form of a technical "subject," then of a "topic," then of a "title."

The first idea for a subject that occurs is likely not to be the most interesting or arresting. The exact wording, therefore, should not be arrived at too hurriedly. A good practice is to draft the subject in several possible forms and then try them out on various

85

people, e.g., one's wife or the members of the church staff. Allow the matter to rest for a while before making the final choice. A short delay in which the subconscious mind is given a chance to work on it will often insure a more intriguing subject than if the first wording is chosen. Select words designed to provoke the listener to think of the subject in terms of his own needs. This has been called the psychological approach to drafting the subject. For example, as someone suggested, "Capitalizing our Calamities" is better than "This Troubled World." Suppose the text is Luke 14:18, "They all alike began to make excuses." "Making Excuses" would be commonplace and less likely to arrest attention than either of two subjects used by different preachers: "Of Course in My Case . . . ," and "I'm Interested, But . . ."

One needs only to read a number of volumes of current sermons every year to realize that Blackwood is right when he says that sermon subjects suffer from "sameness, tameness, and lameness." Frederick Lewis Allen was twitting ministers for their tame sermon subjects when he cited the wording on the outside bulletin board of an imaginary church: "11:00 A.M., Dr. Spilkins. 'Shall We Choose God or Mammon?' " He comments facetiously: "This will bring in crowds of people full of uncertainty as to whether you are going to come out boldly for mammon." Strive diligently on the one hand to avoid commonplace subjects and on the other to create striking subjects that will attract the attention of busy modern folk. But beware of cheap sensationalism.

SUGGESTED READING

Brooks, Phillips. *Lectures on Preaching.* New York: E. P. Dutton and Co., 1877. Pp. 108 ff.

McComb, Samuel. *Preaching in Theory and Practice.* New York: Oxford University Press, 1926. Chapter III.

Stewart, James S. *Heralds of God.* New York: Charles Scribner's Sons, 1946. Pp. 153 ff.

Practical helps on the subjects discussed in this chapter may be found mostly in textbooks on homiletics. The following textbooks, listed in the second section of the Bibliography, are especially helpful: Blackwood, Chapters III-V, VIII-IX; Breed, Part I; Kern, pp. 101 ff. and 247 ff.; Luccock, Chapters IX-XI; Phelps, Lectures I-XV, XX-XXV; and Weatherspoon, Part I.

5. Outlining the Sermon:
General Principles and Procedures

Lack of proper structure is a major weakness of many modern sermons. Too many sermons are thrown together loosely and carelessly without reference to discernible principles. They lack sequence of thought. Their purpose is vague and indistinct. Like summer lightning in New England they flash all over the sky but never strike anywhere. This chapter and the next will deal with the question of structure. Edwin Markham said that the impolite are the best teachers of good manners. By the same token, the best teachers of proper outlining are sometimes those who do it poorly. How to do outlining and how not to do it will both be pointed out, in order to discover some patterns worthy of imitation, some methods by which to judge outlines, and some principles on which to construct them.

What follows in this and the next few chapters may strike the reader as being mechanical. But it is not possible to analyze any skill with a view to discovering how it can best be achieved without making it sound mechanical, or at times even dogmatic. This is true of art, music, creative writing, and public speaking, to name only a few skills, as well as of preaching. The reader should, therefore, keep in mind that while we are dealing with a vital, not a mechanical, process, the limitations in a study of this nature prevent that from being evident throughout.

One preacher explained that he divided his sermons into three parts: "In the first part I tell them what I am going to tell them. In the second part I tell them. In the third part I tell them what I have told them." These three parts correspond roughly to the three main divisions of a sermon: the *Introduction*, that lets the congregation know what the sermon is about; the *Discussion*, that develops the subject; and the *Conclusion*, that in some manner drives home what has been said.

The writers in the field of homiletics generally agree that every sermon, like every public speech, ought to have these three parts, although Willard L. Sperry in his Yale Lectures on preaching objected to having anything like introductions and conclusions. The word "outline," when used in a technical sense, refers to these three main parts of the sermon. But the Discussion itself also requires a detailed outline. The correct word for this is "plan" to distinguish it from the outline proper. In popular usage, however, the word "outline" ordinarily refers to the "plan" of the discussion. This is the sense in which it will be used in the chapters on outlining.

THE NECESSITY OF AN OUTLINE

Outlining a sermon is simply a way of organizing in an orderly sequence what one wishes to say. A speech does not happen: it is designed. An effective preacher does not spray his ideas promiscuously but concentrates them on a limited area, focuses and guides them in the direction he wants them to go. This concentrating and focusing is done by means of an outline. Stephen Leacock facetiously spoke of a person mounting his horse and riding off in all directions. You cannot expect people to understand ideas fanned out in a disorderly manner to the four corners of a room. Human minds grasp ideas when they are presented in some kind of orderly sequence. That is the nature of human minds, the way they function. "Order is heaven's first law." When Paul heard prophesying and speaking in tongues in such confused manner in the early church that no one, not even the speakers, knew what was being said, he laid down a basic principle of sermonizing: "All things should be done decently and in order" (I Cor. 14:40).

Some theological students and preachers have an aversion, if not an actual contempt, for outlining. They regard it as pedantic, as fettering the free expression of a prophetic mind. One theological student is reported to have said that all this "one, two, three stuff" amounts to fiddling while Rome burns. One sometimes suspects this attitude to be a form of rationalizing, or hedging against the hard work and mental discipline involved in putting thoughts down in an orderly fashion. Nevertheless, one can sympathize with those who grow weary with stereotyped outlining. Pleading for a more direct, fresher, less systematic, and less logical approach, some of the younger members of German churches, we are told, have been objecting openly to the uninteresting way preachers have of arranging all sermons into three or four logical parts in the same stilted manner. No preacher should develop all sermons according to the same pattern. Rather, as we shall see later, he should vary the types of outlines and methods of approach as a matter of policy.

But no method of approach, however novel and intriguing, can obviate the necessity of arranging ideas in an orderly manner, if the sermon is to be understood. Beginners especially are likely to suppose that outstanding preachers whose sermons they read or hear have no outlines, because the outlines are not always apparent. But if the meaning and purpose of a sermon are perfectly clear and the trend of its thought easily followed, you can be quite sure the preacher had an outline that guided him, although it may not be discernible. When you cannot make head nor tail of a sermon you can likewise put it down that the preacher himself had no clear conception of what he intended to say or where he wanted to go.

Every successful novelist, dramatist, and short story writer follows a plot. Fielding's *Tom Jones*, said Clifton Fadiman, could be reduced to: (1) boy meets girl; (2) boy wants girl; (3) boy gets girl.[1] An author's plot may not be that simple but it is there as the skeleton of his production, clearly indicated to guide him, although it may not be evident to the reader. In his autobiography John Erskine, the novelist and professor of English, tells how in his early years he learned to write under one of his professors:

He asked us to bring a skeleton of the essay, paragraph by paragraph, each paragraph being represented by a single sentence. By the time we had shaped this outline to his satisfaction and our own, nothing remained but to fill out the paragraphs and smooth away the angularities of the frame. To this day I use no other method in preparing any piece of writing, whether short or long. . . . I do not care to begin a novel or an article before I have worked it out completely in outline. It is easy to write the first sentence when you know what the last sentence will be. I cannot estimate the amount of time I should have wasted, had I not taken that course with George Rice Carpenter.[2]

Yet the reader of Erskine's stories would not detect a carefully planned outline.

[1] Quoted by Gerald Kennedy in *His Word Through Preaching* (New York: Harper & Brothers, 1947), p. 55.
[2] *The Memory of Certain Persons*, p. 98. Copyright, 1947, by John Erskine. Used by permission of J. B. Lippincott Co.

The Advantages of an Outline

An outline is desirable for both preacher and listeners.

ADVANTAGES TO THE PREACHER

1. An outline aids the preacher in development of thought. With the outline as a guide he knows where he is headed. This prevents desultory thinking, or what Goethe once described as thoughts all running away "in a splutter." Many preachers consistently put too many ideas in one sermon and throw them together "without form and void." In a public lecture Julian Huxley remarked that a sea animal without a skeleton, undertaking motion on land, would "collapse gelatinously." Taking hold of that expression, Luccock, in his usual characteristic manner, applied it to preaching. "Who has not seen a sermon collapse gelatinously all over the church auditorium because there was no hard skeleton?" he asked. "The fear of the Lord is the beginning of wisdom in preaching, but the fear of gelatin also helps." [3] The outline confines the sermon within desired limits, controls its course, unfolds it step by step so it will be understandable, and directs it to its intended goals.

Emile Zola, when asked what progress he had made upon a projected book, pointed to a pile of manuscript and said, "It is finished!" "But that is only your syllabus," gasped his friend. "True, but the rest is merely mechanical," said Zola; "it is nothing." [4] All preachers of some years' experience will testify he was right. Once the outline is satisfactorily constructed, the hardest part of sermon preparation is over. After that the filling in is relatively easy. "Outlining is hard work," says McCall, "and few people like to do it; but it is the only road to effective speaking." [5]

2. An outline keeps the preacher on the track. James S. Stewart says:

It is quite fatal to embark on a sermon without having a plainly charted course to follow. . . . Far too many sermons wander erratically

[3] *In the Minister's Workshop* (New York and Nashville: Abingdon Press, 1944), p. 121.

[4] See John N. Booth, *The Quest for Preaching Power* (New York: The Macmillan Co., 1943), p. 44.

[5] *The Fundamentals of Speech*, p. 12. Copyright 1949 by The Macmillan Co. and used by their permission.

from one thing to another, going off at sudden tangents, perpetrating aimless involutions, anon returning upon their own tracks, moving in circles.[6]

The outline keeps one from taking detours, going around in circles, and holds him steadily on the straight road ahead.

3. An outline enables the preacher to keep the parts of the sermon in right proportion. A clearly devised outline is a reminder that no single part should be neglected and no part given disproportionate attention.

4. An outline assures the sermon of movement. If one knows where he is going he can check the outline, as on an automobile trip he consults a map, to tell whether he is moving toward his destination. And, incidentally, he will know when he gets there.

ADVANTAGES TO THE HEARERS

1. An outline enables the hearers to understand what the preacher is saying and where he is headed. They can check on where the preacher has been, where he is, and where he is going next. When a sermon is not clearly planned the hearers may realize they are having trouble following it but will not be able to locate the difficulty. An outline gives order to what is otherwise to the hearers an indistinct, loosely related mass of words, remarks, illustrations, assertions, and questions.

2. An outline prevents the hearers from misunderstanding. At times this is equally as important as their understanding what is being said. At best it is difficult for them to keep up with the preacher's line of thought. They stop a moment to assimilate, or to apply what has been said, wander off the track momentarily, lose a few words or even a sentence, get back on the track again and think they hear what in reality has not been said. If they repeat what they supposedly heard, the results, as many a preacher knows, may be embarrassing or even lead to an unpleasant public controversy. If the preacher follows an outline and indicates each point clearly and skillfully, the chances that the hearers will misunderstand are kept to a minimum.

3. An outline provides the hearers with a needed emotional rhythm. When one point is made they can pause momentarily,

* *Heralds of God,* pp. 134-35.

relax, take a breath, shift position, then settle down for the next lap of the journey. Without these occasional moments of emotional relaxation, listeners become nervously fatigued. The results are comparable to the seventh inning stretch at a baseball game. Sometimes this is spoken of as the "psychological outline" of the sermon. The human mind has distinct attention limits. The curve of attention rises and falls and should definitely be taken into consideration when the sermon is prepared.

4. An outline aids the hearers in remembering what has been said. Sometimes the outline *is* the sermon for them because that is all they take away with them. I heard one minister say to another, "When I was a young man I heard you preach a sermon I shall never forget. Although it has been thirty-five years I still remember it." The older preacher asked, "What was the sermon about and what was the text?" He said, "I cannot remember either text or subject but I distinctly recall the outline. Here it is: (1) Have you got religion? (2) Is it the catching kind? (3) Has anybody caught it from you yet?" Using the parable of the Good Samaritan for his text, Charles Reynolds Brown pointed out that it sets forth three philosophies of life: (1) That of the robbers— "What's yours is mine, I'll take it"; (2) That of the priest and Levite—"What's ours is our own, we'll keep it"; (3) That of the Samaritan—"What's mine is ours, we'll share it." Listeners simply cannot forget outlines as clearly and as strikingly stated as these. To sum it up: the outline makes the sermon more intelligible, more effective, more pleasing, and more memorable to the hearers.

DRAFTING AND ARRANGING THE POINTS

"Points" are the divisions of the discussion. They are variously spoken of as "main heads," "subtheses," and "topical divisions" of the sermon. Taken together they constitute the framework or main body of the sermon.

The problem in outlining is to attain certain qualities recognized as desirable. Speaking in general, these qualities are attained by the form in which the points are drafted and by the way in which these are arranged with reference to each other and to the theme. The qualities most often spoken of as desirable will be listed and explained briefly. Then a principle or rule for the formulation of the points that will help most in attaining the particular quality will be stated and illustrated.

1. An outline should have unity. By the unity of the outline is meant, according to Vinet, that the points are "intimately united, exactly adjusted, and naturally aid and sustain one another like stones of the arch." Every good sermon, like every good speech, story, play, and novel, should be unified around one main idea. This unification is achieved by making each point of the sermon a step or stage in the unfolding of the theme. Bishop Gerald Kennedy, of The Methodist Church, says many sermons are written like dictionaries, "with many interesting sidelights and important observations, but no thread to hold them together." [7]

First Rule: To attain unity each point should be a subthesis of the main thesis. The unity of a sermon can easily be tested by a simple procedure, and this procedure ought to be followed routinely as an exercise before the final wording of the points has been decided upon. Write out the theme of the sermon as a complete sentence, a fully stated proposition. Then, in the same manner, number and write out each point on a separate line, so the whole outline can be seen at a glance. Now ask: Does each point constitute a distinct phase of the thesis? Is each point subordinate to the main thesis? Is any one of them coextensive with that thesis? If necessary draft and revise the sentences until each is clearly a subthesis of the main thesis. These full sentences are primarily for the person preparing the sermon. They need not necessarily be given in that form to the hearers in the delivery of the sermon. If points are written out as complete propositions and kept before one's mind as he proceeds with the preparation of the sermon, it will help insure the unity of the whole.

Text: "What more are you doing than others?"—MATT. 5:47
Subject: "Wherein Are We (Christians) Different?"
Points:
1. Are we Christians superior in the matter of serenity?
2. Are we Christians superior in the matter of behavior?
3. Are we Christians superior in good will and social conscience?
4. We Christians must be different if we are to convince the world of the validity of our faith. [8]

[7] *Op. cit.*, p. 48.
[8] William M. Elliott, *Coming to Terms with Life* (Richmond: John Knox Press, 1944), pp. 40 ff.

The fourth point is not another stage in the unfolding of the thesis but constitutes the main thesis itself. Notice also that it is a declarative statement while the first three points are in the form of a question. As we shall see, this is a questionable practice.

2. An outline should have order. Demosthenes said, "Persuasion is as dependent upon the order of the arguments as upon the arguments themselves." Many preachers have an abundance of good ideas but do not know how to arrange them for the best effects. When an outline has order each point says one thing only and follows the others in a clear continuity of thought. What Horace long ago said of poetry can be said of sermons: "The beauty of order consists in saying just now what just now ought to be said, and postponing for the present all the rest."

Second Rule: To attain order the points of the outline should be co-ordinate. The word "co-ordinate" means "equal in rank," or "not subordinate." According to a rule in logic, subclasses into which genus is divided should be of the same rank. Trees, for example, may properly be divided into *deciduous* trees and *evergreens* but not into *deciduous* trees and *cedars*. Similarly, all points of a sermon should be of equal importance or rank. Someone used the term "bungalow" to describe sermons that are spread out but not built up. Sermons should be built up step by step, each point taking its place and doing its work on a par with the others. Herbert V. Prochnow likens the point of a speech to the members of a relay race team. He says: "Each one takes the token from the one before it and carries it a certain distance where the next section picks it up." [9] These are routine questions to be asked of each point, and answered in the affirmative before it is given final form: Does it carry the truth forward one step and one step only? Is that step of the same importance as each of the other steps?

Text: Not stated.
Subject: "Enemies"
Points:
   1. The worst enemy is a friend gone wrong.
   2. An enemy does himself the most harm.
   3. Do not be any man's enemy.[10]

[9] Reprinted with permission of publishers from *The Successful Speaker's Handbook.* Copyright 1951 by Prentice-Hall, Inc., 70 Fifth Avenue, New York 11, New York.

[10] Sermon by Robert Norwood. Reported by one who heard it.

What is wrong with the third point? Is it not a conclusion to the sermon, or an application of the truth, rather than a co-ordinate point?

Text: "You have seen well."—JER. 1:12
Subject: "Looking at Things Rightly"
Points:
1. We are all apt to make egregious mistakes when we look at our heavenly Father's providential dealings.
2. If we possessed more spiritual discernment, we should not so often torment ourselves with sinful anxieties about the future.
3. A right spiritual discernment will check our impatience in regard to the issue of God's wise dealings and discipline.
4. There is a right way and a wrong way of looking at things.[11]

Again, note the fourth point is not co-ordinate with the other three. The first three points are examples or illustrations enforcing the fourth point. Observe also the first three points are rather long sentences and worded so differently it is difficult to tell readily whether or not they are co-ordinate. Would not the points have been more effective, if, for example, they had all been stated as briefly and as pointedly as the fourth?

3. An outline should have proportion. Proportion means "symmetrical arrangement of whole" or "balance." This applies as much to the actual development of the sermon as to the statement of its points. As stated previously, one should *intend* to give each point its proportionate weight or emphasis both as to time and to space. This prevents throwing the sermon out of balance. But the statement of the points also helps to keep the proper proportion. The phase of the truth embodied in the statement of one point should be of equal importance to the phase in the other points and as important for the development of the main theme as the others. Prochnow suggests that each point may wisely be thought of as a sort of miniature speech by itself and treated as such: constructed with the same care; thought of as having, for the specific matter with which it deals, the same functions as the speech as a whole; and containing its own introduction, discussion, and conclusion. If one handles the points in this manner he will be fairly certain of having a symmetrical whole.

---

[11] Sermon by T. L. Cuyler. Reported by Kern, *op. cit.*, p. 308.

95

Third Rule: To attain proportion, all points should be of parallel construction. Defects in an outline can be spotted more easily if all points are stated in the same form. If the first point is a declarative statement, put all the others in that form. If it is a question, put all the others in that form. The actual phrasing should be similar, with words of the same general type and the sentences of approximately the same length.

Texts: LUKE 24:51-53; JOHN 16:7; EPH. 4:8
Subject: "The Gospel of the Ascension"
Points:
1. It (Christ's ascension) was expedient for the spiritualizing of religion.
2. It was expedient for the universalizing of the gospel.
3. It was expedient for the energizing of evangelism.
4. It was expedient for the fortifying of faith.[12]

This is a perfect example of parallel construction. The sentences are approximately the same length, and the phrasing and words are similar in type.

Text: "Are you he who is to come, or shall we look for another?"—
     MATT. 11:3
Subject: "Is Christianity What the World Needs?"
Points: (Based on the threefold answer Jesus gave to the question of John)
1. Jesus says, Ask those who have tried it.
2. Jesus says, Look at the fruits.
3. Jesus challenges to the venture of faith.[13]

Suppose the third point had been stated, "Jesus says, Try it out for yourself": would that not improve the outline?

4. An outline should have movement. John Watson said the organic whole of a sermon "depends on whether the heads advance, ascend, cumulate, or are independent, disconnected, parallel." [14] The sermon should make progress as it moves toward its conclusion. A judge in a novel-writing contest said two things stood out as he read the manuscripts: First, there was lack of plan,

[12] James S. Stewart, *The Strong Name* (New York: Charles Scribner's Sons, 1941), pp. 46 ff.
[13] Sermon by William P. Merrill. Reported by Luccock, *In the Minister's Workshop*, p. 122.
[14] *The Cure of Souls* (New York: Dodd, Mead and Co., 1896), pp. 41.

and second, there was too much overwriting, repetition, and digression. He observed that there was "scene after scene which did not advance the story, but merely interrupted it, until suspense and interest leaked away." [15] When the movement of a novel or of a sermon is interrupted, interest lags.

Fourth Rule: To attain movement, points should be distinct. Material under one point should not be repeated under other points. Each point should deal with one specific aspect of the subject and only one. A weakness common to many outlines is that of stating points in different words that mean practically the same thing. The moment the preacher begins to repeat himself, or to say from another angle the same thing he has already said several times, the listeners lose interest. Their minds begin to wander, and their attention may be lost permanently. Points carefully distinguished from one another help to prevent retracing steps, circling back, and recrossing ground already passed over.

During the proceedings of the Westminster Assembly the presiding officer said to those who kept speaking several times on the same points, "I desire that you would so order your debates as not to go backwards." [16] One suspects congregations often would like to express that same desire to their preachers. The example which follows is based on a sermon by Jonathan Edwards.

Text: ". . . and confessed that they were strangers and pilgrims on the earth. For they that say such things declare plainly that they seek a country."—HEB. 11:13-14 (A.V.)

Subject: "The Christian Pilgrim," or "The True Christian's Life a Journey Towards Heaven."

Points:

1. That this life ought to be so spent by us, as to be only a journey or pilgrimage towards heaven.
2. Why the Christian's life is a journey, or pilgrimage?
3. Instruction afforded by the consideration, that life is a journey, or pilgrimage, towards heaven.
4. An exhortation, so to spend the present life, that it may only be a journey towards heaven.[17]

---

[15] Quoted by Kennedy, op. cit., p. 48.

[16] S. W. Carruthers, *The Everyday Work of the Westminster Assembly* (Philadelphia: The Presbyterian Historical Society, 1943), p. 49.

[17] See A. W. Blackwood, *The Protestant Pulpit* (New York and Nashville: Abingdon Press, 1947), pp. 40 ff.

A brief study of these points reveals considerable repetition. The repetition is even more noticeable in the subpoints of which there were a total of twenty-two. One wonders if people in Edwards' day, as accustomed as they were to long and heavy sermons, really followed attentively as he retraced his steps again and again.

5. An outline should have climax. A sermon ought to have cumulative effect. That is, it should gather strength as it moves along toward the moment when you hope to move the hearers to decision and action. Someone remarked that beginners commonly make the mistake of bringing up their heaviest troops first. This is also the practice of a few experienced, well-known preachers. Phillips Brooks somewhat consistently presented his main idea first, as does Harry Emerson Fosdick. Rudolph Flesch, the noted writer on effective speaking style, recommends that the main point come early in a speech.

One professor of speech with experience in a number of seminaries, who has made a study of climax in sermons, distinguishes between "intellectual" and "emotional" climax. He says the type of outline employed determines whether the intellectual climax comes first, but "without exception the emotional climax should come somewhere near the close." [18] However, the traditional practice of leaving the climax to the last is observed by most preachers most of the time. The main thing is to exercise care that the sermon does not lose, but rather gains, strength as it proceeds to its conclusion.

Fifth Rule: To attain climax, points should be arranged in an ascending scale. That is to say, the last point should be the major climax to the sermon. That does not mean that minor climaxes may not occur at other places. But the last point should crown what has gone before, begin to bring everything to a focus, gather force and prepare for the final appeal for action. This is done so consistently that examples given will show how the climactic point is left to the end.

a)
Text:　　"*Make to yourselves friends of the mammon of unrighteousness.*"—LUKE 16:9 (A.V.)
Subject: "The Use of Money"

[18] See John Edward Lantz, *Speaking in the Church* (New York: The Macmillan Co., 1954), p. 142.

Points:
1. Gain all you can.
2. Save all you can.
3. Give all you can.[19]

b)
Text: "It is good for me to have been in trouble."—Ps. 119:71
        (Moffatt)
Subject: "Fortunate Misfortune"
Points:
1. Misfortune serves to deepen life.
2. Misfortune is often the means of releasing undreamed-of powers.
3. Misfortune brings enlarged capacity to understand and help other people.
4. Misfortune can make real and vital one's relationship to God.[20]

Miscellaneous Principles

1. The form of the points. This has been touched upon already. For the preacher's guidance in preparation, each point should be a complete sentence, though these need not necessarily be given in full to the hearers. But for the hearer the points should be indicated in a clear, concise, and brief manner. Strive to make the points fresh, striking, and intriguing without being sensational. Avoid odd, smart, merely clever wordings. Endeavor to make them memorable. Alliteration is helpful to these ends but should be used sparingly because it tends to become artificial. Forcing alliteration, like straining for puns, becomes unnatural and is often offensive to those who are obligated to hear it too often. To indicate the artificiality of alliteration, William Chalmers Covert, then professor of homiletics at McCormick Seminary, offered a group of former students the following outline of a sermon on "The Prodigal Son":

I. *His Madness*	II. *His Sadness*	III. *His Gladness*
A. He caviled.	A. He went to the dogs.	A. He got the seal.
B. He traveled.	B. He lost his togs.	B. He ate the veal.
C. He reveled.	C. He ate with the hogs.	C. He danced the reel.

[19] An outline of John Wesley's sermon as reported by Kern, *op. cit.*, p. 292.
[20] Sermon by William M. Elliott, pastor of Highland Park Presbyterian Church, Dallas. Privately printed.

The following outline of a sermon on the parable of the Good Samaritan shows how alliteration may be used in a striking manner:

1. The philosophy of the thieves: "Beat them up."
2. The philosophy of the priest and Levite: "Pass them up."
3. The philosophy of the Samaritan: "Lift them up." [21]

2. The number of main points. There is no standard number. One should use the number of points necessary to treat the subject adequately for the purposes in mind. The number should be varied from time to time to avoid monotony. Frederick W. Robertson, a great preacher, almost always had two points to his outline. Many of the points were commonplace and some of his subjects would have been more satisfactorily and more interestingly developed if he had used more than two points. At least some variation of the number would have added zest for the listeners.

However, there are good reasons why the number of points should be relatively few. Three-point sermons have always outnumbered others because three is a sort of natural number. Aristotle maintained that the "world and all that is in it is determined by the number three. . . . When we use it we but take the lead of nature itself." Our minds seem to operate easily and normally by the use of the number three. We write poems and hymns with three stanzas. We observe things, remember and repeat and teach them more easily, in groups of three. Too many points overtax the mind and are difficult to remember.

3. Subpoints. A sermon is not a law brief nor an outline for a college debate. The numerals and letters used in outlining each point are to aid the preacher in his preparation. They are not for the finished sermon and certainly should not be announced to the people. For the most part only main points should be announced. If the people remember them the preacher will be fortunate. Overanalysis can be hampering to the preacher as well as deadening to the hearer.

Broadus once received a homiletical exercise divided and subdivided until the divisions totaled more than 120. "The analysis was almost faultless," he said, "but it would have made an in-

---

[21] Sermon by Paul C. Payne, reported in *Monday Morning.*

tolerable sermon." [22] John Oman tells of a German professor who had such an elaborate system of dividing and subdividing sermons that he sometimes got bogged down and entangled with his own analysis and had to be pulled out of the quagmire by his students.[23] One can wisely shun overanalysis even in sermon preparation. But assuredly the people should be spared too many groups of "firsts," "seconds," and "thirds."

4. Announcing the points. There are no fixed rules here. Practice among preachers at this point is not uniform. There is an old admonition to preachers: "Don't dangle the skeleton." An outline should not be treated as the primary thing in the sermon. Phillips Brooks advised not to leave the skeleton out but to clothe it with flesh. Announcing all the points ahead of time is not recommended as a regular practice, because it gives everything away, leaves no room for the element of surprise. Here, as everywhere else in sermonizing, variety and flexibility should be the aim. The practice of announcing points as one comes to them is good psychology. As previously mentioned the people need emotional relief or relaxation. This is provided by the way the preacher lets them know they have concluded one lap of the journey and are about to start on the next. This, however, should not be done in the same way each time. How this transition may be made effectively and felicitously is considered next.

5. Transitions. Transitions from point to point keep the sermon moving. They carry the listeners with the speaker as he moves from one place to another. McCall says they are "the glue which holds the parts of the speech together." That is true, but the preacher must remember that he is not gluing pieces of paper together to be printed and read. Rather, he is delivering a live sermon to live hearers.

Movement can be effected by a number of devices. One can indicate by a pause, by the tone of voice, or by a change of manner or of pace that he is passing from one point to another. Some preachers skillfully summarize one point as they move into the next. Everyone needs a supply of what have been called "bridge words," expressions for making transitions, such as: again, still

[22] Quoted in *Preparation and Delivery of Sermons* (New York: A. C. Armstrong and Sons, 1901), p. 289.

[23] *Concerning the Ministry* (New York: Harper & Brothers, 1937), p. 150.

again, in addition, besides, furthermore, still further, moreover, another thing, in the next place, on the other hand, not only this but . . . , once more. Lists of possible expressions for use as transitions should be made, kept handy, and consulted somewhat regularly with the avowed intention of putting variety into this phase of preaching. "Finally" should seldom be used. When used it should always be near the end of the sermon and should actually *be* the last point. Few people listen after that word is once used. If used twice it is fatal.

Two concluding suggestions should be made as this section is brought to a close. First, one should learn to criticize his own outlines on the basis of these rules. A good practice is to place the complete outline before him each week and criticize it objectively, as though it it were someone else's outline to be evaluated. By this method one can provoke himself to see his outlines as a group of theological students are expected to see them in a classroom analysis. If this is done regularly errors can be detected more easily and bad practices checked before they become habitual. If the preacher finds an error occurring two or three times in succession, his subconscious mind is likely to warn him the next time it is about to occur. The subconscious mind is a good partner whose warnings can wisely be heeded. In short, every preacher needs to learn to be his own best critic.

Second, one should remember that these are not rules of thumb, nor laws of the Medes and Persians, never to be altered. Rules are guides to be followed, principles to be observed. They are violated now and then by the best of preachers. A single infringement of a rule does not indicate a poor sermon. But it does mean the sermon would have been improved by just that much if a tested principle had been followed. Eternal vigilance at these points is the price of continuously good sermonizing.

Suggested Reading

Rogers, Clement F. *The Parson Preaching.* London: S. P. C. K., 1949. Chapter II. (Brief but thorough and illuminating.)

Practical helps on outlining may be found mostly in textbooks on homiletics. The following textbooks, listed in the second section of the Bibliography, are especially helpful: Blackwood, Chapter XI; Davis, pp. 224 ff.; Kern, pp. 271 ff.; Luccock, Chapter XII; Phelps, Lectures XXV-XXIX; Rue, pp. 390 ff.; and Weatherspoon, Part II, Chapters I, III, V.

6. Outlining the Sermon: Types of Outlines

Sermons have been classified according to types more often than have sermon outlines. If outlines could be classified satisfactorily into groups to provide a number of different models to follow, it would add variety and freshness to sermonizing. This chapter is devoted to that undertaking. First a few standard or conventional outlines will be identified, described, and illustrated and then special or less customary types will be considered.

Some Standard Outlines

1. "Two-Point" outline. This is sometimes called the "twin" sermon because one half the sermon is usually devoted to one truth, the other half to a contrasting or balancing truth. Often the first half considers the negative, the last half the positive, aspects of the truth. Quite a few of Frederick W. Robertson's sermons, most of which had only two points, were in this form. For example, his sermon on "The Pharisee and the Publican," based on Luke 18:9-14, had these points: (1) The beauty of Christian humbleness; (2) The danger of self-satisfaction. His sermon on "The Irreparable Past," based on Mark 14:41-42, had these points: (1) The irreparable past; (2) The available future.

But a two-point outline is also suitable for other types of sermons. In a doctrinal sermon, for example, the doctrine may be explained or expounded in the first point and applied in the second. Or in the first point the data about a book or character of the Bible may be given, and in the second point lessons drawn from the data. Similarly, in using a secular book or story in a sermon the contents may be given in the first point and the lessons given in the second.

2. "Question" outline. In this type of outline each point is in the form of a question. Introducing an article in which he proposed to discuss a current political problem, Senator Paul H. Douglas referred to a remark by William Graham Sumner, that to understand a social fact we should seek the answers to four questions: (1) What is it? (2) Why is it? (3) What of it? (4)

What are we going to do about it? [1] Asking questions about a subject readily brings out its various phases. One of the easiest ways of building an outline is to make a succession of points out of questions beginning with several of the following adverbs and pronouns: what, why, when, how, where, and who. For that reason it is regarded as a lazy man's device. This type of outline is usually summoned into service when a minister finds it necessary to get up a sermon in a hurry. That may explain why outlines of this kind are so scarce in books of recent sermons. However, they were commonly used by preachers in other generations. For example, Wesley had a sermon on Eph. 2:8 entitled "The Scripture Way of Salvation," with these points: (1) What is salvation? (2) What is that faith whereby we are saved? (3) How are we saved by it? [2]

Question outlines need not be confined to the use of those few words. Arresting sermons may be composed of interrogative sentences beginning with other words. This example was given in an earlier chapter: (1) Have you got religion? (2) Is it the catching kind? (3) Has anybody caught it from you yet? Some time ago I heard of the following outline: (1) Have you done any good today? (2) Did you go out of your way to do it? (3) Was it without thought of return? (4) Was it more than others would have done?

3. "Ladder" or "Unfolding Telescope" outline. These two expressions are placed together because they represent the same general principle, namely: each point grows out of, or builds upon, the previous point. In one case, each point, based upon the previous point, carries the subject up to another level like the rungs of a ladder. In the other case, each point, based upon the previous point, carries the subject out a little farther like the unfolding of a telescope. These outlines are well adapted to argumentative sermons, sermons intended to appeal to the reason or that hope to commit the hearer to something, one step at a time. An example of the "ladder" outline is one based on John 15:11, entitled "The Secret of Happiness," with these points: (1) True happiness is found only in obedience to God's will. (2) God's will is made known to us only in Christ. (3) Knowledge of Christ is of value

---

[1] See *Harper's Magazine*, July, 1953.
[2] Blackwood, *The Protestant Pulpit*, pp. 23 ff.

only as used.[3] An example of the "telescope" outline is one based on Rom. 15:29 (A.V.), "I am sure that, when I come unto you, I shall come in the fulness of the blessing of the gospel of Christ." The subject was "The Triumphant Adequacy of Christ," and the points were as follows:

(1) I am coming to you *with Christ*.
(2) I am coming to you with *the gospel* of Christ.
(3) I am coming to you with *the blessing* of the gospel of Christ.
(4) I am coming to you with *the fulness* of the blessing of the gospel of Christ.[4]

4. "Classification" outline. This is perhaps the commonest of all types. The several points divide people or things into different classes, or apply the truth to different areas of life. For example, Joseph Fort Newton has a classification outline for a sermon on Phil. 1:21, entitled "What to Do with Life Today." He said there are four things a man can do with his life: (1) He can run away from it. (2) He can run along with it. (3) He can take hold of it firmly. (4) He can put his life into the hands of One greater than himself and let Him run it.[5] Phillips Brooks used a classification outline for a sermon based on Ps. 92:1 and entitled "The Highest Help Only Can Satisfy Our Needs." Those needs were listed: (1) In temptation; (2) In sorrow; (3) In doubt; (4) In sin.

5. "Series of Statements" outline. This is another type widely used. The points consist of a succession of statements or observations related to the truth under consideration. The number of points is not intended to exhaust the subject. Additional statements could be made, but the preacher chooses to limit the discussion to those chosen.[6] Luccock labels this "The Roman Candle Sermon," because one point after another is given like the shots fired from a Roman candle. Yet one may have a varying number of points as he may purchase candles that shoot a varying number of times. An example is a sermon on "Achieving an "All-in Victory." The preacher states that to achieve this victory I

---

[3] John McSween, *The Presbyterian Outlook*, June 20, 1949.
[4] Stewart, *The Strong Name*, pp. 90 ff.
[5] See *The Pulpit*, June, 1947.
[6] Lantz calls this a "string-of-beads" outline. *Op. cit.*, p. 132.

must (a) confront myself, (b) consider myself, (c) choose myself, (d) control myself, (e) consecrate myself.[7]

6. "Jewel" outline. Just as you may turn a jewel completely around to view all its facets, so you can turn a truth all the way around to look at its various phases. When you see an outline of this type you feel all has been said that needs to be said on the subject. The subject has not exactly been exhausted but enough has been said to give a well-rounded view of the truth.[8] An example is a sermon on "The Religion of the Incarnation." To understand this religion, the preacher says, we must (a) look backward to the creation of man, (b) look upward to the nature of God, (c) look inward to the soul of man.[9]

7. "Hegelian" outline. Hegel's philosophy revolved around the three ideas of thesis, antithesis, and synthesis. When adapted to a sermon outline these terms bring about a three-point outline in which the first point states the thesis, the second its opposite, the last the truth that emerges from the conflict of the two. Or to put it another way: the first point says, "This is the way things ought to be"; the second point, "This is the way things are"; the third point, "This is the way things may be with God's help." [10] W. M. Clow has a sermon, based on Mark 9:5, with the subject "The Cloister and the Crowd," that has these points: (1) The blessing of the cloister hour; (2) The curse of the cloister life; (3) The keeping of the spirit of the cloister in the crowd.[11]

8. "Guessing Game" outline. This form is suggested by the parlor game, "Is it this?" "No." "Is it this?" "No." "Is it this other thing?" "Yes, that's it." [12] Luccock applies this method to a sermon on "What Is Christian Patriotism?" as follows: (1) Is Christian patriotism flag-waving? Obviously not. (2) Is it loud, swelling words? Certainly not. (3) Is it the kind of devotion that

[7] See sermon by Henry Hitt Crane, *The Pulpit*, November, 1946.
[8] Cf. Luccock, *In the Minister's Workshop*, p. 137.
[9] Sermon by Lynn Harold Hough, *Butler's Best Sermons, 1946* (New York: Harper & Brothers, 1946).
[10] Cf. Blackwood, *The Preparation of Sermons*, pp. 148-49.
[11] *The Secret of the Lord* (New York: Hodder and Stoughton, n.d.), pp. 216 ff.
[12] Lantz's term for this is "exclusion outline," reaching a conclusion by a process of excluding one possible solution after another until the only satisfactory solution is found. *Op. cit.*, p. 140.

Christ had when he cried, "O Jerusalem. . . . How often would I have gathered . . ." Yes, that's it.[13]

9. "Rebuttal" outline. [14] One reads or hears something he considers false or misleading and feels compelled to answer it in a sermon. Under such circumstances the procedure is to find a suitable passage of scripture for a text, formulate a general theme, draft a subject, state points that categorically oppose one by one the important positions taken in what is being refuted, and arrange them in the form best suited for the purposes in mind.

A preacher heard a lecture on humanism by a noted leader of the humanistic society that he felt obligated to answer because so many of his congregation heard it and were asking questions about it. In the address, given previous to Thanksgiving Day, the lecturer had said that religion is a survival of primitive superstition and that men are self-sufficient and no longer need to implore the help of God or render him thanks. Using Col. 3:17 as a text, and taking as a subject "Is Thanksgiving a Primitive Survival?" the preacher devised the following outline: (1) Is belief in God a superstition? (2) Is man self-sufficient? (3) Is prayer foolish?

10. At the 1955 meeting of the Association of Seminary Professors in the Practical Field, the following form for an outline of a life-situation, or "problem-solution," sermon was suggested: (1) Where are we? (2) How did we get here? (3) Where do we want to go? (4) How do we get there? [15]

11. Recently I heard of an older preacher who told a young man preparing for the ministry that one of his standard outlines had always been: (1) Problem—this is the situation; (2) Principle—this is the basis on which it may be solved; (3) Program—this is the way to go about solving it.

This list does not exhaust the possibilities. Undoubtedly many preachers invent outlines and make them standard for them-

---

[13] *In the Minister's Workshop*, p. 143. For this type his term is "chase technique," a term borrowed from H. A. Overstreet.

[14] Cf. Frank H. Caldwell, *Preaching Angles* (New York and Nashville: Abingdon Press, 1954), p. 113. He calls this the "dog-fight" approach.

[15] This was an adaptation of the five steps in a complete act of thought given by John Dewey: (1) a felt difficulty; (2) its location and definition; (3) the suggestion of a possible solution; (4) rational consideration of the suggested solution; and (5) acceptance or rejection of the suggested solution. *How We Think*, ch. vi (Boston: D. C. Heath & Company, 1910).

selves, as did the older minister just referred to. A minister is under no obligation to conform slavishly to a series of outline forms handed down by a professor of homiletics. But he *is* obligated to find ways of saying what he wishes to say in the clearest and most effective manner possible. A supply of possible types of outlines will aid in fulfilling this obligation. No hard and fast lines can be drawn between some of the types suggested. But they may be distinguished from one another sufficiently to provide a variety of models.

All the terms used to describe the types are for the preacher, not for the congregation. These, or other types of sermon plans, should be so firmly fixed in mind that they may be summoned to one's aid readily when he is engaged in sermonizing. As one begins to plan the outline he should experiment for a while with several possible types until he finds the one that best fits the particular subject he is dealing with at the moment. Most preachers could profitably make an occasional check of the types they have been using for several months past to make sure they are not using one type too often, perhaps the one they find the easiest or most intriguing. To avoid getting into a rut at this point, types should be varied intentionally from time to time.

Speaking in general, the plan for the discussion of any particular sermon should be constructed on the same principle throughout. For example, one should not start on the principle of a "question" outline and then switch, in the last point or two, to a "series of statements" plan. To keep the sermon balanced, to follow through on the sequence of thought most clearly, and to enable the people to grasp and remember what is said, the points of each sermon should be stated consistently on the same principle. If a group of various types are etched on the mind, so they may be recalled easily and compared quickly as the drafting of points begins, one will almost automatically compose them in the same form.

Special Types of Outlines

A considerable amount of experimentation with a variety of unconventional approaches to sermonizing has been going on in recent decades. Some of these new approaches necessitate a special form of sermon structure. This section is concerned primarily, not with novel methods of presenting truths as such, but with the type of outlines they require.

EXPOSITORY SERMONS

1. The traditional expository sermon that interprets a chapter or a portion of a chapter of the Bible. The entire procedure in this type of sermon has been fairly well standardized. First, formulate a theme for the main truth or truths contained in the passage. If possible find a key verse in the passage and make it the text. Group the verses under headings, each of which represents a distinct phase of the contents of the passage. Draft and arrange these points so they will provide the skeleton for a coherent unified sermon constructed on sound homiletical principles. True expository preaching is not merely making running comments on the successive verses of a passage: it is preaching a sermon on the passage. Suppose that the passage to be expounded is I Cor. 13. The text might well be vs. 13 of the chapter, and the subject. "The Greatest Thing in the World," the title of Henry Drummond's essay on this chapter. The points could then be: (1) The importance of love—vss. 1-3; (2) The characteristics of love—vss. 4-7; (3) The permanence of love—vss. 8-13.

2. An exposition of a whole book of the Bible. In such a sermon one may wish to group the contents of the book under headings in somewhat the same manner as he groups the verses of a chapter and to treat them in the same way. In this case, each point is stated, then illustrated by appropriate material from the book, and finally applied to modern men. When the sermon is finished the listeners will have a comprehensive grasp of the contents and significance of the book as a whole.

But if one wishes to present the book in a more dramatic manner the handling would be different. The historical setting in which the book appeared may be of major importance for its understanding and also may provide colorful events that can be related in the form of an interesting story. The contents of the book itself, as for example the books of Ruth, Hosea, Jonah, Haggai and Philemon, may be presented in story form and in dramatic fashion. Hence both the setting and the contents should figure in the outline of a sermon on these books.

Let us take the book of Jonah as an example. The text could

be 4:10-11 and the subject, "Modern Jonahs." The points would be:

a) *The historical setting of the book.* The salient facts of the situation would be narrated in some detail. The book appeared after the restoration of the Hebrews from their Babylonian exile, probably about 350 B.C. The noblest among the Jews believed their calamity was a punishment for their isolationism, their narrow nationalism, and their hatred of other peoples. Through their suffering they had been prepared to accept the call of their prophets and to embark upon God's mission for the redemption of the nations. While in exile they had prayed something like this: "O God, deliver us and we will change our attitudes toward other peoples. We will become the instruments of thy salvation instead of thy revenge." But when they returned a great wave of bitterness and hatred toward the Assyrians swept the country. A violent antiforeign movement arose. Dreams of the destruction of their foes and of the realization of nationalistic hopes revived. (Cf. Ps. 137:9; Joel 3:5-14; Isa. 34:2-8; Zech. 14:3-21; and Neh. 13:23 ff.) The book of Jonah appeared in the midst of this situation.

b) *The contents of the book.* Here would be told the story of Jonah, the Jew, called of God to preach to the people he hated. He refused the assignment and came to disaster. In the midst of his distress he cried for deliverance and vowed if given a chance he would perform the will of God. God answered his cry. He went to Ninevah and proclaimed that God would destroy the city. But he carried his old racial prejudices with him. Having delivered God's message he sat on the hillside under the shade of a gourd vine to watch the destruction he longed to see. But the people repented. God spared them. When Jonah realized God had shown mercy to his enemies he was angry. He pouted. He wished to die. He rebuked God for killing the gourd vine that protected him from the sun. God said: "You pity a gourd vine, Jonah? I pity the city of Ninevah with its grownups and its 120,000 little children not yet able to discern their right hand from their left, to say nothing of all the cattle." By this he implied: "I am not an avenging but a merciful God. I love the very people you despise." The meaning of the story for the times is obvious.

c) *The permanent message of the book.* Here would be enforced some such lessons from the book as the following:

110

(1) How little we human beings learn from our social misfortunes.

(2) How desperately we try to escape God's call to the highest.

(3) How difficult it is for us to believe in our common brotherhood.

(4) How stubbornly we refuse to believe in a God of universal love.

If the historical background and story were properly presented, not much time would be left for the actual sermon. The four subpoints under the last main point would have to be driven home quickly and briefly. This produces an unbalanced outline, but the imbalance is justified by the interest aroused by the dramatic story of the book and its setting.

3. An exposition of biblical characters. A particular character under study may stand out as typifying a desirable or undesirable trait, or a personality problem one wishes to use as the basis of a sermon. Once the trait or problem one wishes to stress is identified, that may be made the truth around which the sermon revolves. This provides a *topic* for a sermon, which may then be treated as any other topic. As many points as necessary to unfold the topic satisfactorily are stated, then illustrated by details about the character's life, and supported with other material. Thus one comes out with a standard outline. This method is best suited for characters about whom only a few facts are known.

But if the character is one about whom considerable information is available, a more dramatic and appealing approach may be used. For this purpose two sermon forms are available. First: in the first point tell the story of the character's life and in the second point draw the lessons. Preparing the story is easier if the facts about the person can be arranged in chronological order. Second: tell the story of his life, section by section (these become the points of the outline), and draw the lessons at the end of each section. Or to put this another way, state the lessons as the points and illustrate each with a portion of the story. The sermon will be completed when the last group of facts has been presented. Both of these sermon forms may be illustrated by using Joseph as the character.

First form:
a) The story of Joseph's life

111

    (1) His early life
    (2) His conflict with his brothers
    (3) His rise to power in Egypt
    (4) His reconciliation with his brothers
    (5) His last days

b) Lessons from Joseph's life
    (1) A man with a feeling of destiny
    (2) A man undaunted by misfortune
    (3) A man with a mystical sense of right and wrong
    (4) A man too big to hold a grudge
    (5) A man with a staunch belief in the providence of God

The lessons correspond to the five stages of his life. Because of the large amount of material in the record about Joseph the major portion of time must be spent in telling the story as dramatically as possible. So necessarily the lessons will have to be enforced rapidly and briefly. This does not provide a well-proportioned outline but the advantage of making it interesting outweighs the disadvantage of lack of symmetry.

Second form: This should be composed of the five lessons in the second main division of the preceding outline, each lesson constituting a main point of the sermon. Each point would utilize the particular facts about his life that substantiate it; then the lesson would be drawn and enforced before passing on to the next point. When the points of a character sermon coincide one by one with the several stages of the character's life, the dramatic effect is quite satisfactory. But for the best effect the first form is usually to be preferred because the whole story can be placed before the hearers without its being interrupted each time to enforce the lesson. The first plan has another advantage also. If the story has been properly told, the truths one wishes to enforce will already be so clear that they can be driven in and clinched quickly. Observe that a sermon form of this type about a character is unified around the character, not around a single truth as in a standard outline. Perhaps it should also be said that the person who preaches sermons on biblical characters needs to possess some skill in telling a story interestingly and dramatically. Biographical sermons on nonbiblical characters call for the same general procedures.

NEW APPROACHES TO SERMONIZING

First and last there has been a good deal of experimentation with fresh approaches to sermonizing in our times. One of the most vigorous proponents and exponents of unconventional preaching is William L. Stidger. He is best known for his "symphonic" sermons, to be explained shortly. But he has also broken new ground with suggestions and demonstrations of how to use books, drama, poetry, short stories, art, hymns, and other religious music for novel methods of preaching. The increasing number of untraditional sermons appearing in print in recent years may be attributed partly to the influence of his teaching and writing. A recent practical summary of these new approaches may be found in *Preaching Angles*, by Frank H. Caldwell. He describes and illustrates some thirty angles of approach to preaching. Some of these approaches take place primarily in the introductions to sermons and will, therefore, be considered in the next chapter, which takes up ways of introducing sermons interestingly. Some of them have already been discussed in other connections. But I wish to group others under seven headings, with the main purpose of searching for unusual types of outlines.

1. Symphonic sermons. This type of sermon helped make Stidger famous in the field of sermonizing.[16] His method is to find a few lines of a poem and a text of scripture that contain the same theme and weave them into the sermon somewhat as a melody is woven into a symphony. The structure of the sermon and the manner of using illustrations are ordinarily the same as in traditional sermons. The unusual feature of the sermons is the way in which everything else revolves around the theme, which he repeats dramatically at climactic moments in the sermon. So by the time the sermon is concluded, the theme, and the lines of poetry and the text embodying it, are impressed indelibly on the minds of the hearers. One example will suffice to indicate the procedure.

His subject is "Motherhood and Calvary"; the text "When Jesus therefore saw his mother . . ." (John 19:26 A.V.). The symphonic theme is as follows:

> O Mother, when I think of thee,
> 'Tis but a step to Calvary.

[16] See *Symphonic Sermons* (New York: George H. Doran, 1924) and *Building Sermons with Symphonic Themes* (Doran, 1926.)

After a long, interesting, and effective introduction, in which the preacher draws parallels between mothers and Christ, he weaves his text and theme into his sermon at climactic intervals, as he makes the following points about mother: (1) Her mercy is like His mercy. (2) In her comfort she is like unto His comfort. (3) It was her love that was Christlike love. (4) Mother suffering of pain is like Christ's suffering of pain. All of this is worked out beautifully and interspersed with apt and striking illustrations of many kinds.[17]

There can be no doubt that these sermons are interesting. Nor can there be any doubt that to be effective they must be handled by a person skilled in dramatic techniques. No one should undertake to use this type of approach unless he possesses and has developed dramatic skills to the point of proficiency. Moreover, after reading a number of these sermons in succession one realizes that the constant repetition of theme and text in sermon after sermon, week after week, could become as monotonous as the repetition of texts in ordinary sermons. Hence, this type of sermon should be exceptional and occasional rather than the regular run-of-the-mill sermon. Notice that the basic outline is standard.

2. Imaginary narratives. A number of the new approaches may be grouped under this heading: autobiographical monologue-impersonation, with or without native costume; a story told in the usual manner, or in poetical form, or in the form of an imaginary letter or some other document; a dialogue in the form of an imaginary conversation between two or more characters, or even between a person and an object; or a play with settings and scenes. The number of this type of sermons has been increasing in recent years.[18]

This method of preaching may be effective, as the story sermons of Henry Van Dyke long ago proved. Several of his famous stories, including "The Other Wise Man" and "The Mansion," were preached in their original form as sermons. But this kind of

---

[17] Symphonic Sermons, pp. 109 ff.
[18] See Best Sermons, 1944, sermons ii, iii, iv, xxii (ed. G. Paul Butler; Chicago: Ziff-Davis Publishing Co., 1944). Best Sermons, 1947-48, sermons xxxix, xlii (ed. G. Paul Butler; New York: Harper & Brothers, 1947). The Pulpit, September, 1953, sermons by Clyde M. Allison and John C. Wiley. The Pulpit, July, 1954, sermon by Frederick M. Meek. The Salty Tang, a book of sermons by Frederick B. Speakman, the last four sermons (New York: Fleming H. Revell Co., 1954).

preaching must be done by preachers with considerable dramatic ability, imagination, and skill in the techniques of storytelling, if it is to avoid being insipid and trite. The storyteller needs to know how to handle his voice, change tones and facial expressions, and pause in making transitions from one character to another. Mediocrity is less likely to be tolerated here than in ordinary sermons. Narrative preaching in itself is not intrinsically any more interesting than conventional preaching. The content of the narrative must be significant and as carefully outlined and prepared as the plot of a story or a drama. While the outlines of such sermons may be hidden from the listener or reader, you can be certain the preacher used an outline with a theme, a definite purpose, and a carefully planned sequence of thought leading up to a climax, if the sermon was effective. If the outline could be discovered it would, in all probability, not be different in structure from the outlines of other sermons. Without careful outlining this kind of sermonizing is likely to end in a farce. If it can be done effectively it may wisely be used occasionally to provide variety and spark to one's preaching.

3. Dramatic use of books, poems, and stories. A number of other unusual approaches to preaching may be grouped under this heading. In my pastorates, extending over nearly thirty years, I used such sermons with a fair degree of regularity. At one period I had a series of five or six at intervals of a month each year for several years. At other times they were used only occasionally. Perhaps the most helpful way to treat this topic is to give the results of my own experiences rather than to cite what others have done in this field.

Over the years I used, in all, more than a hundred books of various types. The largest proportion of these were fiction, including both novels and plays. Space forbids making a list of all the titles used, but included were classics and current books by leading American and English essayists, novelists, and playwrights, and similar books available in English by authors of other nations, such as: Balzac, Eugène Sue, Victor Hugo, Tolstoi, Dostoevski, Maeterlinck, Ibsen, Bojer, Hamsun, Silone and Cervantes. Books were not used as the *basis* of sermons, but as *approaches* to sermons and *illustrations* of truths in sermons. The sermons invariably were based upon biblical truth. Generally

115

speaking, both novels and plays were handled in the same manner by the use of four different structural forms.

a) The most common was a two-point outline: first, the story; and second, the sermon, using the story just told as an illustration of the Christian truth or truths listed. Usually the story consumed a disproportionate amount of the time and the points of the sermon were presented in quick succession. For example, Dostoevski's *Crime and Punishment* was used for a sermon on "The Psychic Effects of Sin," based on Num. 32:23, "Be sure your sin will find you out." After telling the story in condensed form and as vividly as possible, I preached the sermon with these points: (1) Sin's greatest punishment is within the soul. (2) Confession of sin is necessary to relieve the soul of guilt. (3) When the sinner confesses and repents God enables him to begin a new life.

b) Sometimes the order was reversed. That is, the sermon was preached first and then the story of the book was given to illustrate and enforce the truth already presented. For example, *The Soft Spot*, by A. S. M. Hutchinson, was used for a sermon on "Playing the Man," based on I Cor. 16:13, "Be watchful, stand firm in your faith, be courageous, be strong." After a brief introduction, which explained the text and emphasized the necessity of playing the man instead of being a weakling in the critical moments of life, a fourpoint sermon was preached briefly: Play the man (i) in life's primary obligations, (ii) in life's temptations, (iii) in life's sorrows, (iv) in life's sins. After that the story of the book was told at length to illustrate and enforce the points already made.

c) Most of the plays were handled in the same way as the novels, but when the play permitted, the outline of the sermon followed the outline of the play. John Galsworthy's *Justice* [19] was used to illustrate a sermon on "Christianizing Our Prison System," based on Heb. 13:3, "Remember those who are in prison, as though in prison with them." This sermon was delivered at the time a prison reform movement was attracting wide attention throughout the state. The points of the sermon were stated in the form of questions and were as follows:

[19] See *Representative Plays by John Galsworthy* (New York: Charles Scribner's Sons, 1924), pp. 161 ff.

(1) What is the Christian way to treat a man who has first been detected in a crime? (Then followed the story of Act I and its application.)

(2) What is the Christian attitude for the court to take when his case comes to trial? (Then followed the story of Act II and its application.)

(3) What is the Christian way to treat him when he is in prison? (Then followed the story of Act III and its application.)

(4) What is the Christian way to treat his relatives and dependents while he is in prison? (Then followed the story of Act IV and its application.)

(5) What is the Christian way to treat him when he is released from prison? (Then followed the story of Act V and its application.)

Incidentally, this is an indication of how carefully a dramatist outlines his play. Plays are among the most fruitful of all books for dramatic sermons because the playwright must organize them for dramatic effect if they are to be successful.

d) In some instances, although the simple two-point outline of first the story and then its lessons was used, the story was so dramatic and forceful as to carry its own Christian message without the need of much actual preaching. "Mercy," a short story by Peter Clark MacFarlane[20] (a most unusual true story of how a whole church forgave a minister who had committed a grave sin), was used for a sermon based on Matt. 6:14-15. The subject of the sermon was "Can We Really Practice Forgiveness?" The story was told to show forgiveness consists (i) in restoring a person to loving favor, (ii) in acting as though his sin had not been committed, and (iii) in giving him a chance to prove his repentance by a new life. These three things needed only to be said by way of summary after the story was finished and an appeal made for the hearers to practice those things in their dealings with one another.

For the most part short stories were employed in one of three ways. First, the story in condensed form was used in the introduction along with the text and theme, to give a new approach to the sermon. This made the introduction longer than

[20] Appeared originally in *Cosmopolitan*, May and June, 1923.

usual but was justified by the interest aroused. The points of the sermon were stated and arranged in the traditional manner. During the course of the sermon occasional references were made to the story already told but other illustrations were also used. This is the method mainly used by Robert E. Luccock in his book of story sermons, *The Lost Gospel*, which has attracted so much attention recently.[21] Second, the story was told in the main body of the sermon and the lessons drawn as points as the story progressed. MacFarlane's "Mercy," already described, can easily be utilized in this manner. Third, now and then, just to vary the procedure, the sermon was preached in the traditional manner and the story used at the end of the sermon to illustrate and enforce what had already been said. This gave a longer conclusion than usual but was justified by the dramatic interest at the climax of the sermon.

Over the years I used books in the nonfiction class, but these were relatively few. These rarely required an unusual type of outline, although at times they were dealt with at such length that the sermon was occasionally thrown out of balance at a particular point by the extensive use of illustrative material from the book. Again, this imbalance was justified by the interest engendered in the minds of those who were eager to learn a Christian minister's judgment of a book which was being widely discussed. These sermons were not book reviews. The contents of the books were used to throw light upon Christian truth. Such books as the following were used: *Singing in the Rain*, by Anne Shannon Monroe; *A Common Faith*, by John Dewey; *A Preface to Morals*, by Walter Lippmann; *The Predicament of Modern Man*, by Elton Trueblood; and books by E. Stanley Jones and James Gordon Gilkey dealing with the psychology of personality.

A few do's and don't's about these dramatic sermons may prove useful. Don't get lost in the details of a book: keep to the main highway. In using fiction especially, don't try to give all the ins and outs of the author's complicated plot. Select the phases of the story suitable to your purposes and courageously and ruthlessly omit all the rest. Make it a biblical sermon: base what you have to say upon an appropriate text. Make it a real

[21] New York: Harper & Brothers, 1948.

sermon: weave the story about the truth and theme of the sermon, rather than the other way around. Familiarize yourself with the story, by going over and over it in your mind, before undertaking to tell it. Tell it offhand, without notes, in as dramatic a fashion as possible. Study and practice the techniques of storytelling until you develop a measure of competence in using them. You will discover quickly by experience that you must read several books to find one suitable for sermons. So plan at the most to preach only a few of these sermons in any year.

4. Sermons on hymns. Hymns are widely used as ordinary illustrations of sermons. Numerous books are available for information about hymns and their tunes, their authors and composers, the circumstances under which they were written, and incidents and experiences connected with their origin and use. Every minister should be studying constantly how to use hymns in worship services and for illustrative purposes. But whether they can or should be used for sermons depends upon whether a particular minister is qualified to make the sermons significant. Hymns are religious poems set to music. Authors of hymns have definite themes and moods they wish to set forth. Each stanza of the hymn is a step in the unfolding of its author's purpose. Many hymns are based upon, or inspired by, specific passages of scripture. Many are associated with interesting religious experiences. Hence, they have settings or backgrounds comparable in value to the backgrounds of books of the Bible.

When used for sermons they may be treated in the same general manner as books of the Bible. Two forms are available as outlines for such sermons. First, after the proper introduction plan a two-point sermon as follows: (1) The setting or background of the hymn; (2) The message of the hymn. The subpoints of the second division would consist of the truths, or phases of the main truth, found in the several stanzas. Second, after giving the general setting or background of the hymn in the introduction, state the points of your sermon so each will consist of the truth or phase of the truth represented by each stanza.

5. Sermons on other musical compositions. Many important major musical compositions have definite religious settings and significant religious values. They may, therefore, be used for sermons in somewhat the same way as hymns. This is a semi-technical procedure requiring some knowledge of musical appreciation, analysis, and interpretation. Superficial, amateurish handling of great musical compositions is of little interest or value at any time or place, and certainly should never be undertaken from the pulpit. If, with the assistance of a devout, technically trained director of music, one can analyze a piece of music, like Stainer's "The Crucifixion" for example, and utilize it in connection with the proper scripture and with the purpose of enriching the spiritual lives and serving the spiritual needs of the hearers, by all means he should do so. If, somewhere in the sermon, one can use some of its magnificent choruses rendered by the choir, that will add immeasurably to its effectiveness. For it is difficult to fully understand the significance of music without hearing it. But nothing could be more banal than the use of a great piece of music without adequate knowledge and skill.

6. **Sermons on art.** Religious art, like religious music, has definite themes and purposes that can be appreciated properly only by the use of special knowledge. If one possesses that knowledge he can use the story of artists and their paintings for sermonic purposes with desirable results. Most religious pictures deal with dramatic scenes from the Bible. They may, therefore, be regarded as characterizations of the people and interpretations of the events with which they deal. Hence, they may be used for exegetical and illustrative purposes.

Here are a few pointed suggestions about their use. If you undertake to use a picture for a sermon, identify and state the general theme of the artist. Study the picture until you understand what the artist was trying to say about the theme through the scene he is depicting. List as subpoints of the theme the several aspects of the picture. Then use these points, either as the main points of the sermon or as those of one main division of the sermon, in somewhat the same way as when using a book, a story, or a hymn. As great music must be heard, so great art must be seen, to be understood and appreciated properly. So if possible the people ought to be able to see a large illuminated reprint, or have in their hands small reprints, while you are explaining the picture. A number of books designed to assist preachers in learning how to study and interpret pictures and use them for sermons are available. But they should be studied with discernment before one undertakes to imitate the procedures suggested.

7. *Sermons on objects.* The ancient prophets of Israel did not hesitate to use objects in their preaching and to act out their parables. Object sermons for children were widely used some twenty-five or thirty years ago but have not been so common in recent years. A few preachers in our day have experimented with the use of objects in their sermons to adults. Many years ago a well-known minister of my acquaintance used a replica of a human brain in a temperance sermon. As he took the sections of the brain apart and explained their functions, he described the effect of alcoholic liquors upon the nerve centers, and therefore upon the behavior of the parts of the body controlled by those centers. According to the report the sermon attracted considerable attention. The use of objects in television programs is definitely bringing this method back into vogue. As yet I have not heard a sermon actually based upon a single object, but I have seen a minister handle the objects mentioned in his illustrations.

Whether the use of objects in television is a passing fad or a more-or-less permanent use of visual aids for purposes of entertainment, advertising, and instruction cannot be now determined. But one feels safe in saying that their regular use in sermons for mature minds is of limited value, that they should be seldom used and then with great restraint. Mature people desire and require something more substantial than object lessons to meet the great issues and problems of life. However, if an object is used for a sermon it could be used in the same manner as a work of art or a piece of music. My suggestion would be to try it out occasionally with caution, but to be sure it is genuine gospel preaching, with length, breadth, height, and depth, not mere allegorizing of objects for immature minds.

In his lectures on preaching Henry Ward Beecher said that when a man has finished his sermon, not a person in his congregation should be unable to tell him what he has done; but as he *begins* his sermon, not a person should be able to tell him what he is going to do.[22] Likewise, James Black thought it a good thing occasionally for a preacher to come to church saying to himself, "I defy anybody in this church to guess how I am going to treat

[22] *Yale Lectures on Preaching*, First Series (Boston: Pilgrim Press, 1872), p. 122.

this subject." [23] All sermons should not be poured into the same mold. Sermon approaches, forms of outlines, and types of material—all should be varied regularly. The congregation had better be shocked occasionally with an unconventional sermon than to presume beforehand to know how their minister is going to handle his subject. But it is unwise to break the habit of using stereotyped outlines and immediately form the habit of using only novel ones.

When Jesus finished his series of parables of the Kingdom he asked his disciples, "Have you understood all this?" They answered, "Yes." He said to them: "Therefore every scribe who has been trained for the kingdom of heaven is like a householder who brings out of his treasure what is new and what is old." (Matt. 13:51-52.) A preacher should not hesitate to experiment with new ways of preaching, but he should not discard the old, tried and tested ways of preaching, validated by the accumulated experiences of countless generations. The use of unconventional sermons will not suddenly revive churches and fill sanctuaries. Used occasionally they can perform the useful purpose of providing variety and interest and of preventing wearisome sameness. But traditional methods of sermonizing, with their diversified forms, will always be the preacher's staple weekly diet for the people.

This chapter has endeavored to emphasize the following points:

1. There is no known way to escape the necessity of planning the outlines of sermons, if they are to achieve their maximum efficiency.
2. No matter what approach one decides upon he will need to arrange in an orderly sequence what he wishes to say.
3. Regardless of the contents of sermons, their outlines will fall consistently into relatively few patterns.
4. Familiarity with a few types of outlines, carefully differentiated from one another, will be of inestimable service in building satisfactory sermon structures and in providing variety in preaching.

[23] Mystery of Preaching, p. 99.

Suggested Reading

Blackwood, A. W. *The Preparation of Sermons.* New York and Nashville: Abingdon Press, 1948. Chapter XII.

Bowie, Walter Russell. *Preaching.* New York and Nashville: Abingdon Press, 1954. Chapters IX and X.

Breed, David R. *Preparing to Preach.* New York: George H. Doran Co., 1911. Parts I and III.

Caldwell, Frank H. *Preaching Angles.* New York and Nashville: Abingdon Press, 1954.

Jones, E. W. *Preaching and the Dramatic Arts.* New York: The Macmillan Co., 1948.

Lantz, John Edward. *Speaking in the Church.* New York: The Macmillan Co., 1954. Chapter IV.

Luccock, Halford E. *In the Minister's Workshop.* New York and Nashville: Abingdon Press, 1944. Chapter XIII.

In the Bibliography may be found lists of books dealing with the use of literature, of art, and of hymns in preaching.

PART III

PREPARING THE SERMON

7. The Weekly Routine

To provide the proper background for the topic in this chapter, it is assumed that the preacher has an accumulation of sermonic materials in his files, notes on a few sermons in process of development, and a weekly work schedule.

Every person must plan his weekly schedule to suit his temperament and to fit his own situation. According to the best information available, many ministers plan to spend five mornings in their study, Tuesday through Saturday. In addition some spend Saturday evening or early Sunday morning making final preparations for preaching the sermon. This schedule provides a maximum of six periods in which the sermon is brought to completion. Some ministers may do the job in less time. But every week one must go through a certain number of steps to produce a sermon. For the purposes of this chapter let us assume that the sermonizing extends through six sessions.

Before the necessary steps are listed, let it be understood that there is nothing fixed and nothing sacred about either the steps themselves or the sequence in which they are placed. Different men would arrange them differently to suit their own types of mind and methods of work. However he does it and whatever the sequence, each person must get all these things done regularly every week before he goes into the pulpit. What, then, are the steps in sermon preparation to be taken each week?

FIRST PERIOD

Get the mind started on the sermon. One of the first steps to be taken is to study the text carefully in its context with the aids available, to be certain it is to be the actual text and contains the truth one wishes to preach about. That truth should then be identified and roughly formulated, after which the purpose or purposes to be achieved should be written down. Ideas that come from this study will, of course, be added to the notes previously made.

Before the time allotted to sermon preparation for this first period has been consumed, two other steps should be taken. First, the sermon should be committed to God. God should be asked to release the creative powers of mind and heart, to stimulate the imagination, to keep one sensitized to the needs of people, and to give new insights into the significance and values of the truth. Second, the subconscious mind should be assigned the definite task of working on the sermon while the minister's other duties are being performed.

The last two steps are closely related and are of sufficient importance to require elaboration. Students of the human mind are convinced we have two intimately related minds: the conscious mind and the subconscious, or unconscious or subliminal, mind. The brain consists of ten thousand million cells that rest neither day nor night. Only a part of the time, however, are we aware of what is going on in our brains. Some of our best thoughts, ideas, and insights flash into our conscious minds suddenly and spontaneously from our subconscious minds. Many of the great inventions and discoveries, in such widely separated fields as religion, mathematics, music, literature, technical invention, and philosophy, have come to men, not when they were consciously working on their problems, but when they were engaged in other activities. This has happened so often with so many people, at work in so many areas of life, that these discoveries are attributed to mental activity that takes place in what William James called the "deep well of unconscious cerebration." Numerous men throughout history, who did creative thinking in various fields, have relied heavily upon this unconscious cerebration.

Experts frankly admit they cannot explain creative ability, that "no one knows at present how integrations of thought take place in the mind, or upon just what principles of nervous action they ultimately depend." [1] But through a study of the experiences of those who do creative thinking, they have fairly well established several important things about how the subconscious mind can be aided to do its best work.

[1] See Eliot Dole Hutchinson, *How to Think Creatively*, Preface (New York and Nashville: Abingdon Press, 1949).

First, there must be co-operation between the conscious and the unconscious mind. The unconscious mind apparently does not originate ideas but only works on what is prepared for it and handed to it by the conscious mind. Men do not suddenly discover bright ideas without reference to what they have been thinking previously. A flash of inspiration from the subconscious mind follows a period of hard work, of deep, vital concern about, and devotion to, a problem on the part of the conscious mind. But unquestionably the subconscious mind takes the seed thoughts that sink down into it from the conscious mind, assimilates and fuses them, and comes forth with a result which the conscious mind alone cannot produce.

Second, the subconscious mind must be given time to produce results. A period of "incubation" or "gestation" is required. "There exists in all intellectual endeavor," says Dr. Joseph Jastrow, "a period of incubation, a process in great part subconscious, a slow concealed maturing through the absorption of suitable pabulum." [2] Graham Wallas identifies four stages in creative thought: conscious *preparation*, unconscious *incubation*, the flash of *illumination*, and the conscious *verification*.[3] This process of incubation was recently publicized in an article for popular consumption in *This Week* [4] in which the author said, "There's a simple secret when you're stuck on a problem: just 'incubate.'" The procedure is not as simple as that statement makes it sound. The act of incubation does not bring results automatically, in fact does not always bring desired results. Nevertheless, it is a definite factor in all creative thinking.

Third, periods of relaxation seem to be favorable for the best results. Many who report sudden insights have indicated that these came outside the hours of their regular work, when they were relaxed—while taking a stroll, playing a game, daydreaming on a couch, or after a long period of sleep. Hence, after working on a problem for a while we should get away from it entirely and relieve ourselves of all tenseness and strained anxiety, if we expect the unconscious mind to do its work most efficiently.

Those who have experienced these creative moments take no credit for them but attribute them to a source outside them-

[2] *The Subconscious* (Boston: Houghton Mifflin Co., 1906), p. 199.
[3] *The Art of Thought* (New York: Harcourt, Brace & Co., 1926), pp. 79 ff.
[4] October 4, 1953.

selves. Emerson and others insisted that their ideas could not possibly have originated in their minds, but they did not presume to identify the source. The ancient poets attributed them to the muses, Socrates to a familiar spirit, Joel Chandler Harris to his "other brother," and Robert Louis Stevenson to "the brownies." A few have felt, as did the poet Blake, that they were "possessed" by an impersonal force against their will. Russel Wallace, who set forth the theory of natural selection simultaneously with Darwin, said, "Ideas and beliefs are not voluntary acts." Some cautiously, and others boldly, have attributed them to God. To stimulate creativeness, Haydn, the noted composer, used to leave his work and go into the chapel to pray. J. B. Priestley, the British novelist, speaks of the experience as "tapping a reservoir of creative energy and skill, which reservoir is really the source of all so-called inspiration. Into my mind came flooding a much greater mind." Sir Isaac Newton, referring to one of his geometrical discoveries, said, "It is plain to me by the fountain I draw it from, though I will not undertake to prove it to others." Gauss said of one of his discoveries in mathematics: "At last I succeeded, not by painful effort, but so to speak by the grace of God. As a sudden flash of truth the enigma was solved." [5]

This "spiritual" explanation, of course, is not strange to Christian preachers, for they have always believed the Holy Spirit to be the source of their finest insights, inspirations, and illuminations. There is no reason why we may not believe our subconscious minds to be the channels through which the vital thoughts of God "get through" to us. By whatever means one tries to explain it, he will be wise to believe that God can do for his sermon what he alone cannot do. Those who have believed this have discovered what has been called "psychic power in preaching." But always remember that these "uprushes from the subliminal" come only when we have done our conscious work well. According to McComb:

The subconscious is no substitute for hard work: it cannot produce what it does not possess. Out of nothing, nothing comes. Only that

[5] For brief treatments of this subject, see the following. Lancelot Law Whyte, "Where Do Those Bright Ideas Come From?" Harper's, July, 1951. Garrison, The Preacher and His Audience, pp. 261 ff. Luccock, In the Minister's Workshop, pp. 201 ff. The reader who wishes to go more thoroughly into the subject of how thinking takes place is referred to Dewey, How We Think, and to Hutchinson, op. cit.

man can have a richly furnished sub-consciousness who has thought and felt, who has grappled with hard questions and has imaginatively brooded upon the undying quests of the soul.[6]

When one leaves his study after the first session with his sermon, he should carry some sort of notebook with him. In it, record should be made of everything that comes into the mind about the sermon while he is conversing, visiting, reading, walking, or otherwise going about the routine of the day. When the sermon idea is handed over to God and to the subconscious mind for the process of *incubation a vital process* is started. Other forces begin to operate for and work with the preacher. His mind and God's mind begin to work together in a spiritual partnership. No idea, thought, insight, or bit of illustrative material should be allowed to escape. Jot everything down! One will again and again be amazed at and grateful for what flows into his hands unsought and unexpectedly, and will want to give God the credit.

SECOND PERIOD

Browse and brood. The first thing one should do as he begins the second period of work on his sermon is to transfer to his sermon notes everything of value he has in his pocket notebook, and to elaborate on his notes as his mind prompts. Then it is time to "browse" or "graze" in the library. Check everything on the subject to be found in filing cabinet and card indexes. Run down every citation and reference to books previously read in the regular course of study. Follow through on every lead picked up in this browsing. To the sermon notes previously made, add all pertinent material discovered in this search.

The next stage of preparation might be to put one's self on the witness stand for cross-examination. Questions such as these should be asked: Precisely what does this subject mean? Is it a vital, practical truth? Who needs it? Why am I preaching it? How many aspects of the truth might conceivably be treated? How many ways could I approach or handle it? In short, walk all around the subject and write down everything that comes to mind as this is done. Questioning the subject in this manner is what James Black called "boxing its ears." [7]

[6] Preaching in Theory and Practice, p. 106.
[7] Op. cit., p. 92.

By this time one will have before him a disarrayed, amorphous mass of material. He should not be concerned at this juncture about its chaotic condition, nor try to unscramble it or bring order out of it. That will come later. An orderly plan should not be forced, or hurried, or arrived at prematurely. The first concern is to collect sufficient material on the subject so there will be something to whip into shape.

Before the second period of work on the sermon is concluded, one should start a process regarded as one of the most important phases of sermon preparation: the brooding process. The process is initiated by detaching one's self from the sermon and letting the mind sweep back and forth somewhat rapidly over the material gathered thus far. This is considered one of the crucial aspects of creative sermonizing. When preachers undertake to describe it for others, they use a number of different terms. "My own preaching," said Bishop McConnell, "comes out of rather prolonged *brooding*." Howard Chandler Robbins says, "Having selected a theme, I *mull* over it for sometime." S. Parkes Cadman assembled all the literature bearing on the subject which he could muster and then, said he, "I *con* over it." Many ministers speak of putting sermons on to *simmer*. Each person must learn by experience precisely what these preachers are trying to explain.

This is a part of the process of incubation previously mentioned. However, one does not completely banish his sermon from his conscious mind but holds it there loosely, or in a state of "free association." William P. Merrill suggested at this stage that the preacher "keep the sermon floating in his mind, somewhere between the conscious and the unconscious amid his varied doings through the day and the week." [8] On this particular morning the brooding should consume only a few moments. At this early stage one can accomplish more by brooding three periods of thirty minutes each than by working on the sermon steadily for three hours. But the brooding goes on at other times and places also until the sermon has been preached. The mind keeps reverting to it at intervals while the preacher is busy at other tasks, or when he finds a few free moments, perhaps before dinner or after going to bed at night.

Again, let us remind ourselves that this is not a mechanical

[8] *The Freedom of the Preacher* (New York: The Macmillan Co., 1922), p. 89.

process of assembling prefabricated parts of a sermon, but going through a life-process of growth. So the notebook should be kept near at hand ready for use. The completed plan of the sermon could come rushing into the mind during one of these periods of brooding though one may not be striving for it.

THIRD PERIOD

Make the tentative outline. The time has now arrived to bring order out of the chaotic mass of ideas and material garnered. First, nail the subject down and formulate the precise theme in accordance with the principles laid down in Chapter IV. Limit the discussion to one truth or one main phase of the truth. Don't undertake too much in a single sermon. Someone has said that beginners and second-rate preachers tend to crowd too much into a single sermon. Second, make an outline for the sermon, keeping in mind the principles and rules in Chapters V and VI. Experiment with several possibilities and settle, at least tentatively, upon the one that is most satisfactory. If this is impossible, try not to get impatient or nervous. Choose two of them and let them lie in the mind together overnight.

The important procedure known as "inventive production" has now begun. The preacher is selecting and arranging ideas into a production distinctively his own. The material has never before been put together in exactly the relationships and for the particular purposes he has in mind. Through his creative thoughts he is bringing an organic unity out of a miscellaneous assemblage of material. In short, he is *inventing* something. E. H. Byington likens this activity to that of God himself as he is pictured in the creation story in Genesis. The preacher's mind at first is like primordial chaos with

text, truths, thoughts, feelings, impressions, illustrations, quotations, applications, tumbling over each other without form and void. On the first day a little light appears and on the second the material begins to divide, above and below. Then the theme appears, like the fertile earth, while soon sun and stars begin to shine. Evidence of life and order manifest themselves, with beauty and fruitfulness; and last of all the truth is fitted for man. Fortunate is he if his creation is completed in time for the seventh day and so well done that the Creator above calls it "good."[9]

[9] *Pulpit Mirrors* (New York: George H. Doran, 1927), pp. 15-16.

This power of invention is so important, says J. B. Weatherspoon, that if a preacher does not have it he has mistaken his business. "Next to character and piety it is the most important element of his outfit." [10] Inventive production, however, is to be distinguished from originality. One cannot expect to originate ideas never before thought of. However much he tried, he could not do that. In the realm of ideas "there is nothing new under the sun." Someone complained, "The ancients have stolen all our best ideas." Every preacher would join Goethe in confessing, "Very little of me would be left if I could but say what I owe to my predecessors." But every one of us is expected to pass old truths through his mind and express them in such ways that they will have new meaning, new force, new vitality for others. Francis Bacon distinguished three types of men of science: those who, like the ant, merely collect and use; those who, like the spider, make cobwebs out of their own substance; and those who, like the bee, gather material from here and there, digest it, and, by a power of their own, transform it into honey. "Do not say that I said nothing new," cried Paschal. "The arrangement is new."

If one is willing to work at it, he can put ideas together in an original way. That is what makes preaching *one's own*. Preaching is not collecting ideas from many sources, but passing on to the people the truth of God as it has been shaped by one's own thinking and tested by his experiences. "We preachers are trying to do one of the most difficult things in the world," says H. A. Prichard. "We are trying to construe through our own personality the meaning of God in other lives." [11] This requires imagination, without a measure of which sermons are doomed to failure.

Wordsworth described imagination as "the faculty of brooding upon some conception until it . . . clothes itself in words and images and trains of thought which are as truly expressive of its real nature as the human face and body are expressive of the human personality which animates them." By using imagination one can "dress up" truth in images others can "see" as surely as they can see people in distinctive apparel. Every person

[10] Revision of Broadus *On the Preparation and Delivery of Sermons* (New York: Harper & Brothers, 1944), p. 77.

[11] *The Minister, the Method, and the Message* (New York: Charles Scribner's Sons, 1932), p. 145.

possesses imagination, potentially and to some degree. But it has to be cultivated by thinking concretely, by working at the job of brooding over truth until its meaning can be seen in mental images, by letting the mind go loose. Christopher Morley once said, "It was a fine day for flying kites: I had no kite to fly so I flew my mind instead." Release the wings of your imagination!

FOURTH PERIOD

Make a complete, detailed outline of the sermon. If the plan was not decided upon definitely during the last period, it should be decided upon now. If it was completed last time it should be rechecked and, if necessary, revised. At this time also an outline of both the introduction and conclusion should be made. The various types of material to be utilized should be chosen carefully. Every item hitherto chosen tentatively for the sermon should be separately scrutinized and its relevancy for *this particular sermon* appraised. However striking a thought or an illustration may be, discard it, if it does not fit the purpose of this sermon. One should be rigid and ruthless with himself at this point. Material should not be used simply because it was picked up at one place or another in the early stages of preparation. Next, decide where and how to utilize the material. Insert items one at a time where they seem to fit best.

When these steps have been taken, it is a good policy to think one's way again through the whole outline as it has been filled in. By this procedure one often discovers that something he decided to use in one place is more appropriate in another. One should go over the outline in this way several times, eliminating and rearranging until he is satisfied with the aptness and pertinency of all the material for the positions chosen. If time permits, the sequence of points, ideas, and illustrations should be viewed as though it were someone else's outline being examined objectively, to make sure it has all the qualities of a good outline. For greater clarification one should stand up and talk the outline aloud as though he were explaining carefully to someone else precisely what it is he is trying to accomplish.

The work on the sermon this period may consume half the morning, but it will pay off. Careful preparation here facilitates the actual drafting of the sermon later.

FIFTH PERIOD

Write out the sermon in full at one sitting. This will probably require the whole morning. Agreement is almost universal that the sermon should be thought through and rethought in some such detail as suggested for the last period, and then mentally composed before delivery. A few preachers consider this mental composition sufficient. The great majority of experienced preachers believe the process of writing out in full to be essential. Writing aids in expressing briefly, accurately, and pointedly what otherwise is likely to be profuse, vague, and loosely stated. Bacon said: "Conversation makes a ready man; reading makes a full man; and writing an exact man." Writing also enables one to determine and control the length of the sermon. After some practice each person soon learns how many pages to write in order to keep the sermon within the allotted time.

Some ministers rapidly write out a sermon in full, then rewrite it for style. A few revise and rewrite three or four times. Ordinarily, one full writing and a penciled revision is sufficient. The chief objection to writing the sermon in full is that it consumes valuable time. The amount of time spent in the actual drafting of a sermon can be reduced to one period of three to four hours, provided the other steps suggested have been properly completed before the writing begins, and provided the preacher learns to use a typewriter with facility. Time spent in writing is well spent. The gain in clarification and condensation of thought is worth all the effort. Even though the manuscript is not used in delivery, the written sermon proves to be one of the best preparations for its effectiveness.

The next three chapters will be devoted to a study of how to utilize illustrative material, how to plan and draft the introduction and the conclusion, and how to compose the sermon to be heard rather than read by the congregation. Hence what has been said about writing the sermon must suffice for the present. But let this be stressed: it is advisable to get the sermon down in its complete form by the end of this period, or by Saturday noon.

SIXTH PERIOD

Give the sermon a final checking and prepare yourself for preaching it. Ministers have different ways of taking the last steps in the preparation for preaching the sermon. Some spend more time than others. Some do the final preparing on Saturday morning, others on Saturday evening, still others on Sunday morning. Much depends upon whether one expects to preach from the manuscript or without notes. But in either case these final steps, if taken in some manner and to some degree, will insure a more effective sermon when it is finally preached.

a) *Read and revise the manuscript.* This final check nearly always results in the shifting of some materials, the elimination of others, and the rewriting of some passages. Only the exceptional person can complete a manuscript at one sitting and then use it without changes.

b) *Rethink the sermon in the light of the congregation.* This is where the imagination performs one of its most useful functions. Playwright Terence Rattigan tells how he invented an ever-present Aunt Edna for his guidance in writing plays. He thinks of her as one of the typical, average theatergoers whose judgment makes or breaks plays. As he works on his plays he keeps wondering what Aunt Edna will think of this and that, and reminding himself that unless he pleases her he will fail. While Jane Taylor was writing her *Poems for Infant Minds,* she conjured up a child into her presence and spoke directly to him in terms he could understand. When she got tired she dismissed him saying, "There, love, now you may go." [12]

Wise preachers do a similar thing, both while drafting their sermon and while getting themselves ready to preach it. They imagine their congregations before them. They call to mind certain individuals and groups and ask themselves as they go over their sermons: What will this person or that person, this group, or that group, think of what I'm saying? Will it fit their needs? Will they understand what I'm saying? This device for putting one's self in the place of his listeners may force some last-minute changes but will keep the sermon down to earth. This has been spoken of as "pastoral clairvoyance," a method of discovering what the people are thinking. "Any man who lacks that," says Fosdick, "has no business to preach anyway."

c) *Get into the mood of the sermon.* This may be done by reading or rehearsing the sermon as though one were actually

[12] See C. F. Rogers, *The Parson Preaching* (London: S. P. C. K., 1949), p. 37.

standing in the pulpit preaching it. It helps to speak it off exactly as one intends to do on the morrow and to gesture as one speaks.

This will stimulate both thought and feeling, make one feel the importance and the urgency of what he is saying, and prepare him to say it with fervor and force. A sermon is more likely to grip the hearts of the people if it first grips the preacher's heart, if it becomes a "fire in his bones."

d) *Commit one's self and one's sermon to God.* Ask God to make both the message and the messenger instruments of his Spirit for the healing and the redemption of souls.

MAIN STEPS IN SERMON PREPARATION

1. Select the text and general subject, or idea, for the sermon.
2. Put the subconscious mind to work.
3. Browse in your library and gather material.
4. Brood over the material.
5. Settle upon specific subject and theme and exact purpose.
6. Make a tentative outline.
7. Prepare a complete, detailed outline.
8. Fill in the outline with ideas and illustrations.
9. Write out the sermon in full.
10. Revise and reshape.
11. Get the sermon in your system.
12. Prepare yourself.

SUGGESTED READING

Chappell, Clovis G. *Anointed to Preach.* New York and Nashville: Abingdon Press, 1951. Chapters III-IV.

English, John M. *For Pulpit and Platform.* New York: The Macmillan Co., 1919. Chapter V.

Macleod, Donald, ed. *Here Is My Method.* New York: Fleming H. Revell Co., 1952.

Mears, A. G., *The Right Way to Speak in Public.* New York: Emerson Books, Inc., 1953.

Newton, Joseph Fort, ed. *If I Had Only One Sermon to Prepare.* New York: Harper & Brothers, 1932.

Prichard, Harold Adye. *The Minister, the Method and the Message.* New York: Charles Scribner's Sons, 1932. Chapters IV-VI.

Stevenson, Dwight E. *A Road-Map for Sermons* (pamphlet). Lexington: The College of the Bible, 1950.

8. Preparing Illustrative Material

The word "illustrate" means to make clear, to illuminate, to throw light upon a subject. Illustrations are essential because of the way the human mind functions. Abstract statements of truth, detached from the practical experiences of real people in live human situations, have little power to convince ordinary minds. Matthew Arnold said: "A correct, scientific statement of rules of virtue has upon the great majority of mankind simply no effect at all." That statement may be too sweeping, but nevertheless it is safe to say that the great masses of the people do not think—are not prepared to think—in exact, carefully worded formulas. They think in terms of their practical problems. If they are to be moved by the truth they must be shown, in terms they understand, how the truth meets their need and fits into their daily activities. Illustrations are instruments for accomplishing these ends.

Ordinarily before anyone begins the discussion of a subject in theoretical terms, a problem in semantics must be settled. A definition of terms must be agreed upon by teacher and hearers before communication can take place. Unquestionably, Jesus chose deliberately to use a method of teaching that bypassed the necessity of this definition of terms, for he neither defined terms nor attempted to prove the truth with close-knit arguments. He took a short cut to the minds of his hearers. He taught in concrete rather than in abstract terms. He certainly never heard of the modern psychological term "apperception" but nevertheless understood the mental process which that term describes, namely: that people interpret what they hear and see in terms of what they already know. If they possess no knowledge with which to interpret new ideas, no communication of those ideas can take place. Alien ideas are in exactly the same category as a foreign tongue. Paul declared, "If I do not know the meaning of the language, I shall be a foreigner to the speaker and the speaker a foreigner to me." (I Cor. 14:11.) Unfortunately preachers and congregations are often foreigners to each other because preachers are not using language that "registers" in the minds of the people.

Every preacher ought to make a detailed study of Jesus'

method of teaching for the light it will throw upon his own method of preaching, especially upon his method of using illustrations. Jesus expressed himself largely in figures of speech. Someone has estimated that more than one-half of his public instruction was given in the form of parables or comparisons. One scholar found 164 metaphors in the Synoptic Gospels.[1] Fifty-six metaphors have been found in the Sermon on the Mount alone. These figures of speech suggested pictures of things the people were familiar with in their daily life, such as: bread, salt, light, water, and patches on old clothes. He compared the difficult heavenly mysteries with well-known earthly things, such as the farmer planting seed in his field, the fisherman dragging his net filled with all kinds of fishes, and a man arousing his neighbor from sleep to borrow a loaf of bread. In parable after parable he gave brief characterizations of individuals and groups acting in human situations with which his hearers were closely acquainted and in which they could easily identify themselves and their neighbors.

Even now, when we read Christ's words, pictures of objects and people form in our minds almost automatically. His words were alive. To use Kipling's expression, "They walked up and down in the hearts of the hearers." By means of these illustrations an immediate understanding was established between his mind and the mind of his hearers. Without further explanation he and they were in rapport. There can be no doubt that this method of teaching accounts in part for the profound impression his words have made on people of all classes and of all ages throughout the world. Wise is the preacher who adopts the Master's method in his preaching!

FUNCTIONS OF ILLUSTRATIONS

How can we formuate the reasons for using illustrations?

1. Illustrations are used to make the truth concrete. The right kind of illustration provokes a mental picture in which the hearer actually sees the truth. "The Word became flesh and dwelt among us . . . ; we have *beheld* his glory." (John 1:14.) When Jesus appeared the truth was no longer mere words, mere theory, mere theology: it came to life. The people *saw* God's

[1] Benjamin W. Robinson, *Some Elements of Forcefulness in the Comparisons of Jesus* (Chicago: University of Chicago Press, 1904), p. 114.

Word walking among them in human form, acting out the truth. I once heard J. H. Jowett explain the meaning of the expression "Be transformed by the renewal of your mind" (Rom. 12:2). Explaining that the word "renewal" literally means "refurnishing," he proceeded to draw a word picture of a person refurnishing his mind by taking out one set of ideas and putting in another, as he would refurnish a room by taking out one set of objects and bringing in another. I can never forget that truth because I *saw* it as clearly as I saw the people about me.

2. *Illustrations are used to make the truth interesting.* Jonathan Swift claimed, "Dullness is the sin against the Holy Ghost." Whether one would go that far or not he surely will agree that preaching interestingly is at the same time a virtue and a necessity. Referring to preaching, John Bright, the British statesman, once said, "Nothing that I can think of would induce me to undertake to address the same audience once a week for a year." That is a heavy responsibility, but, as experience proves, it can be done successfully if the preacher continuously uses interesting illustrations. After writing a weekly article for the *Westminster Gazette* for a year, H. G. Wells quit because the strain of turning out an article a week was too much for him. In his final article he said, "If there is anything worse in this way than periodic journalism it must be preaching and having to go into a pulpit with half an hour's supply of uplift fresh and punctual every Sunday." The freshness of the preacher's weekly uplift will be provided to a great extent by his ability to find striking, arresting ways of illustrating his subjects.

3. *Illustrations are used to make the truth impressive.* An illustration is a device, not only for making the truth easy to understand, but for making it easy to remember. Thomas Guthrie, the noted Scottish preacher, used to ask the children of his congregation on Sunday evening what they remembered about his morning sermon. He discovered they remembered the illustrations better than anything else. So he decided thereafter to preach pictorially for the benefit of children and adults alike and did so with success. Beecher insisted that a preacher could safely repeat a sermon within six months if he changed his illustrations. Illustrations, he said, are remembered longer than any other part of the sermon. They are frequently the only parts of

the sermon remembered by some people. Illustrations that embody the truth in a pictorial way must be used if one wishes to impress that truth permanently upon the minds of his listeners.

4. Illustrations are used to make the truth persuasive. Shortly after the end of the last World War the United States Office of War Information published a book entitled *Persuade or Perish*. That ought to be said to preachers, though in slightly different form—"Persuade or fail." A sermon is not a sermon if it does not move the listeners to do something about the message it contains. Much of the persuasive power of every sermon is found in its illustrations. One need only recall his own experiences and check the experiences of others to prove that illustrations are the most effective way of convincing the judgments, arousing the emotions, and moving the wills of congregations.

5. Illustrations are used to make the truth practical. They bring the truth down into common life. We preachers become so familiar with eternal truths we sometimes forget that those truths have to be lived by the people amid the finite and the material things of earthly existence. Our hearers must carry the precious "treasure in earthen vessels" (II Cor. 4:7). Illustrations are designed to show how the truths of the divine order may be put to work amid the temptations, trials, drudgery, and complex relations of the human order. Martin Luther took the preachers of his day to task for "aiming at high and hard things" and "neglecting the saving health of the poor unlearned people." Then he added, "When I preach I sink myself deep down." And so should we all—deep enough to see clearly, and to devise ways of helping folk see clearly how the gospel fits their needs.

But devising illustrations that fulfill these functions is not easy. Spurgeon tells of a great scholar who prayed, "Lord, give me learning enough that I may preach plain enough." Preaching the profound truths of the gospel so plainly that even an unlearned man can understand them requires prolonged brooding, vivid imagination, and skill. Jesus could preach concretely only because he thought his way into the experiences, the minds, and the hearts of people. His pictorial teaching was never mere word painting or entertainment but a way of conceiving the truth, a quality of thinking. Truth was *embodied* in his illustrations.

There are three basic rules to remember at this point: (1)

Never tack an illustration onto a sermon. (2) Never use one that attracts attention to itself and away from the truth. (3) Use illustrations *through* which the hearer can see to the truth, as he sees through the window to the world outside.

One of the preacher's subtle temptations is to use illustrations for their own sake, to become enamored with their sheer artistry, their dramatic interest, their moving power, and to forget that they should be embodiments of the truth he is preaching. Edwin H. Byington said he once heard a sermon in which the illustrations reminded him of the supplement to a Sunday newspaper. They were folded into the sermon, not an integral part of it. Illustrations should be structural rather than decorative—built into the sermon, not added as an ornament. Richard Baxter, the illustrious Puritan preacher, expressed this forcefully and vividly in words that still stir our hearts:

> What skill doth every part of our work require, and of how much moment is every part. To preach a sermon, I think, is not the hardest part; and yet what skill is necessary to make plain the truth, to convince the hearers; to let in the irresistible light into their consciences, and to keep it there, and drive all home; to screw the truth into their minds, and work Christ into their affections; to meet every objection that gainsays, and clearly to resolve it; to drive sinners to a stand, and make them see there is no hope, but they must unavoidably be converted or condemned; and to do all this for language and manner as beseems our work, and yet as is most suitable to the capacities of our hearers. This, and a great deal more that should be done in every sermon, should surely be done with a great deal of holy skill. So great a God, whose message we deliver, should be honoured by our delivery of it.[2]

INVENTING ILLUSTRATIONS

Illustrations which the preacher invents for himself are the most effective because they are part and parcel of his own thinking. Now and then a sermon subject will be a vivid illustration. That is one reason for an effort to make the subject as arresting as possible. Occasionally one will devise an outline, each point of which is a good illustration of the truth being presented. Some of the most illuminating illustrations come from the study of the etymology of words. Many of the most helpful things a preacher

[2] *The Reformed Pastor* (New York: Robert Carter and Bros., 1860), p. 75.

says are conveyed through figures of speech that come to him after long brooding over the truths he yearns to explain clearly: metaphors, similes, allegories, exclamations, interrogations, apostrophes, personifications, hyperboles. A good way to stimulate the imagination in forming figures of speech is to read regularly "Toward More Picturesque Speech," a department in *Reader's Digest* that contains unusual figures of speech taken from current writings. Brief, pithy biographical sketches delineating types of people, or desirable and undesirable qualities of personality, also make fascinating illustrations.

If humor comes naturally, it can be used with good effect. Often a whimsical turn to a subject, a touch of humor, can drive home a truth better than a serious statement. One can hardly conceive of more vivid and impressive ways of expressing the truth than the exaggerations Jesus used to describe the man who meticulously strained his water to avoid swallowing a gnat but gulped down a camel without so much as batting an eye; and the man who was gravely concerned with the speck in another's eye but unperturbed by the log in his own eye. These statements must have provoked laughter from his hearers. But if humor has little or no relevance to what is being said; if, so to speak, it is dragged in by the feet merely to provoke laughter—it is an interruption, a diversion, and an impertinence. Furthermore, "Laughter that grows out of disparagement, and at the same time fosters feelings of superiority, may be strongly anti-Christian in its effects. There are sadistic, vindictive elements in many forms of humor." [3] The desire to tell a funny story that contains the slightest tinge of vindictiveness should always be inhibited. Even if a person is endowed with native wit, he should use his ability with restraint.

'Tis pitiful
To court a grin when you should woo a soul;
To break a jest when pity should inspire
Pathetic exhortation; and to address
Skittish fancy with facetious tales
When sent with God's commission to a heart.[4]

The experiences and observations of the preacher are probably the most prolific source of illustrations. Preachers continually

[3] Garrison, *The Preacher and His Audience*, p. 205.
[4] From "The Task," by William Cowper.

convert into brief illustrations what they see, hear, read, and experience. The old word for such illustrations was "anecdote," which is from two Greek words meaning "not given out" or "not published." The word simply means a brief narrative, or an interesting or amusing incident or event. We are reluctant to use the word in our day but there is no satisfactory substitute for it. Anecdotes always have constituted, and perhaps always will constitute, the largest percentage of illustrations for sermons. They come from the very stuff of life itself.

The person who wishes to invent worth-while illustrations needs to cultivate the ability to see things in pictures and to help others see them. This requires the expenditure of energy and the development of skill. Ruskin rightly said:

The greatest thing a human soul ever does in this world is to see something, and tell what he saw in a plain way. Hundreds of people can talk for one who thinks, but thousands can think for one who can see. To see clearly is poetry, prophecy, religion—all in one.[5]

Seeing the truth clearly and telling it in pictures plainly is far more effective than telling what someone else saw. "Surely the Lord is in this place," said Jacob: "and I did not know it." (Gen. 28:16.) One function of the preacher's weekly illustrations is to show his congregation that God is—or ought to be—in many ordinary places where they have not yet detected his presence. While Paul was waiting for his traveling companions at Athens, he moved about the streets. Later when he addressed the curious crowd he said, "As I passed along, and observed the objects of your worship, I found also an altar with this inscription, 'To an unknown god.' What therefore you worship as unknown, this I proclaim to you." (Acts 17:23.) (Italics mine.) As the minister moves in and about his parish, he should keep his eyes open for illustrations to make God more real to the people.

> Earth's crammed with Heaven,
> And every common bush afire with God;
> And only he who sees takes off his shoes—
> The rest sit round it and pluck blackberries.[6]

[5] Modern Painters, Vol. III, Part IV, ch. xvi, sec. 28.
[6] From Aurora Leigh, by Elizabeth Barrett Browning.

The following miscellaneous suggestions about inventing illustrations are listed for consideration.

1. *Beware of overindulgence in figures of speech.* Watch especially for mixed metaphors. Too many figures of speech, like too many puns, are irritating. Strive to attain what has been spoken of as "unconscious freedom of allusion."

2. *Avoid putting yourself at the center of too many illustrations.* Jesus invented his stories, but carefully avoided relating them as his own experience. He kept himself out of the pictures. Preachers can wisely do likewise in most instances. However, it is advisable occasionally to relate experiences in the first person. People sometimes are more impressed by the preacher's experiences than by what he tells of the experiences of people in fiction or in faraway places and ages. John Oman believes the relating of personal experiences to be permissible so long as one does not make himself the hero round which it all turns. But he warns against the danger of embellishing stories related in the first person, dressing them up for the glorification of the narrator, and telling tall personal experiences that challenge the credulity of the hearers.[7] These warnings are worth heeding. A wise basic rule to lay down is this: never strain the credulity of the hearer!

3. *Avoid passing references to long lists of names, authors, and books.* For example: "This truth was exemplified in the lives of such illustrious men as the apostle Paul, Augustine, Calvin, Lincoln, and Dr. Grenfell"; or "This is effectively illustrated by Dante's *Divine Comedy*, Milton's *Paradise Lost*, Browning's *Saul*, and George Bernard Shaw's *Saint Joan of Arc*." Passing references of this sort are not illustrations. They are parades of reading. Either tell enough about persons or books mentioned so the people will understand specifically what it is about them that illustrates what is being said, or omit them.

4. *Carefully prepare the anecdotes used.* Make a study of the parables of Jesus. Each is a literary gem, with no superfluous words, no inadvertences. Each illustrates one main truth and does it with precision. When an incident is related, don't dawdle. Get into the story quickly. Leave out all asides, all extraneous matter, all casual remarks. Don't get lost in the details. Use quick strokes. Be brief. Tell the story in simple and picturesque language.

[7] Concerning the Ministry, p. 164.

143

5. Use dialogue to provide vividness and movement, but use dialect sparingly. Few people can use dialect naturally and sincerely. An impersonation may provoke laughter at the expense of someone else or of his group and thus make an unfavorable impression. In most instances it is more effective to tell a story in ordinary language and in an ordinary manner.

6. Study the techniques of storytelling, but adapt them to sermonizing. The two are to be distinguished. A good sermon illustration must have a plot, action, climax, and an application. Don't hesitate to apply an illustration. A preacher is not telling stories as such but trying to unfold the truth of the gospel.

7. Remember the injunction of Augustine: "Make the truth plain! Make the truth pleasing! Make the truth moving!"

BORROWING ILLUSTRATIONS

Since no one can read everything, experience everything, and go everywhere, every preacher finds it necessary to borrow some illustrations from others. Jesus quoted from Jewish writings, repeated familiar proverbs, and borrowed from the prophets the ideas for at least two of his parables: the parable of the vineyard and the parable of the shepherd. So borrow, but keep in mind the following suggestions.

1. Use compilations of sermon illustrations with extreme caution. A large number of preachers would say, "Never use them!" A distinction needs to be made between compilations of sermon illustrations and compilations of choice poems, passages from literature, and excerpts from writings of various kinds. The latter serve a useful purpose, provided they supplement, rather than substitute for, one's general reading. In these general compilations may be found much material that can be adapted.

But in the collations of sermonic materials the illustrations are ready-made. A person uses these at great risk. They soon become common property and commonplace. Since they do not grow out of one's own experiences, and the context in which they originally appeared is unfamiliar to him, he runs the risk of misunderstanding and misusing them and of making them sound unreal. Continuous reliance upon books of illustrations stifles one's imagination, powers of observation, and ability to see relationships, and hinders creative thinking. These books are a lazy man's device. Used habitually they make for hasty, careless preparation. They provide a shallow, superficial, and artificial background for sermons. They had better not be used even as a crutch. "Be your own anthologist," wisely advises James S. Stewart.

2. *Learn how to use quotations wisely.* Quotations provide a fairly large proportion of effective illustrations. But they need to be used with discrimination. They should be used to support and stimulate one's thinking, not to substitute for it. "Enough of quotation," cried Emerson; "tell me what you think." People in the congregation begin to share Emerson's feelings when too many quotations are used by the preacher.

Quotations should be apt. They should really illustrate and, as we shall see later, be worked into one's train of thought. A good policy is to "use a quotation when it comes as if it were inevitable." [8] Also, guard against using more than are necessary to further the argument or to elucidate the point being made.

3. *Do some straight thinking on the ethics of borrowing.* Learn to distinguish between legitimate use and plagiarism.

As indicated in the previous chapter no one can hope to be original in the absolute sense of that term. But this should give one no concern. S. Parkes Cadman advised young ministers:

Do not vex yourselves about originality, for Emerson laid that specter when he said that all literature since Plato was a quotation. You cannot turn to any essay of the Sage of Concord without finding numerous citations from the best works. His frequency and suitability in appropriating the words of earlier writers provoked the comment of Oliver Wendell Holmes, that Emerson's quotations were like the miraculous draught of fishes. He was a striking illustration of Bacon's axiom that reading makes a full man.[9]

Everybody borrows. Borrowed ideas should be incorporated into one's own thinking, formulated in his own words and categories. They are then his own, as nearly as anybody's ideas are ever his own. When someone asked Charles Lamb where he got the material for one of his essays, he said he had milked three hundred cows for it, but the butter was his own.

[8] See Black, op. cit., p. 128.
[9] *Ambassadors of God* (New York: The Macmillan Co., 1920), pp. 255-56.

The preacher should be concerned when he incorporates the words of others into his sermon and leads the congregation to think they are his own. That is plagiarism. According to Webster's dictionary, to plagiarize means: "to steal or purloin and pass off as one's own (ideas, writings, etc., of another)." It is derived from a Latin word meaning "kidnaper," which, in turn, comes from the Greek word meaning "oblique" or "crooked." A person can avoid a great deal of inner turmoil as well as the possibility of public misunderstanding and criticism if, at the beginning of his ministry, he lays down a few basic principles about the use of another's material and sticks to them without arguing with himself about them. Some suggestions, representing the common ethical judgment of generations of preachers, follow.

a) Never put a quotation, long or short, in the manuscript of the sermon without using quotation marks and indicating the source, if the source is known. That protects against the charge of dishonesty if someone should see the manuscript, and provides the source of the quotation if it should ever be put in print.

b) Never preach another man's sermon, even if it is acknowledged. That is a dereliction of duty. God calls each person to do his own preaching and the people come to church to hear his sermons not another's.

c) Never appropriate the complete outline of another's sermon without letting the congregation know it is being done. If the preacher is well known, identify him. If his name would mean nothing, simply state a minister once devised an outline of a sermon on your text that you wish to make use of.

d) Never incorporate into your sermon any major portion of a sermon or of any other writing by another without indicating in some way that it is a quotation. The source and author of every extended excerpt should be revealed clearly.

e) Never describe experiences of someone else as though they happened to you. Clearly this is intellectual dishonesty.

4. Exercise discriminating judgment and good taste about acknowledging. As indicated earlier there are good reasons for using quotation marks and citing sources in the manuscript of a sermon. But it is not necessary always to do this in delivering the sermon. A few general suggestions are offered as guides.

a) Identify the author and source if it will add weight to what is being said or will provoke the hearer to read something of value.

But continually citing exact sources may become an objectionable and irritating form of pedantry. Too much of that makes hearers feel one is attempting to impress them with his learning. Dawson C. Bryan tells of a brilliant young minister who kept citing the sources of his numerous quotations. Afterward one young person remarked, "His messages are helpful, but I get so distracted by his mention of Dr. So-and-So, Professor Whatnot, and the eminent writer Whosit." [10]

b) There are satisfactory ways of utilizing another's material in a sermon without citing sources as one is expected to do in a scholarly article or book. Austin Phelps said, "Put the signs of quotation into your delivery as well as into your manuscript." [11]

c) Incidents told by others can be related in such a way that the hearers will know without being told they are not original with the speaker. One can always introduce the material with a few stock phrases, such as: "Someone has said . . . ," "It has been said . . . ," "The story is told that . . . ," "So-and-So tells of . . . ," and "I heard (or read) recently . . ."

d) Poetry is in a class by itself. As a general rule poetry should be used without indicating it is a quotation. Unless a person writes poetry himself, the people will know it is not his own. Ordinarily, citing the source of a quotation from classical poets is superfluous. By all means avoid the hackneyed expressions, "As the poet has said . . . ," "As the great Shakespeare says . . . ," etc. On the other hand, the congregation will often want to know, and the minister will often want them to know, who wrote the lines of less familiar poetry used. To mention the name of the author is usually sufficient, although one should always be prepared to give interested inquirers (of whom there will always be many) the exact sources.

e) The use of copyright material in the pulpit is not usually considered an infringement of copyright laws. The standard rule for the use of copyright material over the radio is: permission must be secured to quote poetry of any length and to quote more than forty-five words of prose. However, there are so many aspects of the problem that the reader is referred to *The Pastor's Legal Adviser,* by Norton F. Brand and Verner M. Ingram, Chapter XX.[12]

Every minister can well afford studiously to avoid running the

[10] *The Art of Illustrating Sermons* (New York and Nashville: Abingdon Press, 1938), pp. 193-94.

[11] *Men and Books* (New York: Charles Scribner's Sons, 1882), p. 199.

[12] New York and Nashville: Abingdon Press, 1942.

risk of injuring the cause of Christ by the use of another's material that could remotely be classified by his hearers as plagiarism. Weatherspoon suggests this general rule that is worth remembering: "Never use another's contribution in a way that would be embarrassing to confess in public or that would be embarrassing if the author were present." [13]

How to Make Use of Illustrations

Whether the illustration is one's own or another's, and whatever its type, it must be "worked into" the sermon. Illustrations cannot be inserted ready-made into sermons, as pieces are inserted into a jigsaw puzzle, and expected to fit. All illustrations should be woven into one's train of thought. If the illustration is his own the preacher should compose it, not as a thing in itself, but for the specific place he expects to use it in the sermon. If it is a quotation, that also must be woven into the purposes in view. Seldom can an illustration be satisfactorily inserted abruptly without reference to what precedes and what follows.

A good way to understand what is meant by working illustrations into a sermon is to read a few sermons by outstanding preachers and observe precisely how they do it. When this is done watch for three things: (1) How the illustration is prepared for. The thought must be prepared for the illustration and the illustration for the thought. (2) What formula is used for presenting the illustration. (3) How the illustration is concluded or applied.

Let us look at an example or two of how one preacher does it. The preacher is making the point that we can turn our misfortune into opportunity. His last sentence, before bringing in his illustration, says that instead of allowing a misfortune to trample him down a man can surmount it and guide it to useful ends. Immediately he introduces his illustration with this formula: "Have you ever heard how the Braille system of reading for the blind was invented?" Then he tells how Braille invented the system when he was totally blind and what it meant to him and to countless other blind people. Finally comes his conclusion, or application: "Thus Louis Braille turned his misfortune into opportunity." In another sermon he says that adversity rounds out and enriches character, explains in a sentence or two what this

---

[13] Op. cit., p. 92.

means, and adds that Edwin Markham was right when he wrote,

> Defeat may serve as well as victory
> To shake the soul and let the glory out.[14]

In this case he made his application before he gave his illustration.[15]

Preparation for the illustration is not the same thing as a preface, so often referred to. By the "preface" is meant talking about an illustration before it is given. For example: "Let me illustrate this with one of the most fascinating and moving stories it has ever been my privilege to hear"; or, "For this fine illustration I am indebted to Dr. So-and-So's book, entitled . . ."; or "I will now relate an incident, not only because it is a good illustration, but because it has its own intrinsic worth." Joseph Parker called this sort of talk a lot of "painful nonsense." All such prefaces should be omitted. The illustration is usually prepared for by a brief statement or two that explains the point being made. Then the illustration is introduced to throw light upon what has just been said. Rarely should an illustration be inserted and left dangling without either introduction or conclusion.

Formulas for introducing an illustration are many. Here are a few taken at random from a number of printed sermons: "Do you remember . . . ?" "You will remember . . ." (these are poor devices, for in most instances the listeners do *not* remember); "We say with Kipling . . ."; "Just take one example . . ."; "Dr. Stanley Jones gives eloquent testimony . . ."; "As Charles R. Brown says . . ."; "In Thackeray's *Vanity Fair*, Becky Sharp says . . ."; "As one of our wise contemporaries has put it . . ."; "Did you read in the newspaper the other day . . ."; "We have in modern times a vivid illustration of this truth . . ."

The most effective way to introduce the illustration is to do it directly and quickly, thus: "In a bitterly contested golf tournament Walter Hagen . . ."; "It was reported recently in England . . ."; "A few days ago I saw a man, long unemployed, who had just received a letter calling him back to his old position." In this connection remember two important things: avoid hackneyed formulas and strive for variety. In other words, keep out of a rut.

[14] From "Victory in Defeat." Used by permission.
[15] Elliott, *Coming to Terms with Life*, pp. 19, 20, 25.

Ways of applying illustrations likewise are many. Remember: the application is the statement that follows immediately upon completion of the illustration. Here are a few also taken at random from several printed sermons: "Such an attitude will not do . . ."; "Now that is not only a great thing to say . . ."; "How all of us need to learn this art . . ."; "How true this is . . ."; "Something like that needs to happen in the lives of a good many of us"; "Well, are you willing . . . ?" "There are few things that we American Christians need much more to learn than the lesson of that"; "Similarly . . ."; "This is not true simply about individuals but about generations . . ."; "He was voicing, was he not . . . ?" "That is true to experience, is it not?" "That may very well symbolize for us a truth . . ."; "Just so . . ."; "Precisely so . . ."; "Exactly so . . ."; Again, variety in concluding illustrations should be the goal.

The use of poetry deserves special attention. Poetry has a universal appeal. For this reason it is probably more widely used than any other type of illustrative material. Before using any part of a poem one should familiarize himself with the poem as a whole. If lines are quoted out of context and without understanding the poet's purpose and mood, they are likely to be misused or misinterpreted. Only the lines relevant for one's purpose should be used. Often for the sake of one or two lines of a poem, a preacher finds himself quoting many other lines that have no bearing upon, or perhaps contradict, what he is saying. Hence too much cannot be said about the wisdom of quoting poetry briefly. The listener, unlike a reader of poetry, has no time to stop and think about the poet's line of thought, images, and intricacies of rhythm. Too many lines divert attention to the poem itself, to the speaker's dramatic ability, or to his unusual memory; and the hearer loses sight of the purpose of the illustration. If at all possible, the poetry used should be memorized. This should invariably be done with poetry used to conclude a sermon. By study and practice a modest competence in both reading and speaking poetry can be developed.

Some concluding suggestions are listed about the use of illustrations, partly by way of summary:

1. *Search until an apt illustration is found.* Be adamant in this respect. Discard an illustration if there is any question as to its aptness.

2. When quoting from any source, quote accurately. Don't garble what is intended to be a carefully chosen, carefully worded quotation.

3. Avoid illustrations that require too much explaining. Such explanation stops the movement of the sermon, interrupts the progress of thought, and diverts attention from the thought to the illustration itself.

4. Exercise restraint in the number of illustrations used. Giving one illustration after another, like stringing beads, becomes monotonous and less effective the further one proceeds.

5. Never illustrate the obvious. Samuel L. McComb tells of a person who said of the sermon he had just heard, "I would have liked it if Dr. ——— had not insisted on piling upon me a mass of illustrations in support of a truth which it never occurred to me or any other Christian to doubt." [16]

6. Seek always for variety. Don't ride a hobby by using illustrations week after week from a favorite field of interest.

7. Make the illustration subordinate to the truth which is being preached. An illustration should be primarily structural rather than decorative. Never use an illustration for its own sake or one that attracts attention from the theme of the sermon.

SUGGESTED READING

Beecher, Henry Ward. *Yale Lectures on Preaching*, First Series. Boston: Pilgrim Press, 1872. Lecture VII.

Bryan, Dawson C. *The Art of Illustrating Sermons*. New York and Nashville: Abingdon Press, 1938.

Garrison, Webb B. *The Preacher and His Audience*. New York: Fleming H. Revell Co., 1954. Chapter VI.

Macartney, Clarence E. *Preaching Without Notes*. New York and Nashville: Abingdon Press, 1946. Chapter II.

Sangster, W. E. *The Craft of Sermon Illustration*. Philadelphia: Westminster Press, 1950.

Spurgeon, Charles. *The Art of Illustration*. New York: Wilbur B. Ketcham, 1894.

Some of the most helpful treatments of the subject of illustrations may be found in textbooks on homiletics. The reader is referred to the list of textbooks in the Bibliography, nearly every one of which has material of value.

[16] *Preaching in Theory and Practice*, p. 54.

9. Preparing the Introduction and Conclusion

"It is generally agreed," says McComb, "that the two parts of the sermon most easily ruined are the Introduction and the Conclusion." [1] Without doubt they are consistently the weakest parts of the average sermon. This chapter seeks to discover how they may be made to perform their functions effectively.

THE INTRODUCTION

1. The purposes of the introduction. Few would insist that every sermon of every type requires an introduction. But the consensus of opinion is that most sermons need introductions for the following reasons.

a) *To avoid abruptness for both preacher and people.* Broadus believes sermons ought generally to have an introduction because "there seems to be in people a natural aversion to abruptness and delight in a somewhat gradual approach." [2] That explains why there are preludes to musical compositions, prefaces to books, porticos to buildings, and entrances and pathways to gardens, as well as introductions to sermons. John Oman's position is sound:

> While it is better to have no introduction than one which oversteps its business, it is seldom that you have a subject into the middle of which you can plunge with profit. And even if your subject need no introduction, your audience does. If for nothing else, they need a little time to settle down. [3]

Someone has said an introduction to a sermon should be just that. That is, it should say, "Sermon, this is my audience! Audience, this is my theme." That little courtesy paves the way for minds to meet more easily.

b) *To gain the good will of the hearer.* Political speakers customarily take time before beginning their speeches to gain the

[1] *Op. cit.*, p. 72.
[2] *Preparation and Delivery of Sermons*, p. 266.
[3] *Op. cit.*, p. 155.

good will of their audiences or to remove prejudices against what they intend to advocate. While it is presumed people do not come to church in an antagonistic mood, nevertheless they are not always in a receptive mood, eager to listen. The introduction should be designed to allure them to the preacher and to his subject.

c) *To arouse the interest of the hearer.* The introduction should act as an an appetizer to make the listener want to hear what is to follow. "There is no room for debate as to what the introduction ought to be," insists Gerald Kennedy. "We are simply trying to get our people to want to hear what we have to say." [4] They will want to hear it if they are quickly convinced it is of some importance to them.

d) *To let the hearer know what the sermon is about.* The hearer should not be asked to go on a journey blindly but should be given an indication of where he is going and a hint of what he may expect to see. The introduction to a sermon may be compared to the chart which the ranger draws on the blackboard before he takes a group of tourists over a trail through a national park. This chart is not merely to help them decide whether or not they wish to take the trip, but to give a prospectus of what is ahead. The preacher is assured that the hearers will travel with him "more hopefully if they can survey the scene a little before taking the road." [5]

2. The component parts of an introduction. What is put into an introduction to help it achieve its purposes? What are its constituent elements? All introductions need not and should not be composed of exactly the same elements. But since the introductions of so many sermons consistently contain the same materials, we are justified in saying that an introduction ordinarily should contain the following five parts.

a) *The text.* If, as stated in an earlier chapter, Christian preaching ought to be based squarely upon the Bible, the introduction is the logical place for the scriptural basis of a sermon to be indicated. That basis need not, indeed should not, be indicated the same way nor in the same place in every introduction. But somewhere in the introduction, and in an appropriate manner, the truth to be presented should be given a scriptural foundation.

[4] *His Word Through Preaching,* p. 58.
[5] Oman, *op. cit.,* p. 155.

The traditional way of using the text is simply to announce it at the outset. But if that procedure is followed regularly it becomes wearisome to the congregation. Speaking from the viewpoint of the lay listener, George Wharton Pepper suggested that preachers find a way of opening a sermon other than announcing a text of scripture.[6] Some of those other ways will be suggested shortly.

b) The subject or theme. Some preachers announce their text and immediately thereafter state their subject abruptly. W. E. Sangster commends this practice:

> Some able preachers make a practice of announcing their text and saying at once, "My subject is . . ." They give the theme in their first phrase. No small part of their toilsome preparation has been the making of that one fecund phrase. They announce it, therefore, right away and the sermon has begun. No winding drive to the front porch. No porch. They step in.[7]

This method, while effective if used occasionally, is too abrupt for regular use. Most of the time the people ought to be prepared for the theme before it is presented. Suggestions as to how this may be done will be made in the next paragraph. Whatever the preacher's method of approach, the congregation should know before the introduction is finished what he is going to talk about, but not what he is going to say about his subject. The purpose of the introduction is to prepare for what is coming, not to say it ahead of time. Or, as Oman puts it: the introduction should *really* introduce and *only* introduce.

c) An explanation of the connection between the text and subject. Sometimes that connection may be so obvious the mere announcement of the text and theme together is all that is necessary. But usually it is a mistake to assume hearers can see the connection as clearly as the preacher sees it after having mulled over it for some hours. There is little justification for using a text at all unless the people can see clearly that it contains the sermon theme. This can be made clear in either one of two ways: first, present the text and then lead up to the theme; or second, present the theme and lead up to the text. In the first method the text is explained in its context. Seldom is it advisable or fair to rip a single

[6] *A Voice from the Crowd*, p. 19.

[7] From *The Craft of Sermon Construction*, p. 119. Copyright, 1950, by W. L. Jenkins. Used by permission. The Westminster Press and The Epworth Press.

text from its setting and proceed to preach on it without any reference to what it meant originally. But seldom is it necessary to go into a long, tiresome, drawn-out explanation of the setting in order to get at the truth of the text. The whole process may be, and usually should be, done swiftly. In the second method, the theme is explained or illustrated briefly: then the text is approached in such way the people will see the connection between them. Whatever the method, the relationship of the two should be unmistakable.

d) *An indication of the relevancy or importance of the subject to contemporary life.* This is equivalent to saying that every introduction ought to show the hearer how the truth applies to him, or why it is important to him. Doing this skillfully from week to week without doing it the same way every time, is the secret of an effective beginning. All the powers of one's imagination and ingenuity will be taxed to devise a variety of ways to do this.

The one unbreakable rule: one should never permit himself to fall into the habit of introducing the sermon the same way every time, and never permit the congregation to come to expect him to do so. Just for a change and as a surprise, one should begin once in awhile with an abrupt, blunt introduction. Henry Sloane Coffin once read Ps. 11:3 for his text: "If the foundations are destroyed, what can the righteous do?" glanced up, lifted his glasses from his eyes, and, looking his congregation squarely in the face, said, "Why, they can go on being righteous, of course!" Those two sentences, plus his dramatic action, constituted the whole of his introduction. The person reporting it indicates that it was quite effective and also stated that many people anticipated Coffin's sermons eagerly partly because of the variety of unexpected ways in which he introduced them.

e) *Some interesting material designed to arrest the attention of the hearer.* The best way to arouse the interest of the congregation regularly is to use a variety of interesting materials in various ways. The materials that may be used are many and include: an incident from life or literature, a brief story, an aphorism, a letter, a quotation, a news item, a cartoon, lines from a poem or hymn, reference to a book, a bit of conversation or dialogue, reference to the season or to the occasion, a problem, a difficulty, a question. This interesting material is most often used at the beginning of the introduction, but may be equally effective when used in the body of the introduction or at its close.

One of the best ways to achieve variety is to shift the sequence of the component parts of the introduction. These parts should not be *labeled* as one proceeds. They may often merge. Just as occasionally one may wish to have a sermon without an introduction, so he may wish to have an introduction without one or more of these elements. Most of the time all should appear, but not in the same sequence too often in succession. (1) Begin with the text. Give its setting, its explanation, its exposition. Move to the contemporary human situation, problem, or need. Illustrate with a bit of interesting material. Then set forth the theme. (2) Begin with a human situation: problem, need, difficulty, or question. Give some interesting illustrative material. Present the theme and conclude with the text. (3) Begin with the theme: a direct statement of subject and purpose. Present the text. Follow that with illustrative material, and conclude with the importance of the theme for the hearers. (4) Begin with a bit of interesting illustrative material. Then follow whatever sequence is desired. As a matter of principle and policy, arrange the parts in different sequences upon different occasions.

Let us examine two introductions, one that begins and the other that ends with the text, to see how the sequence of the parts may be varied with equally good effects. Here is the introduction to a sermon entitled "Subversive Inactivity" by Frank B. Fagerburg, based on Matt. 12:30, "He that is not with me is against me."

Suppose that on last election day an officer had visited the home of an American citizen and said, "You did not vote today. You are summoned to court to defend yourself against the charge of contributing to the destruction of democracy." Or suppose someone should go on Sunday morning to an American father who, comfortable in bathrobe and bedroom slippers, is reading the newspaper and say to him, "Why have you chosen to help destroy religion and the church?" Suppose, again, that we should go to someone perfectly able to make a gift to the community chest, who instead joins the majority of citizens and does nothing about it, or to someone who is perfectly able to act as a solicitor of such gifts and does not, and say, "What do you have against the little children who are helped by clinics and hospitals?" or "Why are you aiding the cause of juvenile delinquency?" Every such imaginary individual would be amazed, forgetting for a moment that he should be greatly angered. Yet in each case the charge is a just one. We have talked a great deal about subversive activity. What about subversive inactivity?

Surely, this is what Jesus meant when he said, "He that is not with me is against me." Was he not in other words saying, "In the business of faith and righteousness there is no such thing as neutrality. You are either for or against, and hesitation between the two means that you are against"?

I should like to apply this principle of Jesus in two realms—democracy and the Christian cause.[8]

Notice: he begins with imaginary situations, announces his theme, and connects it with his text which he then proceeds to explain.

Halford E. Luccock has a sermon entitled "Parlor or Living Room?" based on Moffatt's translation of John 15:10, "Remain within my love." The introduction began with the quotation of the text. Then followed:

In other words—move in and live there!

A remark frequently made by visitors to New York, so frequently that it has become part of the great American ritual of trite remarks, and yet always spoken with an air of having made a fresh contribution to the world's wisdom is this: "New York is a fine place to visit, but I would hate to live there." It would be hard to imagine words which could more accurately describe the attitude of a great host of people to Christianity—"a fine place to visit, but I would hate to live there!" And they don't.

Yet Christianity is not a museum, an art gallery, a point of interest to be visited. It is a great "living room." The thing to do with it is to live in it. Yet that is often the last thing we ever think of doing with it. We talk about it, we measure it, we visit it in a sight-seeing car, we photograph it and paint it, eulogize and disparage it—do everything with it, except the one thing it was designed for—live in it.

Jesus said, "Abide in me." He offered the spacious hospitality of his truth and himself to the whole race as a "living room." In the very suggestive translation of Doctor Moffatt, he said, "Remain within my love." Jesus says to us: "Live there. Let my love be the four walls of your life, close and dear and intimate enough for a sheltered hearthside; wide and far-ranging enough that the whole family of earth may find place within it." [9]

[8] *The Pulpit*, November, 1951. Used by permission.

[9] *The Haunted House* (New York: Abingdon Press, 1923), pp. 155-56.

Notice: he begins with his text as translated by Moffatt, then immediately states his theme but does not label it, follows this with an interesting illustration and comment, and at the end comes back again to his text and its significance for his hearers.

3. The importance of a good beginning. This cannot be exaggerated. Often the first sentence or two, and always the first paragraph, are crucial. If the preacher does not grip the interest of the people by that time he may fail to grip it at all. For this reason most capable preachers spend a good deal of time devising arresting, unusual ways of beginning their introductions. Sangster commends and justifies the use of "shock tactics" if necessary in beginning an introduction. Then he adds:

Yet people can be arrested sharply by other than "shock" tactics. There is the piquant opening. A sharp paradox can arrest. An incisive question thrust at the heart of the text the moment it is uttered can do it. It can be done by contradicting the text immediately, from the superficial standpoint of worldly wisdom, and then fighting back to the Bible truth again. Or, if one does not contradict it, one can cast doubt upon it in an opening phrase. None of these are oratorical "tricks."

To illustrate what he means Sangster tells of the last sermon preached by J. N. Figgis before the University of Cambridge, on June 2, 1918. After four years of war the Allies were being driven back again. In that tense moment of great national fear the preacher started with the text: "The Lord sitteth upon the flood; yea, the Lord sitteth King for ever" (Ps. 29:10 A.V.). Immediately he asked tensely, "Does he? Does he?" Then he plunged into his sermon.[10]

Charles Reynolds Brown started a sermon by quoting his text: "Am I my brother's keeper?" (Gen. 4:9), and then saying:

You expect me to say "Yes." I say "NO." I am not my brother's keeper. I have no desire to be. There is something officious and patronizing about being any man's "keeper." I want no man to set himself up as my keeper; and I must do unto others as I would have others do unto me. When the position of keeper, therefore, is offered to any right-minded person, he declines. I am not my brother's keeper —I am, however, my brother's brother. And that is another pair of

[10] Op. cit., pp. 126-27.

shoes altogether . . . I am my brother's brother, first, last and all the time.[11]

One should not hesitate to give his sermon an unexpected twist at the very outset. He should always work hard on the first sentence or two. Let it be said again: deliberately and intentionally search for an arresting, striking, and if necessary a "shocking" way to begin. Avoid triteness and platitudes. Don't let anyone call you "Dr. Obvious." Avoid any slavish adherence to the mere conventional and traditional in the way to begin. Practice variety, variety, variety!

4. The length of the introduction. There is no standard rule here. The preacher's controlling purpose, the type of sermon, the length of the entire worship service, the time allotted to the sermon, and the attention span of the congregation—all will be factors in deciding the length of the introduction. But in these days when everybody works on schedules, and under pressures, hears so many competing voices, reads picture magazines quickly, and listens to brief programs over radio and television, one cannot expect an audience to be interested in a sermon unless he knows how to say what he has to say quickly, briefly, and to the point. Whatever else is said pro and con about introductions, all seem to agree they should be brief.

Watch "wearisome preliminaries" in the introduction. "Resist, as you would resist the devil," said Sangster, "that awful tendency to drag." [12] Be specific and concrete. Be direct. "Gentlemen," advised Spurgeon, "don't go creeping into your subject as some swimmers go into the water: first to the ankles, and then to the knees and then to the waist and then shoulders: plunge in at once over head and ears." Nothing will kill interest more certainly than a laborious beginning. An old woman said of John Owen, the famous Welsh preacher, that he was so long spreading the table she lost her appetite for the meal. Every dull, uninteresting, wearisome, complex introduction fails Christ and the people whom he loves. In his name we should learn how to entice the people to hear his gospel gladly.

[11] The Gospel for Main Street (New York: The Century Co., 1930), pp. 24-25.
[12] Op. cit., p. 125.

5. The time to prepare the introduction. Writers are practically unanimous at this point. While one works on his sermon, he should make rough notes about ways of starting it. But before deciding upon the exact nature of the introduction he should have the entire sermon worked out in such detail that he knows precisely what his goal is to be. Once he settles down to drafting the sermon, the introduction should be the first thing composed. Or, as Dr. Blackwood puts it, in writing as in delivery one should start with the opening sentence and go straight through to the end.

THE CONCLUSION

Rhetorically, psychologically, and spiritually the conclusion is, next to the introduction, the most vital part of the sermon. It is not an addition to the sermon but an organic part of it, necessary to its completeness of form and effect. It gathers up the various ideas and impressions of the message for one final impact upon the minds and hearts of the hearers.[13]

Yet conclusions are consistently the weakest parts of sermons. Far too many sermons ravel out at the ends. Every poor conclusion is a lost opportunity, because there the sermon should come to its final climax, there its main purpose should be achieved, there the preacher's supreme effort should take place. More attention should therefore be given to the problem of how to make conclusions effective.

1. The purposes of the conclusion. There is little difference of opinion as to what the conclusion is expected to do, in spite of the fact that so many ministers seem not to work at the job of learning to do it well. Mainly those purposes are the following.

a) *To bring the sermon to an effective close.* As obvious as this is, many do not know how to do it. They hesitate, meander, and flounder, spoiling otherwise good sermons by conclusions that are long, drawnout, and thrown together loosely. After one of his earlier speeches William Jennings Bryan asked his mother, who was present, what she thought about it. "William," she said, "it seemed to me you didn't improve all your opportunities." Somewhat surprised, he asked, "How do you mean?" She replied, "Why, you had several opportunities to sit down before you did." Many regular attendants at church say to each other what they do

[13] Weatherspoon, *op. cit.*, p. 123.

not say often enough to their pastors, "He missed several good stopping places." Perhaps the more critical feel what they are too kind to say, "He's done and we're all done, but he can't stop." [14] The conclusion should be designed to stop a sermon in the right way and at the right place. George W. Chadwick, the American composer, used to tell his students when they were laboring fretfully over their music, "Never finish a thing after it is done." A preacher should learn to stop when he has finished the sermon instead of cruising around looking for a landing place. Or, to change the figure of speech, he should end the sermon with concentrated force and power instead of letting it unravel like a rope and dangle at loose ends.

b) *To apply the truth.* This, too, is obvious. But too many of us do not know how to do it forcefully. Richard Storrs, the noted Brooklyn preacher, told of a fellow student in the seminary who said he liked to discuss subjects but didn't know what to do with them after they were discussed. "I could only leave them and go along," he said. Discussing subjects and leaving them with the hearers may be good lecturing but it is not good preaching. Preaching is discussion *plus*—and that plus distinguishes sermons from every other form of public address. Part of that plus consists in showing the hearer how the truth applies to him. The application may be distributed throughout the whole of the sermon but should be compacted in the conclusion.

c) *To lay the truth on the hearer's conscience.* This is closely related to what has just been said. In fact, it may be considered as implementing the application. Another part of the *plus* of sermonizing is to focus the claims of the truth on the moral judgments and wills of the hearers. A sermon is defective until that is done. Every proven and tested truth carries a divine obligation to do something with it. Storytellers are instructed never to tack a moral onto a story. This principle does not apply to preaching. Unless the "moral" is attached to the sermon it cannot be called a sermon. Moralizing, in the sense of laying upon the consciences of the hearers their obligations concerning the truth, has been called the "consummation of preaching." That consummation is reached in the conclusion. Cotton Mather advised the ministers of his day: "Let your perorations often be lively expostulations

[14] Oman, *op. cit.,* p. 157.

with the conscience of the hearer; appeals made and questions put unto the conscience and consignment of the work over into the hands of that flaming preacher in the bosom of the hearer." [15] That is still good advice for ministers. No sermon is finished until it has been turned over to the consciences of the people to go to work on.

d) *To move to action.* This is the last, and one of the most important parts, of the *plus* of preaching. "Quintus Quiz," in one of his articles in the *Christian Century,* told of a preacher who warned his younger brethren not to leave the arousement to the end. He said if they did, some of the hearers, knowing it was coming, would "put up their mental umbrellas and let the dripping fall upon their neighbors as though to say to them, 'This will do you good.' " Even so, that's a risk the preacher takes. But it is not so much of a risk as some imagine. People not only want to know before the preacher finishes what he thinks they ought to do about the sermon, but expect him to exhort them to do it. They are disappointed, consider the sermon incomplete, if he fails to do so. A preacher should not permit himself to forget that from beginning to end he is out for a verdict, a commitment, a choice, an action on the part of the hearers. Pressure on their wills, an effort to arouse their emotional response, is definitely an integral part of the conclusion. No preacher should ever apologize for endeavoring to move—feelingly move—his hearers to action as he closes his sermon.

If the reader will reflect a moment upon these four purposes he will realize they are not to be separated with hard and fast lines. They merge and in many instances may be achieved simultaneously, or gathered together in one or two sentences at the close. Occasionally a single bit of material may serve to apply the truth, lay it upon the hearer's conscience, and move him to action.

2. *The component parts of a conclusion.* Can we identify the constituent elements of a conclusion as we did with the introduction? For purposes of study we may identify five parts, with the understanding that they are not necessarily to be thought of in isolation from but in conjunction with one another.

a) *A proper transition or connective.* A transitional phrase

[15] *Manductio Ad Ministerium* (New York: Columbia University Press, 1938), p. 106.

is needed at the beginning of the conclusion as a "bridge word" to tie it to the body of the sermon. Without it, the conclusion comes as a surprise, or even a shock, to the congregation. Some think it far better for the congregation to awake suddenly to the fact that the conclusion is not only under way but ending rather than be told it is about to begin. Announcing the conclusion, they feel, is a signal for the hearer to put his mind on getting ready to leave, and therefore a sure way to lose his attention. But there is another side to the question. In a previous chapter it was suggested that transitions aid the listener in following more easily the progress of thought and at the same time prepare him psychologically for the next stage of the journey. If that be true, there is every reason why he should know he has arrived at the last lap of the journey. If that lap is interesting it not only holds his attention but brings him to his destination with appreciation, inspiration, and aspiration.

"Finally" and "Now in conclusion" are so commonplace as to be almost trite and had better not be used, especially if either has been used to announce the last main point of the sermon. "Keep faith with your people when once you awaken the joyful expectation of the end," advised Charles R. Brown. Certainly, if one does not conclude quickly after he says, "In conclusion," he risks losing the hearer's attention. "Now, my dear brethren, for a few words of exhortation and practical application" is too casual and therefore weak and ineffective. The transition can sometimes be made satisfactorily by a pause, a vocal inflection, or a change of pace. Just a word or two, such as "and now," "so," "thus," "therefore," "surely then," are usually sufficient; but they should be the opening words of as striking and arresting a sentence as possible. Phillips Brooks once began his conclusion: "Thus, then, I have passed through the ground which I proposed. See where our thoughts have led us." Fosdick is especially adept at making smooth, felicitous transitions to his conclusion. These are a few examples taken at random from one volume of his sermons: "It is going to be a long hard haul . . ."; "Friends, the call now is for spiritual militancy . . ."; "If thus by our deepest nature we are made for religion, let us . . ."; "Thus we come to the consequences of the matter . . ."; "Let us say this to ourselves now . . ."; "Friends, I appeal to you this Easter morning . . ." [16]

[16] *On Being Fit to Live With* (New York: Harper & Brothers, 1946).

b) Some reference to the truth just unfolded. Such a reference may be made in more than one way. The subject can be restated in a single, brief, comprehensive sentence that reproduces the truth of the entire discussion. Or a brief résumé of the sermon can be given. The word "résumé" is to be preferred to either the word "summary" or the word "recapitulation," because it means not a formal summary, but a brief restatement of the main points in different forms and in a freer way. This résumé may constitute a major portion of the conclusion. But it should be more than a mere academic summary: it should be an appeal both to the mind and to the emotions and should look forward as well as backward. And above all, it should not be laborious and tedious. Fosdick effectively combined résumé with appeal in an apostrophe to Christ with which he concluded a sermon:

Ah, Christ, still calling commonplace fishermen from their nets, and counting in the end on getting enough of them to change the world, call us today, and let no appalling contrast between the size of the world's problems and the littleness of our resources blind our eyes to the fact that forever and forever the individual matters—the soul of all reformation the reformation of the soul! [17]

c) Some material designed to drive the truth home and clinch it. This may be of the same varied kinds used to make the introduction interesting: an incident from life or literature, a brief story, a passage of scripture, an aphorism, a letter, a news item, a bit of conversation or dialogue, a question or series of questions, an apt quotation, or the lines of a poem or hymn. But remember! the material is being used at this point for a purpose different from its use in the introduction. The purpose there was primarily to interest the hearer in the truth and its importance. Here the purpose is to fasten the truth in his mind as one would drive a nail into a plank and clinch it. So the material must be pertinent to one's immediate purpose, must be apt or pat, must fit the truth and the purpose like a glove fits the hand.

d) Some material designed to persuade the hearer to accept the truth and do something about it. Said H. H. Farmer:

A sermon has failed, indeed it has not been a sermon, unless it carries to the serious hearer something of a claim upon, or summons

[17] *Ibid.*, p. 184.

to, his will, to his whole being as this gathers itself together in the will. A sermon . . . should have something of a quality of a knock on the door.[18]

Be personal! "When a man preaches to me," Daniel Webster said, "I want him to make it a personal matter, a personal matter, a personal matter." The preacher should talk directly to each person. He should make each listener feel, "I mean you!" He should not hesitate to use the pronouns "I" and "you" in phrases such as: "I beseech you," "I wish I could persuade you," "I invite you," "I challenge you," and "I appeal to you."

e) *A strong concluding sentence.* A fairly large number of conclusions end with poetry—far too large a number in the judgment of many. If the poetry is brief, if the verses quoted are strictly in line with the truth, and if they are quoted well and from memory, they may make the kind of appeal with which a sermon should close. But the most appropriate way to close is with a strong sentence. Just as the introduction should have an arresting first sentence so the conclusion should have a forceful last sentence. Ordinarily this sentence should be the preacher's own. Because he is speaking person to person, heart to heart as their pastor, his words will carry more weight then the words of any other person. Someone observed that closing a sermon with a quotation is equivalent to saying, "Now I have come to the most crucial part of my sermon and I feel unequal to it. I shall, therefore, turn you over to Tennyson or James Russell Lowell."

The closing sentence may be a declaration, a searching question, an exhortation, a practical direction or command, a verse of scripture, or an address to God expressing a hope or prayer. I once heard an effective appeal to a sermon end with the question, "Can God count on you? Can he?" Here are a few concluding sentences from some sermons by Ralph W. Sockman. "Choose life, then, that you and your children may live, by loving the Eternal your God, obeying his voice and holding fast to him" (a portion of his text). "Therefore, before we cross the threshold of tomorrow, the counsel that comes to us is, 'Choose you this day whom ye will serve.'" "Thus we shall rise above ourselves and be ready for a day demanding greatness." [19] McComb concludes a sermon

[18] *Servant of the Word,* p. 65.
[19] *Now to Live* (New York and Nashville: Abingdon Press, 1946).

to young people by appealing to them to choose the right guide for their souls. The appeal ended, "I think you know that Jesus Christ has a right to that place. Then put Him there—not to-morrow—today!" [20]

3. Some miscellaneous rules and suggestions for the conclusion.

a) *Prepare the conclusion carefully.* "If you prepare nothing else, my boy, be sure that you know how you are going to end," A. P. Herbert, editor of *Punch*, advised speakers in the House of Commons. That is also good advice to preachers. Plenty of time should be spent on preparing the conclusion. When preaching, time should not be permitted to run out so the conclusion has to be slighted. Before the sermon is put into final form, determine the purpose of the conclusion. But do not draft it until the body of the sermon is finished. One cannot know ahead of time exactly how to put a conclusion together, because he cannot tell how he is going to feel or precisely what his appeal should be until he gets to that point in the preparation.

b) *Use no new ideas in the conclusion.* To bring in new ideas is diverting and weakens and dissipates the effect of the central message. The conclusion is supposed to enforce and bring to a focus what has already been said.

c) *Make the conclusion brief and pointed.* When the time for the conclusion has arrived, go about its business with dispatch. Don't meander. Practice word economy. Take into account the relentless law of diminishing returns. Drive straight ahead. Keep moving. Leave off "elaborate perorations," "florid self-conscious climax," "literary fireworks," "declamatory pyrotechnics." [21] Proceed with determination but with restraint, at times even with quiet power, to the goal.

d) *Make the conclusion positive.* All negative aspects of the subject belong to the body of the sermon. The conclusion ought to stimulate people to follow their noblest impulses and resolutions. Clovis G. Chappell says, "No man has a right so to preach as to send his hearers away on flat tires. Every discouraging sermon is a wicked sermon. . . . A discouraged man is not an

[20] *Op. cit.,* pp. 215-16.
[21] See Stewart, *Heralds of God,* p. 137.

asset but a liability." [22] Send the people out with the thrill of determination, decision, exaltation, and hope. In effect, every conclusion ought to say to each hearer: "Arise, shine; for your light has come, and the glory of the Lord has risen upon you" (Isa. 60:1).

e) *Use no distracting materials or movements in delivering the conclusion.* Don't apologize. Don't use humor. Don't take off your glasses, wipe them, and replace them. Don't close the Bible, or reach for the bulletin to locate the number of the closing hymn, or look at your watch. Don't once break eye contact with the people. Memorize the entire conclusion. Here, if nowhere else, be completely free from manuscript or notes. Let nothing divert your attention or the attention of the people from your final effort. Know where and how you are going to stop. Even the sudden impulse of a brilliant new idea, or the excitement generated from speaking, should seldom be allowed to change your mind.

f) *Make it the conclusion to the whole sermon.* A surprising number of conclusions are not conclusions to the sermon but to the last point of the sermon. If, as previously insisted, each point is one and only one step in the unfolding of the central theme, and if all points should be co-ordinate, then all need to be drawn together at the end. As stated in Chapter V each point of a sermon may wisely have its own conclusion. But such conclusions do not obviate the necessity of a conclusion to the sermon as a whole.

g) *Vary the types of conclusions.* Sockman reports a young college woman as saying, by way of acute criticism of conventional sermons, that no matter where preachers start into their sermons she always knows where they are coming out. Heed that criticism! Do not end all sermons in the same easy way. Avoid platitudinous, stereotyped, rubber-stamp endings. Vary the types of material used. Vary the ways in which they are used. Vary the sequences of the several parts. Vary the manner both of beginning and ending. Here, as in the introduction and in the form of the structure, outwit and surprise anyone who dares to say he knows what you are going to say and how you are going to say it.

[22] *Anointed to Preach* (New York and Nashville: Abingdon Press, 1951), pp. 62-63.

Suggested Reading

Blackwood, A. W. *The Fine Art of Preaching*. New York: The Macmillan Co., 1937. Pp. 125 ff.

McComb, Samuel. *Preaching in Theory and Practice*. New York: Oxford University Press, 1926. Chapter IV.

Stewart, James S. *Heralds of God*. New York: Charles Scribner's Sons, 1946. Pp. 122 ff.

The most thorough treatment of introductions and conclusions is found in textbooks on homiletics. Of those listed in the Bibliography the following are especially helpful: Blackwood, Chapters X and XIV; Breed, Part I; Davis, pp. 217 ff.; Kern, pp. 327 ff. and 340 ff.; Oman, Chapter XX; Phelps, Lectures XVI-XIX and XXXII-XL; and Weatherspoon, Part II, Chapters II and IV.

10. The Style of the Sermon

"When one has found out what to say and in what order," wrote Cicero, "there still remains by far the greatest thing, namely, how to say it." The "how" includes both style (the type of words and sentences used in composition) and delivery (actually saying it). This chapter will deal with style. The next section of the book will deal with delivery.

Factors That Determine Style

There are four important things to keep in mind while composing a sermon.

1. A sermon is composed for listeners. That fact should affect how it is done. Composing to be heard is to be distinguished from composing to be read. The hearer and the reader occupy different situations. The reader can stop to think about what he is reading, look up unfamiliar words in the dictionary, untangle long and involved sentences in order to get at their meaning, or retrace his steps if he discovers his mind wandering. The hearer can do none of these. He hears once and from that single hearing must grasp instantly the meaning of what he hears and simultaneously keep his ears open for the next sentence. He can ask no questions and make no comments. The reader sets his own pace. The preacher sets the pace for his listeners. If the reader gets tired he can rest for a while and later pick up where he left off. If the listener tires and stops listening he cannot recover what he missed.

The writer's "center of gravity" is the written or printed page. The speaker's center of gravity is the listeners out in front. The writer can insert parenthetical statements and explanatory footnotes. The speaker uses such devices only at the risk of switching his hearers completely off the track. The writer uses punctuation marks to stop or slow down the reader and get him to separate words and phrases, or, as the case may be, to tie them together. The writer uses italics and underscoring for emphasis. For these devices the speaker substitutes pauses, changes of tones, and gestures. Both use words and sentences but use them somewhat differently. In short, the different situations of readers and listeners require the attitudes of writers and speakers to be different.

An effective speaking style may appear somewhat deficient when put in print and an effective writing style may seem heavy when spoken. The problem of the speaker is to produce a style with maximum "listenability," the problem of the writer to produce a style with maximum readability. Perforce the speaker must use a briefer, more direct, and more easily understood, way of expressing himself. Some ministers forget this and compose their sermons for a future reading public rather than the present listening public. Thus they miss the primary objective of the sermon.

To avoid this temptation some ministers refuse to write their sermons until after they are delivered. Joseph Fort Newton said, "My sermons are seldom, if ever, written until after they have been preached—else I see or feel the flutter of a paper between me and my people." [1] Likewise Chappell says:

I always prepare a sermon before writing. . . . A sermon, being a spoken address, ought to sound spoken. The minister who first prepares and preaches his sermon, then writes it, is more likely to attain this end. Such a minister writes as he speaks instead of speaking as he writes. Thus his sermon seems spoken even when read.[2]

As we shall see later, it is not necessary to wait until after a sermon is preached to draft it in a speaking style. There are satisfactory ways of composing to be heard as surely as there are satisfactory ways of composing to be read. But the point here is: it is necessary to distinguish between the two.

2. A sermon is composed for a mixed group of people. That fact also should affect how it is done. Normally a congregation will contain people of all ages, from all walks of life, and from all levels of education. If the preacher wants all his hearers to understand his sermon he must present it in a style common to all. If he speaks in the terminology familiar only to one part of his audience the others will not know what he is talking about.

Some preachers address themselves primarily to the adults in their congregations. A vicar in Leeds, England, solved the problem of his restless choirboys by providing them with juvenile

[1] See Prichard, *The Minister, the Method, and the Message,* p. 179.

[2] *Op. cit.,* pp. 85-86.

170

thrillers to read while he preached. When some people objected and suggested he deal with the situation by making his sermons shorter and more interesting, he is reported to have said: "Our sermons are preached primarily for the benefit of adult members of our congregation. The Faith is too large to be put over in five-minute doses."

Some preachers act as though they are addressing a group of ministers. At least they talk in the specialized language of theological seminaries. The judge of the court of appeals in Kentucky censured the preachers of his denomination for talking to their people in the technical terminology of their profession. He said:

If a lawyer or doctor or other professional should address the average audience in terms of his profession, I doubt that even a preacher would understand much of it. So it is that many in your congregation do not understand. The fodder is placed too high for them to reach. It is certainly so for the casual attendant, for the "man in the street." [3]

A layman said to a ministerial friend of Chappell, "Why don't you stop using that pseudo-scientific jargon and speak to your people in English?" [4]

These laymen are intelligent and educated but simply are not familiar with theological terms just as they are not familiar with the professional language of doctors, physicists, and philosophers. The author of a recent article about his life with a Brooklyn gang of youngsters known as The Cougars attached a glossary of gang terms so his readers could understand what he was saying.[5] Teenagers everywhere often use a lingo that requires an interpreter before they can be understood. In his recent lectures on preaching Luccock points out the danger of preachers' preparing their sermons for a coterie, using a private language understood by only a small segment of their congregations. That, he says, is what small groups of people in the arts, in scholarship, in music, and in painting do: they write and create for one another, instead of for the people, or the public. In so doing, he says, they elevate obscurity

[3] The Presbyterian Outlook, August 10, 1953.
[4] Op. cit., p. 55.
[5] Harper's Magazine, November, 1954.

to the rank of a primary virtue. . . . Much preaching has suffered from the same opaqueness. It is a contagious disease. . . . There is a classic story that used to be a joke. It is funny no longer. It is that of Douglas Jerrold, reading Browning's *Sordello* and then crying out, "My God, I am losing my mind." [6]

The implication is that preachers should beware of addressing their sermons only to those students of literature who are capable of understanding Browning.

No preacher would prepare a sermon in the lingo of teenagers. Then why should he prepare it in the style of a highly selected group of intellectuals or a specialized group of professional preachers? Sermons should not be prepared for theological audiences, literary audiences, adult or youth audiences, or any other small percentage of congregations, but for the whole audience—the "public" audience. Webb B. Garrison reminds us that "given only a pulpit and a preacher, it is possible to have a monologue but not a sermon. Preaching cannot exist without the listener as well as the talker." [7] The preacher who preaches in an "unknown tongue" is deceiving himself if he thinks he has listeners. Beecher said that in his early pastorate in Indiana he preached in the language of the Bible with discouraging results. Every Sunday night he had a headache and went to bed vowing he would quit preaching and buy a farm. Then he decided to talk in the language of the Hoosiers who sat before him rather than the language of the ancient Hebrews. Immediately the whole situation changed: his congregation not only increased but sinners were converted.

3. *A sermon is composed for the people of the present generation.* The style of communication prevailing in our age should affect our style of preaching. If one wishes to be heard he must speak in the contemporary vernacular. For a long time New Testament scholars were puzzled by the fact that the Greek of the New Testament was so different from classical Greek. Then by comparing it with some old papyri they discovered it was the common, not the literary, language of that period, the vernacular. The gospel was taken to the people in their own tongue.

[6] *Communicating the Gospel* (New York: Harper & Brothers, 1954), pp. 19, 21.

[7] *The Preacher and His Audience*, p. 21.

That has to be done afresh in every age. The new version of the Bible is in the direct, straightforward language characteristic of our times. For example, Heb. 13:16 in the American Standard Version of 1901 reads, "To do good and to communicate forget not." The recent revisers made it read, "Do not neglect to do good and to share what you have." That illustrates the change of style that has taken place in the last fifty years. Preaching style must undergo a similar revision.

Our generation uses a direct conversational manner of speaking. Old-fashioned, silver-tongued oratory is outmoded. All sorts of speaking have had to be shortened and simplified. The tempo and complexity of living have increased until everything moves faster. Preaching methods must be adjusted to the prevailing moods, methods, and mediums of communication. Long sermons, with long sentences and heavy, orotund style of some of the older preachers, are listened to inattentively and often impatiently by modern congregations. If Chalmers, Beecher, Spurgeon, and Brooks were alive today they would have to adopt a new style of preaching and would be among the first to do so.

In his last interviews with Henry L. Stoddard of the New York Sun shortly before his death, Calvin Coolidge said:

We are in a new era to which I do not belong, and it would not be possible for me to adjust myself to it. . . . When I read of the new-fangled things that are so popular now I realize that my time in public affairs is past. I wouldn't know how to handle them if I were called upon to do so. That is why I am through with public life forever.

That was an honest statement characteristic of the man. No one should be expected to adjust to error or wrong. But every public leader must wrestle with the problems and face the issues of his generation in the thought-terms and the language of that generation. If he does not know how to adapt to the situation, he had better step out of the picture and turn the job over to someone who does. "Adjust or die," the severe law of nature, applies to preachers as well as to other public leaders.

4. The document being composed is a sermon. Sermons have always been the most direct form of public speech. Genuine preachers who have the yearning heart do not speak to please literary critics but to please God. They do not try to entertain

173

their hearers but to bring them face to face with God. They are never content with glittering generalities. They have a personal message which they deliver personally—man to man, heart to heart. They are out for individual verdicts. George A. Gordon told of a parishioner who commented after a Sunday sermon, "I want your preaching to be searching, Doctor, but is it fair to point to me?" The preacher does not ask whether that is fair or not. On the contrary he considers it a divine obligation. All prophetic preachers symbolically point their fingers at individuals saying, "Thou art the man." This requires a style that provides the most direct path to the minds, hearts, consciences, and wills of the listeners.

AURAL STYLE

The style of speaking that best fulfills the functions of a sermon is now referred to as aural style. The word "aural" literally means "of or pertaining to the ear." Applied to a style of speaking it means speaking or writing that is tailored to the needs of the listener. It is direct, personal, conversational. Martin Luther said we ought to speak in the church "as we do at home, in plain mother tongue, which everyone is acquainted with." That is a good description of aural style. Rudolph Flesch calls it "shirt-sleeve" English.

William Lyon Phelps, the well-known professor of English at Yale, made a name for himself partly because of his informal, natural method of classroom instruction. He utilized that same method effectively in his public addresses. When asked about his technique of public speaking he said the only technique he knew was to talk to large groups the same way you talk to small groups. "Whether I am talking to two persons or to two thousand," he said, "my manner is exactly the same. . . . I never begin with conventional platitudes and generalities; no matter how large the audience may be, I always feel as if I were talking to each one separately." [8]

Even so, some distinctions must be made between conversation in a small group and conversational public speech. In a group of three people a good deal of three-way dialogue takes place. In a group of two thousand people the speaker does all

[8] Autobiography (New York: Oxford University Press, 1939), p. 284.

the talking. In fact he engages in a monologue. In the chitchat of a living room, informality, unstudied expression, and relaxed demeanor prevail, which in a public address would appear too casual or perhaps careless. This is especially true of preaching that takes place as part of a formal, dignified worship service. Nevertheless, the preacher should speak to the large group in the same *direct* manner in which one person addresses another in private conversation.

The sharp line once drawn between colloquial style and literary style is fast disappearing. Literary style in our day is becoming less and less classical and more and more colloquial. Formal, stilted grammar is being replaced by functional, common-sense grammar. Splitting infinitives and ending sentences with prepositions are now acceptable practices. Writers are as anxious to be understood by the common people as are public speakers. Hence, instead of discouraging colloquial English, both teachers and writers are now advocating its use within reasonable limits. The *American College Dictionary* states outright, "That English is good English which communicates well the thought of a given speaker to a given audience." However, this should not be taken as a commendation of careless, incorrect, or low speech at any time, much less in a sermon. A conversational style of preaching, therefore, means a style above the level of informal, casual street talk but below the level of old-fashioned literary composition. A preacher with a serious purpose and a sense of the fitness of things need not trouble himself too much about being either too colloquial or too formal if he keeps his speech simple and direct.

> In words as fashions the same rule will hold.
> Alike fantastic if too new or old:
> Be not the first by whom the new are tried
> Nor yet the last to lay the old aside.[9]

An effectual aural style is achieved mainly in four ways.

1. By the use of simple words. These should be words commonly understood by all groups. Edward L. Thorndike says, "Until it gets into the mind, a word is only puffs of air or streaks

[9] Alexander Pope, *Essay on Criticism*, Part II.

of ink." [10] Unfamiliar words are worse than wasted. They not only fail to penetrate the listener's mind but prevent him from getting any meaning out of the sentence in which they occur. A man, leaving a service where he had heard a candidate for the pulpit of his church, remarked, "For many years I have been coming to this church with my Bible. Today I find I have brought the wrong book, for in reality I needed a copy of Webster's Unabridged Dictionary." Now and then one hears of a pedantic preacher who delights to make use of unfamiliar words and to quote phrases in Latin, German, or some other language unknown to most of his congregation. This display of learning may impress the people with the minister's scholarly attainments but leave their souls unfed. They do not come to church to be introduced to big words but to be introduced to Christ.

When still a lad, Benjamin Franklin said to his mother, "Mother, I have imbibed an acephalous molluscous." Supposing he had swallowed something poisonous his mother forced him to take a large dose of an emetic. When he got over the effects of the medicine he said to her, "I had eaten nothing but an ordinary oyster." At that his mother proceeded to give him a sound thrashing for deceiving her. Then and there Benjamin vowed he would never again use big words when little words would do. Every preacher could well make a similar vow early in his ministry.

2. By the use of few words. Never use two words where one will suffice. Leave off all empty, meaningless, unnecessary words. Eliminate as many prepositions, conjunctions, adverbs, and adjectives as possible. "The superfluous adjective," says Farmer, "is to your message what barnacles and seaweed are to the clean straight lines of a ship designed to cut through the water like the edge of a knife." [11] The same could be said of superfluous adverbs and all other unnecessary words. The father of a young minister offered to bear the expense of a regular Saturday night telegram giving in fifty words the gist of the sermon he expected to preach the next day. The necessity of using fifty words, no more and no less, to make clear to his father the heart of his sermon was a discipline for which he was forever grateful. The effectiveness

---

[10] "Psychology of Semantics," *American Journal of Psychology*, LIX (1946), 613.

[11] *Op. cit.*, p. 61.

of a sermon often depends as much upon what is left out as upon what is put in. "If I knew how to omit," said Robert Louis Stevenson, "I should ask for no other knowledge."

Many a sermon is cluttered up with meaningless phrases that make noise to no purpose, such as: "as you may or may not know . . ."; "If you will permit me, I should like to say . . ."; "One or two of you may have heard me tell this anecdote, and I hope you will forgive me for repeating it . . ."; "Without objection, I propose to develop this topic in greater detail . . ."; "The text is found, as I believe you will discover upon looking it up, in . . ." Such phrases, according to Garrison, not only "fill up brief space with sound that signifies nothing," but give "the listener an opportunity to shift his mental gears and turn to a stimulus more compelling than the cliche." [12]

3. By the use of expressive words. Specific words are always more expressive than general words. Emerson described the specific language of the drivers and teamsters in Concord as "words so vascular and alive they would bleed if you cut them, words that walked and ran." Use words with action in them: concrete rather than abstract nouns, transitive verbs in the active voice. Use pictorial words, words that bring pictures to the mind. Speak of sounds, of things that can be touched and seen. These are known as "visual, auditory, motor, and tactile images." Samuel McComb tells of a "student of Tennyson who discovered that in a thousand lines of his *Idylls of the King*, the poet used eighty-three visual, forty-eight auditory, one motor and seven tactile images." McComb examined

a sermon by Robertson and one by Brooks, each consisting of about four thousand words, and found Robertson used thirteen visual, four auditory, three motor and three tactile images, whereas Brooks used fifteen visual, seven auditory, eight motor and two tactile images.[13]

All such words bring pictures of action, of things, of people, of human situations, to the minds of the hearers.

4. By the use of simple, basic sentence structures. Simple subject and predicate sentences sound like conversation. Learn the basic rules of grammar. They are designed to help one ex-

[12] *Op. cit.*, pp. 105-6.
[13] *Op. cit.*, p. 111.

press himself clearly and to assist the hearer in grasping what he hears. "Grammatical processes are the working tools of rhetoric, too useful, too necessary, to be neglected." [14] Proper grammatical construction is also a working tool of communication. But occasionally one must ignore a rule in order to avoid a stilted, awkward way of saying what he wants to say. Winston Churchill's secretary changed a sentence in one of his famous wartime speeches because it ended with a preposition. Churchill crossed out the change and wrote, "This is the kind of arrant pedantry up with which I will not put." [15]

Avoid the use of jargon, involved sentences with excessive amounts of words that have little meaning and add nothing to clarity of thought. Quiller-Couch says jargon has two main vices: First, it uses "circumlocution rather than short straight speech"; and second, it habitually chooses "vague, woolly abstract nouns rather than concrete ones." As examples he mentions a minister in the House of Commons who needs to say "NO," but instead says, "The answer to the question is in the negative." That is jargon! You read in the newspaper, "He was conveyed to his place of residence in an intoxicated condition." That is jargon! In plain speech it means: "He was carried home drunk." "When you write in the active voice, 'They gave him a silver teapot,' you write as a man. When you write 'He was made the recipient of a silver teapot,' you write jargon." He tells of someone asking, "What would have become of Christianity if Jeremy Bentham had had the writing of the parables?" [16] We might appropriately ask, "What would Christianity become in our present age if preachers spoke to their congregations with the simplicity and directness Jesus used in his exquisite parables?"

An American politician [17] coined the word "gobbledygook" to describe the obscure verbiage he found in the pronouncements of the various departments of the national government. The word means "after the gobbling of turkeys," just a lot of "sound and fury signifying nothing." William Lyon Phelps once said of Henry James's writing and conversation, "He wrapped his mean-

---

[14] Weatherspoon, op. cit., p. 227.

[15] Garrison, op. cit., p. 97.

[16] Sir Arthur Quiller-Couch, On the Art of Writing (New York: G. P. Putnam's Sons, 1916), pp. 100 ff.

[17] Maury Maverick.

ing in layers of words but did not tell you much, and you had to dig it out for yourself." For that method of speaking he coined the term, "verbose reticence," [18] which means "uncommunicative silence [reticence] abounding in words [verbose]." By all means a preacher should avoid wrapping up his thoughts in layers of words that mean nothing to his hearers because they do not have time to take off the wrappings. To all preachers who tend to use jargon or obscure verbiage by that or any other name, Halford Luccock gives this injunction: "Discocoon yourself."

Canon Liddon wrote a letter to a friend in which he said, "London is just now buried under a dense fog. This is commonly attributed to Dr. Westcott having opened his study window at Westminster." Keep out of mental fogs while you are composing your sermons. Scientific experiment, so we are told, has determined that a bank of fog three feet thick, six feet high, and one hundred feet long contains less than a half glass of water. Quoting those figures to a group of ministers, Bishop Edgar Blake of The Methodist Church said, "You cannot slake thirst with fog. There is only one safe thing to do with it and that is to keep out of it."

MEANS OF ACHIEVING AN EFFECTIVE PREACHING STYLE

There is no easy way to attain an effective speaking style. No one can teach the "tricks of the trade" in a dozen short lessons. The bald fact is: there are no tricks. One develops a style by continuous study and practice. Vinet stated the matter pointedly:

The experience of all times, and the testimony of all teachers, present to us as inseparable, these two propositions: (a) That we must not flatter ourselves that we shall have a good style, without an interesting fund of ideas. (b) That even with an interesting and substantial supply of ideas, we must not flatter ourselves that style will come of itself.[19]

Any man who is willing to pay the price, however, can achieve his goal.

1. Study. Make a study of words, grammar, composition, and rhetoric. Even if a person somehow bypassed these subjects in

[18] *Op. cit.*, p. 553.
[19] *Homiletics* (New York: Ivison and Phinney, 1866), p. 353.

his college course, he need not be dismayed. His college course taught him how to locate books he wants, how to read, and how to think for himself. So he need only search for the right books and go to work with them, not with the intention of becoming an authority on all phases of the subject, but of getting hold of some fundamental principles for his practical purposes. If one needs to start at the bottom, let him ask the teacher of English in his college or in the local high school to direct him to a good book on the basic principles of grammar. Or, let him purchase *English Grammar Simplified*, by James C. Fernald, revised edition.[20] This book is inexpensive, brief, and satisfactory for quick study of the subject.

All preachers should have a good dictionary—a G. and C. Merriam's, *Webster's* or Funk & Wagnalls' *Standard* are both regarded as standard—and a book of synonyms. Two splendid recent books of synonyms are *Standard Handbook of Synonyms, Antonyms and Prepositions*, by J. C. Fernald, revised edition,[21] and *Webster's Dictionary of Synonyms*.[22] These books will be all one needs to begin his study of style.

If one feels he already has a fair grasp of the elementary principles of the use of the English language, let him secure a few books that will bring him quickly to the heart of his problem. For example, let him read the chapter on "Jargon" in Quiller-Couch's *On the Art of Writing*. This is one of the earliest popular explanations of the more direct way of writing and speaking. The most zealous advocate of that method in our day is Rudolph Flesch. His *Art of Plain Talk* [23] and *The Way to Write*,[24] on which he and A. H. Lass collaborated, give all the details about the various types of words, phrases, and sentences necessary to familiarize one thoroughly with the inns and outs of the method.

The most thorough general treatment of style from the specific viewpoint of preaching is found in Weatherspoon's revision of Broadus, *On the Preparation and Delivery of Sermons*, pp. 223-78.[25] An excellent brief treatment of the same subject may be

[20] New York: Funk & Wagnalls Co., 1946.
[21] New York: Funk & Wagnalls Co., 1947.
[22] Springfield, Mass.: G. & C. Merriam Co., 1951.
[23] New York: Harper & Brothers, 1946.
[24] New York: Harper & Brothers, 1947.
[25] New York: Harper & Brothers, 1944.

found in Luccock's *In the Minister's Workshop*, in a chapter entitled "Words Are the Soul's Ambassadors." [26] A splendid and extended treatment of the preacher's style from the viewpoint of the listener may be found in Garrison's *The Preacher and His Audience*.[27] His chapter on "Problems and Opportunities of Style" not only gives a good introduction to the various aspects of the subject but offers many detailed suggestions about precisely what to do.

Do not undertake too much at one time. Take it in small doses. Do not buy too many books that cover the same ground as though you were preparing an exhaustive treatise on the subject. Aside from reference books, buy one book at a time and work your way through each before purchasing another.

2. Practice. Once one gathers together a few suggestions he should put them into practice a little at a time in his weekly sermonizing. That will bring better results than trying to master the subject by wide reading. One learns to compose sermons only by composing them. Some theorizing about it is unavoidable. But the theories should be put into practice on actual sermons, not on classroom exercises. A preacher's best laboratory experience will be the time spent in preparing his weekly sermon.

Draft and redraft, until you are satisfied you have hit upon the simplest, most direct way of saying what you have in mind. Reject flowery, florid expressions. "Murder your darlings," urges Quiller-Couch. Prune! Discard! Eliminate! Substitute! Rephrase!

James S. Stewart advises:

Shun everything stilted, grandiose, insipid or pedantic. Do not be like the learned preacher who in the course of a sermon in a village church remarked, "Perhaps some of you at this point are suspecting me of Eutychianism." . . . It is sheer slackness to fling at your people great slabs of religious phraseology derived from a bygone age, and leave them the task of retranslation into terms of their own experience: that is your task, not theirs. . . . If you have a tendency toward purple passages, suppress it sternly.[28]

By a little practice one can learn to talk to people through a pencil or through a typewriter. One helpful procedure is to

[26] New York and Nashville: Abingdon Press, 1944
[27] New York: Fleming H. Revell Co., 1954.
[28] *Heralds of God*, pp. 38-39.

imagine one's self up on his feet before the congregation talking to particular people and then write down what he mentally says. James Black explained to a group of theological students how he did that very thing. As he began to write he thought about the people—needy, troubled, tried people—he had encountered in his pastoral visiting. Then he would write a sentence or two, look across the desk at the imaginary person opposite and ask, "Is that any help to you? It cannot be." He would try again, and ask, "Does that bring anything to you? Not likely." He would scrap that and try again and, if necessary, still again until he had written what he was sure would strike home to his listeners.

When the sermon is finished satisfactorily and one is going over it for the last time, let him speak it aloud imaginatively to his people again. If something doesn't at that time speak well, drop it, or revise it until it does. Even if one does not actually rewrite it, he should recompose it mentally and speak it that way when the sermon is delivered. Working this way on real sermons, for real people, in real human situations, gives one the feel of his words, puts him into the mood of the sermon, and provides him an atmosphere that stimulates a speaking style.

But be reminded again: one should avoid trying to do too much work on style in any one week. He should work on the style of the sermon the allotted time only and then preach it as best he can. If he does that week after week for a few months he will be surprised and the congregation will be pleased at the results. After a while some things will become more or less habitual, the intensity of the effort on style can be somewhat lessened, and less work can be done on the composition of sentences and more on the expansion of general knowledge.

THE STYLE AND THE MESSAGE

The style should never be confused with the message. Hard work on words and sentences will not in itself assure an effective sermon. One must have something to say, something that grips his heart until he feels it must be said at all costs. Matthew Arnold once exclaimed, "People think that I can teach them style. What stuff it all is! Have something to say, and say it as clearly as you can. That is the only secret of style." [29] Actually

[29] Quoted by Stewart in *Heralds of God*, p. 149.

that is not the sole secret of style, but without that, style misses its mark. "Preach not because you have to say something, but because you have something to say," advised Archbishop Whatley. Style is a means to an end, not an end in itself. Words, as Luccock so forcefully says, "are the soul's ambassadors." They are not the message: they only convey the message.

What the preacher has to say is always more important than the way he says it. Any style is defective that calls attention to itself and away from the sermon. That occurs if the style is offensive to good taste. A listener told Henry Ward Beecher he had used incorrect grammar in his sermon. Beecher replied, "Did I? Well, all I have to say is—God help the grammar if it gets in my way when I'm preaching." We can sympathize with Beecher's feelings. He was irked that a listener could be more concerned about a single mistake in grammar than about the message into which he had poured his soul. But Beecher was not minimizing the importance of grammar. Ordinarily he went to great trouble to have correct grammatical constructions. A preacher is derelict in duty who permits his careless style to get in the way of his message.

Style may also take attention away from the message by being too artistic, too beautiful. When that happens the style becomes the center of the attention of both the preacher and the congregation. The best preaching style is designed to make the message stand out so clearly that the style itself is invisible. "The best style is like plate-glass, so transparent that in looking at the objects beyond it you forget the medium through which you see them." [30]

The primary thing is that the minister be on fire with his message. He must believe it and want—desperately want—the people to believe it. Once he gets up to preach, that should be first and foremost in his mind. A prominent layman who declares he has qualified from long experience as a leading authority on poor sermons says they result from three things: "insufficient mental effort, hasty superficiality and the absence of spiritual urgency." [31] The chief offender of the three causes listed is the last. The feeling of spiritual urgency is the prime requisite of effective

[30] E. G. Robinson, *Lectures on Preaching* (New York: Henry Holt & Co., 1883), p. 155.

[31] *The Presbyterian Outlook*, August 10, 1953.

preaching. Nothing else can make up for the lack of it. Paul said to the Corinthians: "When I came to you, brethren, I did not come proclaiming to you the testimony of God in lofty words or wisdom. . . . My speech and my message were not in plausible words of wisdom, but in demonstration of the Spirit and power." (I Cor. 2:1-4.) Every sermon should convince the congregation that above everything else the preacher is concerned about the importance of his message.

One of the recurring notes in Edwin Arlington Robinson's poems is reference to the shallowness and hollowness of preaching. He speaks of the preacher who adds

> . . . one thundered contribution more
> To the dirges of all-hollowness.[32]

He refers to "glacial sermons" that "like the man who fashioned them" were "too divinely thin." [33] We can almost feel his pulsing righteous indignation as he writes:

> . . . for there be none that shall indite
> So much of nothing as the man of words
> Who writes in the Lord's name for his name's sake
> And has not in his blood the fire of time
> To warm eternity.[34]

Consider these lines a voice from the crowd reminding all preachers that without a message that sets their souls on fire their words are but a "noisy gong or a clanging cymbal" (I Cor. 13:1).

Suggested Reading

Baxter, B. B. *The Heart of the Yale Lectures.* New York: The Macmillan Co., 1947. Part II.

Chrisman, Lewis H. *The English of the Pulpit.* New York: Geo. H. Doran Co., 1926.

Farmer, H. H. *The Servant of the Word.* New York: Charles Scribner's Sons, 1942. Chapters IV and V.

[32] *Collected Poems of Edwin Arlington Robinson*, p. 154. Copyright 1937 by The Macmillan Co. and used by their permission.

[33] *Ibid.*, p. 215.

[34] *Ibid.*, pp. 466-67.

Garrison, Webb B. *The Preacher and His Audience*. New York: Fleming H. Revell Co., 1954.

Handy, Francis J. *Jesus the Preacher*. New York and Nashville: Abingdon Press, 1949. Chapters III-IV.

Jones, E. W. *Preaching and the Dramatic Arts*. New York: The Macmillan Co., 1948.

McComb, Samuel L. *Preaching in Theory and Practice*. New York: Oxford University Press, 1926. Chapter VII.

Stewart, James S. *Heralds of God*. New York: Charles Scribner's Sons, 1946. Pp. 118 ff. and 149 ff.

The reader is also referred to the list of books on style in the Bibliography.

PART IV

PREACHING THE SERMON

11. Methods of Delivery

Strictly speaking, a sermon exists only when it has been delivered. Previous to that it has been only gestating. Not until it has been preached can its function of communicating the gospel be fulfilled. Hence all the labor of preparation awaits the hour on Sunday when the sermon comes to birth. That hour determines whether one shall "see the fruit of the travail of his soul and be satisfied" (Isa. 53:11), or whether the sermon will be stillborn. In the process of delivery the words go forth from the preacher's mouth either to accomplish their purpose or to return to him empty (Isa. 55:11).

Here is the final test! Here you win or lose! All that has gone before helps or hinders, as the case may be, but the proof of the pudding is the eating. Here in the delivery of your sermon the nourishment which you have brought for a hungry congregation is either eaten with relish, satisfaction and resultant strength, or it is left on the plate as a bit of cold victuals, useless and repellant. Take heed therefore how you deliver.[1]

The manner of delivery, of course, is not the sole factor in determining whether or not communication takes place. Optimum conditions for communication must prevail. The hearers have a responsibility. The physical settings of the sermon—acoustics, lighting, and ventilation—play their part. Stimuli other than the preacher and the sermon enter the picture. The arrangement of the sanctuary determines whether congregation-preacher relationships suitable for communication exist. These factors are important but over most of them the preacher has little control. However, he has exclusive control over the communication factors involved in his method of delivery. That responsibility he must carry faithfully.

[1] Charles R. Brown, *The Art of Preaching* (New York: The Macmillan Co., 1922), p. 155.

For the purposes of this study five types of sermon delivery will be distinguished from one another: extemporaneous preaching, reading the sermon from a manuscript, reciting the sermon from memory, free preaching, and a composite method of delivery that combines elements of each of the other types.

EXTEMPORANEOUS PREACHING

The words "extemporaneous" and "impromptu" are treated as synonyms in Webster's dictionary. Literally, extemporaneous means "from the time," or originated for the occasion. The literal meaning of impromptu is "in readiness" or "at hand." Both are defined as "made or done without previous study or preparation," or on the spur of the moment. The colloquial expression for this is "speaking off hand," the image being that of shooting without a rest. The Germans have a corresponding expression that means "speaking from the stirrup," as when one shoots on horseback without dismounting. In current usage, impromptu more nearly retains its original sense of speaking without advance preparation. Extemporaneous applies to addresses of which the thought has been prepared but the language and incidental treatment are left to the suggestion of the moment.

Very few important speeches are invented in whole while the speaker is on his feet. Someone commending Daniel Webster for a magnificent speech in Congress expressed surprise that he could deliver such an excellent speech on the spur of the moment. Webster replied, "The material for that speech has been in my desk for months." That is, though the speech had apparently been put together quickly while he was on his feet, he had been shaping his thoughts and gathering material on the subject for a long period of time. That speech was extemporaneous in the sense in which the word is being used here.

Beecher did extemporaneous preaching. He used to say that a dozen or more topics were lying loose in his mind every week. He was always hard at work reading and studying subjects and texts. But his ideas about a particular sermon crystallized only a few hours before it was preached. On Sunday morning he would choose one subject from among those he had been brooding over throughout the week, analyze it, write about it for a while,

187

then hurry off to the church, carrying his unfinished notes with him. But when he arose he laid the notes aside and spoke freely.

Spurgeon followed a similar procedure except he said he never composed a sentence in advance. Gaius Glenn Atkins, the well-known Congregational preacher of our day, said:

> I have never written, because I could always remember enough of what I wrote to trip up the creative side of my mind and not enough of it to give it as it was written. . . . I never took any notes into the pulpit and for a long time never put pen to paper—I just thought it out.[2]

Dwight Bradley, another noted Congregational preacher of our time, said:

> I never write a sermon before its delivery, and I do not even prepare an outline in notes. . . . I go into the pulpit charged with the thought and the feeling of the hour and of the subject, and let the preaching take care of itself. . . . I memorize poetry, however.[3]

This way of preaching is effective for a few men who, like Beecher and Spurgeon, have unusual abilities for speaking often and for putting their thoughts together quickly, but who nevertheless are all the time working hard at the tasks of reading, gathering ideas and putting them into proper form, and improving their methods of expressing themselves clearly and forcefully. But it is a dangerous method for the average preacher. As described above, it sounds like hasty and careless preparation. In the hands of less capable men, this sort of sermon preparation *is* careless. In fact it is the kind of preparation that has sometimes brought extemporaneous preaching into disrepute. But that was emphatically not the case with the preachers mentioned. Their preparation, though almost exclusively mental, was thorough and congealed quickly at the end of the week into a well-organized, effectively delivered sermon. In this type of preaching, the degree of the thoroughness of the general preparation and of the special thinking done beforehand determines the quality of the finished product.

[2] Joseph Fort Newton, ed., *If I Had Only One Sermon to Prepare* (New York: Harper & Brothers, 1932), pp. 181-82.

[3] *Ibid.*, pp. 171-73.

READING THE SERMON FROM A MANUSCRIPT

The meager information available on the subject leads us to believe that the practice of reading sermons has not been widespread at any period in Protestantism. Weatherspoon says the practice seems to have originated in the reign of Henry VIII in protest against the impassioned preaching of the Independents. He reports the case of a preacher being driven from his pulpit in London merely because he raised his eyes from his manuscript while preaching. Previous to that time, preaching, both in England and on the Continent, was more or less free speaking. He quotes a letter found in the statute book of the University of Cambridge, dated in 1674, showing that Charles II attempted to persuade both court and university preachers to discontinue the practice of reading their sermons. The letter informs the university of the King's desire

that the said preachers deliver their sermons, both in Latin and English, by memory, without books; as being a way of preaching which his Majesty judgeth most agreeable to the use of foreign churches, to the custom of the university heretofore, and to the nature of that holy exercise.

Furthermore, the letter says the King had

commanded . . . that the names of all such ecclesiastical persons as shall continue the present *supine and slothful way of preaching* [italics mine] be, from time to time, signified to him by the Vice-Chancellor for the time being, on pain of his Majesty's displeasure.[4]

The General Assembly of the Church of Scotland in 1720 declared that the reading of sermons was "displeasing to God's people and caused no small obstruction to spiritual consolation." We cannot now determine the extent of the practice in England and Scotland nor how successful were the efforts to discourage it. We know only that it was practiced to some extent in other days and at present it is common among only a few Protestants here and abroad.

Reading from a manuscript has some advantages. Preparation for reading a sermon requires much less time and energy than for free speaking. Knowing he will be able to present his sermon

[4] *Op. cit.,* pp. 315 ff.

exactly as he planned it, the preacher can approach its delivery with more relaxation. He is relieved of all fear of forgetting or of breaking down. He is assured of a more precise, accurate, and polished style. He can avoid diffuseness, volubility, and verbosity. R. W. Dale once told Joseph Parker that he read his sermons to keep from talking too much. "If I spoke extemporaneously," he said, "I should never sit down. My command of words is such that as a young man I could preach standing on my head. To be condensed is my object in writing my sermons." Reading is easier on the nerves than free speaking. By reading the preacher can control the expenditure of emotions and thus avoid a large measure of nervous exhaustion that so often follows extemporaneous preaching.

But observe! these benefits apply most to the preacher. The determining factor in the choice of a method of delivery is not which is easier on the preacher but which best communicates his message to the people. Considered from the viewpoint of effectiveness in communication, reading has a number of disadvantages.

Take the lack of nervousness, for example: that is not always an advantage. A certain amount of nervousness beforehand is so nearly universal as to be regarded as normal. Numerous public speakers have confessed they approached their speeches with tenseness and often with fear and trembling. But they learned from experience that nervousness can be an asset instead of a liability. This nervousness is believed to be due to a tenseness of the muscles of the abdomen, throat, legs, arms, and face, resulting from one's sensitiveness to the importance of his speech and his eagerness to deliver it. This is nature's way of providing a speaker with extra energy for vigorous action. If a speaker is too relaxed he deprives himself of that extra energy for speaking and reduces somewhat the effectiveness of what he says. But if that extra energy is expended in normal bodily movements to go with earnest speaking, nervousness soon passes away.

Carl Schurz, a noted orator, asked Oswald Garrison Villard in his early speaking days if he had been frightened when he spoke a day or two previously. Villard said very emphatically, "No." "Then I know you made a poor speech," said Schurz. "If you are not frightened you cannot make a good one. That

190

has always been my experience." [5] Few worthwhile speeches were ever delivered forcefully, without some nervousness at the start.

Or, consider the problem closely related to nervousness: the dread of forgetting that sometimes leads to stage fright. One can avoid that by reading, but he may do so at the expense of his effectiveness. This is the thesis of Webb B. Garrison in a thoughtful book referred to previously.[6] His explanation is as follows. Stage fright is a physiological condition resulting from extreme self-consciousness. As just explained, normal tenseness is relieved by throwing one's self naturally into the delivery of his message. Now, suppose one is overanxious to win approval and keeps feeling inside, "I must make good. I cannot afford to fail." This brings two desires into conflict: the desire to win approval and the desire to get the message across. This conflict short-circuits the normal outlet for the body's increased energies and stage fright results. Reading will relieve the fear of failure sufficiently to avoid panic, but it may not release the energies into better speaking. The remedy for the difficulty is to give one's exclusive attention to his speech and throw himself with complete self-forgetfulness into its delivery. That relieves the physiological-emotional conflict, drains off excess nervousness, and increases speaking effectiveness.

Reading merely to avoid anxiety may also produce fear of speaking without a manuscript, or even result in the inability to do so. Clarence E. Macartney tells how T. DeWitt Talmage was cured of dependence upon his manuscript. One day his manuscript slipped through the opening in the back of the horsehair sofa which adorned some pulpits in those days. While the congregation sang a hymn he had to get down on his hands and knees before their eyes to retrieve it. That raised some doubts about the advisability of using the manuscript. But it took one more bitter experience to cure him. Upon a subsequent occasion the church was plunged into darkness as he was nearing the end of his sermon. He was forced to dismiss the congregation, saying, "It is impossible to proceed." At home he thought the matter over. He said later he was so humiliated that a message from God

[5] Oswald Garrison Villard, *Fighting Years* (New York: Harcourt, Brace & Co., 1939), p. 227.
[6] *The Preacher and His Audience*, pp. 239 ff.

should depend on gas meters and a paper mill, he vowed to do without notes from then on.[7]

Reading also breaks audience contact. Every time the speaker looks at his manuscript, contact is broken and the attention of the hearers is momentarily interrupted. Dawson C. Bryan writes that one Sunday after dinner his wife said to him, "How many times do you think you looked at your notes during the sermon?" "Not very often, I am sure," he confidently replied. "I knew that sermon better than usual." "You looked down at them forty-seven times in less than thirty minutes," she said. "And for a man as tall as you are, you lose the congregation's attention each time." [8]

As we shall see in the next chapter, the eyes are an important part of one's speech mechanism. Continuous eye contact is necessary, not only to keep the attention of the hearers, but to give them opportunity to stimulate the mind and the emotions of the preacher. Both these things are essential if the full impact of the preacher's personality gets behind his message. Some experts question whether complete person-to-person speech, the impact of mind upon mind, living encounter of personality with personality, are possible without speaker and hearers looking each other squarely in the eyes. Sir Walter Scott emphasized the importance of face-to-face talking when, in *The Heart of Midlothian*, he made Jeanie Deans explain her decision to go in person and plead before the king and queen for her sister's life rather than to write a letter.

Writing will not do it—a letter cannot look, and pray and beg and beseech as the human voice can do to the human heart. A letter's like the music that the ladies have for their spinets—nothing but black scores, compared to the same tune played or sung. It's word of mouth must do it, or nothing.[9]

Does all this mean that a person cannot really preach by reading? Some think so. Weatherspoon, for example, says reading is one thing and preaching another. Reading can be done effectively. But reading is not speaking and should not be re-

---

[7] *Preaching Without Notes* (New York and Nashville: Abingdon Press, 1946), pp. 162-63.

[8] *The Art of Illustrating Sermons*, pp. 246-47.

[9] The Scottish dialect of the original is given in English.

garded as such. He suggests, if one means to read, that he determine to do it well, but not try to disguise the fact he is reading or to convert reading into speaking. Reading before a large congregation is different from reading to one person, but it is still reading. His advice is: be as good a reader as possible, do it openly, and do not try to assume postures, gestures, looks, as though you were speaking.[10]

The Duke of Windsor tells of being advised on public speaking at this very point by Winston Churchill. Churchill said to him: "If you wish to read your speech out, I should do so openly, reading it very slowly and deliberately, and not making the least attempt to conceal your notes. Of course, it is better if you can find time to memorize it." Then he went on to say, somewhat facetiously, "Rather a good way of dealing with notes at dinner is to take a tumbler and put a finger bowl on top of it, then put a plate on top of the finger bowl and put the notes on top of the plate; but one has to be very careful not to knock it all over, as once happened to me." [11] Incidentally, the last remarks were his way of emphasizing one of the disadvantages of using a manuscript.

But others insist that reading can be preaching. For example, Farmer says:

Merely to read a sermon is fatal. It is worse than fatal; it is a culpable repudiation of one's task and calling. . . . The alternative to reading is not dispensing entirely with notes or manuscript in the pulpit. The alternative to reading is preaching, and you can preach from notes and even from the full manuscript, if you have taken the trouble to do what I spoke of earlier, namely to absorb it, and if your mind is dominated by the sense of this central I-thou relationship of which we have been speaking.[12]

Thomas Chalmers is often cited as an example of one who really preached by using a manuscript. He held his manuscript in his left hand and followed each word with the index finger of his right hand. But that was not the worst of it. He had a rough, harsh voice that broke at times. His articulation and pronunciation were poor. He started his speaking in a drawl. His movements

---

[10] Op. cit., pp. 320 ff.
[11] Quoted from "A King's Story," Life, May 22, 1950.
[12] Servant of the Word, p. 59.

were clumsy and awkward. But once he got well started the whole situation changed. All constraint, awkwardness, and feebleness of voice disappeared. One hearer said, "His whole being seemed to rush into his preaching." Another said, "His eyes were afire with intelligence and rapture and zeal." Undoubtedly he achieved some of the best effects of direct speaking. In spite of the reading his personality broke through to the people.

But one person who heard him regularly said his "extempore discourses delivered to operatives in the outskirts of Glasgow were far more effective and more truly eloquent than the sermons which he delivered with so much applause in the Tron church of that city."

Jonathan Edwards is frequently cited as an example of a great preacher who read his sermons. Yet, in later life, he regretted the practice and tried to improve his delivery by using both the extemporaneous and the *memoriter* methods. Unquestionably there are outstanding ministers in our day who preach from manuscripts. But certain questions always arise: Are men who use manuscripts effective because they read their sermons or in spite of it? Are they men of such strong personalities that they can break rules with impunity and cancel out all disadvantages? Is their method of delivery one that can safely be recommended to average preachers? No certain answer can be given to these questions. Some light may be thrown upon the answers after the other methods of delivery have been studied.

However, before turning to other methods, one more important factor in the situation needs to be dealt with. A preacher's delivery should be adapted to the needs of his age. As previously stated, the tempo and trends of our times require public speech to be direct, personal, conversational. Lay men and women of all walks of life are taking courses in how to make public addresses. Practically all of them are taught to speak directly to their audiences without the use of a manuscript. High-school and college young people who take public speaking are given the same instruction. When these lay people listen to their ministers preach from a manuscript they begin to wonder.

Professors of homiletics in theological seminaries now and then receive letters from laymen who ask, "Why don't you teach your students to preach without a manuscript?" Every time laymen are given a chance to express themselves they vote against the reading of sermons. A prominent layman, addressing himself to the ministers of his denomination through a church magazine, reflected the feelings of laymen of all denominations when he pleaded, "Please, oh please, Mr. Preacher, don't read your sermons."

In colonial days church boards occasionally included clauses in the contracts of ministers forbiding them to preach "from the book," an old expression for using a manuscript. One wonders how many laymen of our day, accustomed to seeing other public speakers make their addresses without being tied to a manuscript, would include a similar clause in the contracts of their ministers if they had a chance. In the House of Commons if a member begins reading his speech another member has the right to arise and say, "Mr. Speaker, may I call attention to the fact that the honorable member is reading his speech." This, they tell us, usually finishes that speech. A modern Protestant minister would be shocked if someone in the congregation should arise soon after the sermon began and say, "Mr. Preacher, in behalf of the entire congregation, I call your attention to the fact that you are reading your sermon." This probably would finish that particular sermon but it might make him aware of the desire, and perhaps the right, of the people to have sermons preached to them in the direct manner to which they are accustomed everywhere else but in the church.

Can ministers as a group and the seminaries that train them how to preach afford to ignore the current attitude of laymen in this matter? There is a growing conviction in many quarters that they cannot wisely do so. The time has come when the opinion of the church's lay "public" in this regard must be given serious and thoughtful consideration.

As a matter of actual fact, what in our day is spoken of as "manuscript preaching" does not always mean the preacher reads every word of the manuscript. Many so-called manuscript preachers are so thoroughly acquainted with the contents of their manuscript they do not have to read all of it. Parts of it are spoken from memory, and parts are spoken extemporaneously. For a large portion of the time their audience contact is good. Nevertheless the manuscript is closely followed and pages are turned or laid aside one by one as they are finished. The amount of the reading determines the degree of many of the disadvantages of this method of delivery, and the amount of the free speaking provides some of the advantages of other methods.

RECITING THE SERMON FROM MEMORY

This method of delivery requires the sermon first to be written in complete form, then committed to memory, and finally delivered word for word just as it was originally composed.

The minister who recites his sermon from memory shares at least one—perhaps only one—advantage with the minister who reads his sermon. He is assured of delivering it in the same completed, carefully worded, polished manner in which he wrote it, provided, of course, his memory does not fail him. Preparation for this form of delivery requires more time and energy than for reading, unless one possesses an unusual memory like that, for example, of Lord Macaulay or of Rufus Choate. Macaulay could repeat a long poem accurately after hearing or reading it once. In his day it was said that if all the copies of Milton's *Paradise Lost* were destroyed he could restore the poem in its entirety from memory. He read everything he could get his hands on: well-known books, obscure books, and manuscripts. Years afterward, if he needed information from what he had read he could recall the exact place—volume and page—where he read it. Rufus Choate was able to write a speech, leave it at his desk, and deliver it exactly as he had prepared it.

If a minister possesses a memory like these men he can doubtless prepare his sermon for delivery with but little more labor than would be necessary to prepare it for reading.

If he could read his sermon over once and repeat it verbatim he also would have little dread of forgetting it. But if memorizing does not come that easy, his dread of forgetting, and the nervousness accompanying it, will be worse than if he planned to read the sermon.

But the chief disadvantages of this method stem from the fact that the preacher is placed in the position of a child reciting a piece he has learned "by heart," or of a college student delivering an oration rhetorically *before* an audience. Both he and his congregation are aware of that fact. His chief concern must be with his remembering and this inhibits him from throwing his whole personality into his message. Thus, reciting from memory may act as a barrier between him and his hearers to the same extent as does the manuscript of the reader.

Louis Bourdaloue, one of the great pulpit orators of France in the late seventeenth century, used to keep his eyes shut throughout his sermons to avoid the possibility of seeing something that would distract his attention and cause him to forget his speech. Ministers who recite their sermons can accomplish the same thing without actually having their eyes shut.

Luccock says if the preacher's attention is centered "in the hippodrome of his mind, around which he is chasing a fleeting idea or form of words, instead of out in front of him in the audience—his voice and eyes will show it. The audience will know it, and the interest will drop." [13] Like all other professors of homiletics he has seen that thing happen in the classroom. Theological students sometimes deliver their sermons with a sort of glassy stare in their eyes. They are so wrapped up in the act of recalling what they have memorized they do not see the people before them. Others achieve the same result by looking toward the back of the room a few inches above the heads of their audience. Now and then a student peers sidewise out the windows as though he is thinking on his feet. But he always fails to deceive his listeners: they know he is avoiding their eyes for fear he will forget what he has memorized.

Under such circumstances the preacher is not free. His chief concern cannot be to get his message over but to recall the next word or sentence. This keeps his gestures from being natural— makes them stiff, mechanical, and artificial. Practically the only faculty of the mind in operation is memory. He is shackled to a written manuscript he left on his study desk. Physiologically and emotionally he is in the same predicament as the speaker struck with stage fright. Like that speaker he needs to throw himself with abandon into the effort of getting his message across, to give his sole attention to speaking *to* his audience instead of *before* them.

The tragedy of it is, the people are aware of what is going on before them. They *feel* they are witnessing a type of performance. If the preacher succeeds in repeating perfectly his beautifully written sermon, they will want to applaud, not so much

---

[13] *In the Minister's Workshop*, p. 198.

for what he says, as for the artistic way in which he says it. I once heard an after-dinner address by an orator who had achieved notoriety in his section of the country for his flowery speeches. He was called upon to deliver his orations at various kinds of community gatherings where oratory was expected and relished as part of the entertainment. At one place when he was in the midst of a series of sentences of beauty uttered with great eloquence the audience burst into applause before he had completed the series. They were applauding his skill in memorizing, not the value of what he was saying. The applause was exactly the same kind that greets a person on a stage who performs skillful and difficult feats. The audience breaks out in applause before the act is finished. They are expressing their appreciation of art. The orator was giving an exhibition: he knew it and the audience knew it. He was invited for that purpose. He had nothing vital to advocate. He was not dealing with life-and-death issues. He was not out for a verdict.

This is not intended to cast reflections upon the preacher's motives nor to put him in the class of professional performers. The parallel is drawn to call attention to the situation that prevails when a preacher recites a sermon from memory. The people quickly, almost instinctively, sense that he is reciting a piece instead of talking to them. There are plenty of places in community life where artistic speech fills a need. But the pulpit is not one of them. In the pulpit a man is engaged in speaking the truth of God to the hearts and consciences of men. He is out for a verdict on important issues. He is pleading, entreating, beseeching men in behalf of Christ to be reconciled to God. He cannot achieve his persuasive purpose adequately if he gives the people the slighest impression he is demonstrating his artistic abilities instead of pouring out his soul.

FREE PREACHING

"Free preaching," as used in this study, means sermons that have been more carefully prepared as to structure, content, and language than in extemporaneous preaching, but are delivered, as in extemporaneous preaching, without use of manuscript or notes. The popular expression to describe it is "preaching without notes." The preachers who use this method agree it requires a great deal of thorough preparation beforehand.

The steps in the weekly preparation are similar though not precisely the same with all preachers. Some prepare an outline in detail but do not write the sermon out in full. As shown in the last chapter, this was the practice of the late Joseph Fort Newton, and is the method used by Clovis G. Chappell. This is also Clarence E. Macartney's method. He makes an outline with a few divisions and a statement at the beginning indicating where he intends to go and how he intends to get there. He gets this outline well in mind. "Those heads and subheads," he says, "can be written on your mind just as indelibly as on a piece of paper." He leaves this outline behind when he goes into the pulpit.[14]

Others outline the sermon in detail, then write it out in full, and from the completed manuscript make a condensed outline. Often the second outline is made on the margin of the pages of the manuscript. This final outline is thought through until it is clearly in mind. The sermon is then freely preached without the use of notes or manuscript. This was the method used by Bishop George Craig Stewart of the Episcopal Church, except that he did a bit of actual memorizing. He described his method briefly thus:

I make no attempt to memorize anything except the outline, any poetry and quotation that may occur, and the exact phrasing of the introduction and conclusion. I never take the sermon into the pulpit, not even a note.[15]

Frederick W. Robertson, who was thought of as doing free preaching, seems to have taken more than the usual number of steps in his preparation. He made copious notes from which he prepared an outline. Using this as a guide he wrote out his thoughts to be sure he was expressing himself clearly. From his written document he made what he called a syllabus. From the syllabus he made a skeleton of an outline which he took into the pulpit for reassurance. Many ministers who take a brief outline into the pulpit with them really do free preaching. They may glance at the notes a few times to be sure they are moving along the tracks as planned. But practically all of the time they are

[14] *Op. cit.*, pp. 154 ff.
[15] Newton, *op. cit.*, p. 158.

composing their thoughts as they go and keeping perfect eye contact with the congregation.

There are several things in the week's preparation invariably emphasized by those who use this method. The first is the necessity of a clear, solid structure for the sermon. According to Robertson, everything depends upon method, which he described as "correct arrangement" or "truthfulness of arrangement." Without that, he says, memory is useless. But if the thoughts have been "methodized beforehand," memory can easily recall them. The words and sentences will then take care of themselves during delivery.

James S. Stewart believes that freedom of delivery depends upon "carefulness of construction" beforehand. He specifies what he means as follows:

Clarity of logical structure; well-defined divisions and subdivisions; exclusion of irrelevances; short paragraphs, with a single clear-cut thought in each, not long unbroken stretches, where a dozen ideas jostle; balance and progress and development; with one or two strong and vivid illustrations marking out the track. The point is that freedom of delivery will tend to vary in direct proportion to accuracy of construction. If you can fashion a sermon which stands out clearly in all its parts before your own mind, the tyranny of the manuscript is broken.[16]

As emphasized by both these preachers, the right kind of structure is an invaluable aid in recalling the sermon as it was carefully prepared in the study, thus making notes unnecessary. This is what is known as "logical" instead of "verbal" memorization. By the psychologists this is regarded as the highest use of the memory. Logical memory is the power to recall the organization and orderly arrangement of ideas because one has thought them through clearly for himself. Ministers who use free preaching testify that once the outline and sequence of thought have been firmly established in mind much of the exact words, sentences, and even long passages can be reproduced in delivery as they were originally prepared. Hence, they stress strongly the necessity of concentrating for a while each week upon mastering the structure of the sermon so that the main and subdivisions,

[16] *Heralds of God*, pp. 181-82.

the position and content of illustrations, and narrative and descriptive passages can be pictured vividly before the mind.

Likewise, the necessity of composing the sermon for speaking style is emphasized as an important part of the preparation. George A. Buttrick insists: "This question of diction and clarity is not academic: it is moral! A preacher is under indictment who does not ask and answer these questions: 'What do I wish to say? Why do I wish to say it? How can it be said with vividness, compulsion and tenderness?' " [17] Thomas Guthrie used to put a blank page beside each written page of his sermon. A passage difficult to memorize was regarded as obscure. He would then rewrite it until it became "luminous." A luminous or clearly stated passage, he discovered, was easy to recall. Intensified work on style for a brief time each week, therefore, aids in getting the sermon in mind for free delivery.

The other thing consistently stressed as essential for preparation beforehand is absorbing the message into one's soul until he feels its importance and urgency and has a yearning desire to persuade the people to believe it, accept it, and live by it. That is not only a main factor in saying it well but in being able to say it, and wanting to say it, without notes.

Richard Storrs studied law before deciding to become a minister. He observed that Rufus Choate and other members of the bar in Boston presented their arguments to judge and jury without notes. When he became a preacher he said to himself, if the lawyer with a man's temporal interests at stake would not think of reading his speech, then the preacher with a man's immortal soul at stake should not read his sermon. So he learned to preach without notes.

George M. Gibson asks the students in his classes in homiletics if they can imagine "the trial lawyer battling for his client's life, the salesman bent on getting the name on the dotted line, the lover pressing his attentions on his lady," using notes or a manuscript or demonstrating their ability for memorizing. Then he urges them to learn from all such people this basic lesson: first and foremost the preacher must have "a passionate concern with what he has to say and a burning determination to move the other to agreement." [18] All other factors in free preaching are

[17] *Jesus Came Preaching* (New York: Charles Scribner's Sons, 1931), p. 160.
[18] *Planned Preaching* (Philadelphia: Westminster Press, 1954), p. 138.

201

secondary to a person with a sense of divine mission on fire with with a divine message. A preacher with a burning determination to get his message accepted and acted upon will not want, nor likely need, and may not permit any barrier to come between him and the people.

Free preaching has its disadvantages. One chief disadvantage has already been stressed: if done properly it requires more time in preparation than other methods. Since sentences must be formed while one is on his feet he is likely to make occasional grammatical errors. He cannot control the accuracy of his statements, or prevent some profuseness of style as can the reader of sermons. Since some memory work is required, especially as far as the sequence of thought is concerned, there is a certain amount of risk of forgetting something important and of becoming disconcerted. The preacher who uses this method is probably more dependent upon moods and feelings of the moment than if he used other methods. Unquestionably it takes something out of him. Often it leaves him in a state of nervous exhaustion. Hence, it is probably the most costly, most exacting form of preaching.

Free preaching also has advantages. These may be summarized in this single statement: it has the possibilities of fulfilling all the essential functions of effective public speaking. Potentially it gives full scope and perfect freedom to the personality of the preacher and provides modern congregations with the conditions of "listenability," and the direct conversational style they desire in public speech. In free preaching the preacher's voice, bodily actions, and display of emotions can be perfectly natural and attain their maximum power. Preachers who use this method testify that despite its exhausting demands it gives unusual exhilaration to their spirits. There is no joy greater than the *feel* of the response of the people to the personality of the preacher. Practically all professors of public speech recommend free delivery without qualification. Many of them consider it the only *complete* form of *real* speaking.

COMPOSITE METHOD OF DELIVERY

In preaching, as in all other fields, the ideal is rarely, if ever, attained. Hence, the average minister is likely to work out a method of delivery composed of some aspects of each of the methods of delivery. Even those who think of themselves as doing extemporaneous and free preaching may make use of notes, read an occasional passage they want to give accurately or lines of poetry they cannot memorize, or recite portions of the sermon they have committed to memory. Many who think of themselves as manuscript readers do varying amounts of free speaking.

All men are not born with the same capabilities and temperaments. All cannot attain the same degree of skill. Different men have different work habits and different methods of achieving the same ends. Two ministers equipped with disparate abilities and using diverse methods may have equally successful preaching ministries. Protestant congregations are generous, patient, and tolerant. They often put up with many of the limitations, weaknesses, and mistakes of the preacher who feeds their souls and whom they respect and love and recognize to be a genuine, sincere, devoted servant of God. Each person must dedicate *himself* to God.

In the matter of delivery every preacher must "work out [his] own salvation with fear and trembling" (Phil. 2:12). Each must study himself and his congregation and adopt for himself the method of preaching that promises, in the light of all known factors, including the will of God, to be the most effective for *his* ministry. But all should be seeking constantly to grow in ability to communicate the gospel and be willing at all times to discard old methods that have proved ineffective and to adopt new ones that promise better results.

SUGGESTED READING

Baxter, B. B. *The Heart of the Yale Lectures*. New York: The Macmillan Co., 1947. Part II.

Brown, Charles R. *The Art of Preaching*. New York: The Macmillan Co., 1922. Chapter VI.

Kirkpatrick, R. W. *The Creative Delivery of Sermons*. New York: The Macmillan Co., 1944.

Macartney, Clarence E. *Preaching Without Notes*. New York and Nashville: Abingdon Press, 1946. Chapter V.

McComb, Samuel L. *Preaching in Theory and Practice*. New York: Oxford University Press, 1926. Chapter IX.

Stewart, James S. *Heralds of God*. New York: Charles Scribner's Sons, 1946. Pp. 176 ff.

12. Speech Mechanism

The acceptance of God's call to the ministry carries with it the obligation to do everything in one's power to learn how to utilize his speech mechanism effectually and to keep it operating efficiently. The fulfillment of that obligation requires him to correct defects in the mechanism, learn the techniques of operating it, and perfect the skills in its use.

As regrettable as it may be, the facts indicate that a large proportion of men who go into the ministry seem not to take this obligation seriously. Some time ago Robert Schock, public speaking instructor at the Army and Air Force Chaplain School at Carlisle Barracks, Pennsylvania, on the basis of several years' experience in the school, expressed the opinion that numerous clergymen in our country have bad public speaking habits. The students were from all denominations and of several faiths. One-fifth of them were chaplains and four-fifths of them civilian ministers commissioned in the Reserve and National Guard. He feels sure, therefore, that the number who passed through the school were a representative cross section of clergymen in the nation. Most of them had basic faults of one kind or another and seemed surprised when these were pointed out.

One radio listener, who wrote under the pseudonym "The Listener" in the *Atlantic Monthly* a few years ago, expressed considerable vexation with the poor voices of the preachers heard. He (or she) said:

The tradition of the "holy tone," the tradition of reading or citing the Scripture as hollow, throaty chant, instead of the bravest language ever written, hangs damp and heavy upon most preachers. Some talk on tiptoe. Some bark, roar, howl and bemoan. Some croon. Some lisp. They can and do read the greatest prose in the language as if it were a garble. They speak not as Demosthenes spoke, with pebbles in their mouths, but with soft-boiled golf balls. They do not speak like ordinary men and women; they do not speak even like their own parishioners.

The preachers (to judge them by their voices, which are after all the only instruments by which they can be judged on the radio) have mostly made no effort to master the basic principles of a simple technique which opens to them the doors of thirty-one million homes containing fifty-four million church members. One wonders why and one worries. . . . For a small sum, or for less, or for nothing at all, any preacher's voice on the air can be recorded and played back to him. How many preachers have thus heard their own voices? How many preachers have said to themselves: "I've got to do something about this at once!" How many have sought the calm professional guidance of the people who know how radio sounds in the nine hundred radio stations of the country? [1]

Discount this as the judgment of one person—and that a vexed person—if you wish, but the fact remains that the average preacher does not know how his voice sounds to others. Some years ago the mayor of Louisville, Kentucky, had a recording made of one of his speeches and later fell asleep while listening as it was played back to him. One wonders how many preachers would fall asleep, or lose interest, or perhaps stop listening altogether, if they had to listen to themselves preach week after week. The preacher has an obligation to discover the effect of his speaking and, if necessary, to do something about what he learns.

Fortunately the person who wishes to do so, and is willing on his own initiative to work at the task, can learn how to speak effectively enough to insure a successful preaching ministry. Pat Kelly, the supervisor of announcers for NBC, said a while ago, "Only five persons out of a hundred are born with good voices. The rest of us have to work for one." The encouraging thing is, we can work for a good speaking voice and achieve it. Thousands of people are doing it every year by making use of the practical aids now available for home use. More than twenty-five years ago, J. R. P. Sclater, in his Yale lectures on preaching, said, "The art of reasonable, coherent and audible public speech may be acquired by anyone, who has a voice, some self-control and an average intelligence." [2] That could be said with even more assurance now because of the many helpful books, recording machines, and other aids not available a quarter of a century ago.

To be sure, some speech difficulties are due to actual physical defects that require the attention of a physician, or a speech specialist, or perhaps a psychiatrist. For this reason anyone with serious speech abnormalities should consult a specialist to discover

[1] "The Preacher on the Air," December, 1943. Used by permission.
[2] Op. cit., p. 93.

whether he has organic trouble. But according to experts, speech difficulties are nearly always due to bad habits that can be corrected by the individual himself with proper practice and a little guidance.

The first thing one should do is to have a recording made of his sermon, preferably one actually preached in connection with public worship. As it is played back he should study it objectively and critically with a view to understanding his own habits. Then he should acquaint himself with the various parts of his speech mechanism and how they operate. A thorough and scientific description of the physiology and the functioning of the speech mechanism may be found in Roy C. McCall's college textbook *Fundamentals of Speech,* Chapter IX.[3]

Next, he should purchase a book designed to aid the average person who, on his own responsibility, is willing to improve his speaking habits. Fortunately a number of books have been published in recent years for that express purpose. The following are two of the best recent books of this type that I know: (1) *The Successful Speaker's Handbook,* by Herbert V. Prochnow,[4] which devotes six chapters to every phase of delivery, including the voice, breathing, articulation, pronunciation, and bodily action; (2) *How to Make Better Speeches,* by William G. Hoffman,[5] which contains five chapters on the same general topics.

Paul Robeson once said to a noted singing teacher, "I don't want you to make me a professional singer. Just show me how to use my voice without ruining it. I'll do the singing." Any person who is willing to work at it diligently enough and long enough can learn not only how to keep from ruining his voice but how to use it properly. Once he learns a few fundamentals he ought to be able to do his own preaching and do it well. The suggestions that follow are made for such a person and are intended to be a summary of the important facts one needs to know about the various aspects of the problem.[6]

The speaking mechanism has four parts, each of which plays

[3] New York: The Macmillan Co., 1949.

[4] New York: Prentice-Hall, Inc., 1951.

[5] New York: Funk & Wagnalls Co., 1948.

[6] I am greatly indebted to the three books mentioned above. From them I have borrowed and quoted extensively. The reader is referred to them for exercises and suggestions of inestimable value in forming good speech habits.

an important function in producing effective speech. Each will be considered in some detail.

SOUND PRODUCTION

First, the human voice is a wind instrument. The wind that operates it is breathed into the lungs and then pushed out of the lungs through the windpipe into the voice box, thence out through the mouth and nose. The lungs rest upon the diaphragm. As the air expands the lungs, the diaphragm is pushed out and down. As the lungs exhale the air, the diaphragm pushes in and up and propels the outgoing air more rapidly. The muscles of the diaphragm are capable of expelling the air with considerable force. Sometimes the diaphragm is spoken of as the bellows and sometimes as the air pump. Learning how to use the diaphragm properly in breathing is the first and basic step in learning how to speak effectively. Its proper use affects the force or volume of the vocal tones and determines whether or not they are properly sustained for speaking whole sentences between breaths.

One voice teacher used to say to his students, "You can put your mind into your sermon, and you can put your heart into it; but until you put your diaphragm into it, it won't amount to much." Ordinarily, breathing is automatic and unconscious. But in learning how to speak one must give conscious attention to its control. Practice diaphragmatic breathing for awhile: breathe deeply, from the bottom of the lungs. Start every word from the diaphragm and put firm breath pressure back of it. Be careful that the intake is not excessive, that it does not fill the lungs to capacity. Then learn to store up the breath, to hold it long enough to say a sentence and let it out slowly until a natural pause is reached. The secret of breathing for speaking is to control the smooth flow of the air through the vocal cords.

Second, sounds originate in the larynx, a boxlike structure at the top of the windpipe composed of muscles and cartilages, and popularly spoken of as the voice box. Inside this are two flexible membranes called vocal cords that vibrate as the air is pushed through them. As they vibrate they release sound waves, just as the strings of a harp or piano release vibrations when touched. These sound waves may be of different lengths or frequency and account for the variety of tones the human voice is capable of making. The pitch of the voice, its inflection, and modulation and the range of tones are determined by the frequency of the vibrations. Every person has tonal range limits. Some people have a naturally high or tenor (soprano) voice, others a low or baritone (contralto) voice. But within one's natural range he is capable of producing tones of high, medium, and low pitch.

The quality of the tone is affected by the tongue and the muscles of the neck, jaw, and face. When not being used in articulating words, the tongue should be relaxed and lie flat on the floor of the mouth. Othewise it gets in the way of the tones. The muscles of the neck and jaw should be relaxed; otherwise they pinch or constrict the larynx and interfere with the vibrations of the cords. When the sounds are restricted by tight muscles, then harshness, huskiness, roughness, or raspiness result. One teacher advises, "Learn to take the steel wool out of your voice." That is done by learning to relax the muscles that affect it. A perfectly relaxed throat and face are likely to make smoother, more melodious tones. When Billy Rose listened to a recording of his radio script he said, "Take it away! That's an impostor. It sounds like a nail file rubbing a cheesegrater!" Part of his trouble was due to muscular constriction that choked off the sound.

The second step in learning how to speak, therefore, is to learn how to relax these muscles so the tones can get through the passages and out into the air without interference. Let the sounds flow out easily. Push them out with the diaphragm. Don't try to push them out with the muscles of the throat or neck. If loudness is desired, do not holler but let the volume come primarily from breathing. "Thunder is not lightning," said Spurgeon. "Men do not hear in proportion to the noise created." The tonal quality is the main thing. Some voices seem to have better penetration or carrying power than others. But anyone can give his voice its maximum carrying ability by permitting sound to flow out freely.

Third, as the sound comes from the vocal cords it must be reinforced by the resonators—the nasal cavity back of the nose, possibly the sinuses and the mouth cavity. The hard palate, or roof of the mouth, acts as a sounding board to give the tone a final push out of the mouth. If one concentrates attention on it awhile he can actually feel the sound hitting the roof of the mouth at the edge of the upper front teeth. As the sound emerges from the voice box it must be resounded in both nasal and mouth cavities, if it is to be full and pleasing. If it is cut off from the nasal cavity and forced to come through the mouth cavity only, the tones are shrill. If it is cut off from the mouth cavity and forced to travel up into the head only, the tones are heavy and thick. That causes "cold-in-the-head" or "talking-through-the-nose" tones—muffled and metallic.

When Beecher was in college he talked as though he had pudding in his mouth. With the assistance of an elocution teacher and by practicing "exploding" vowels through his resonators, he was able to overcome the trouble and to achieve his unusual speaking voice. The resonators are of great importance. They reinforce volume. Because they are flexible they can shape and change sound. They actually create the vowel sounds. Speech teachers sometimes advise speakers to forget their vocal cords and think of their voices as being in their heads not in their throats.

The chief sounds not properly resonated are m's, n's, and ng's. Take series of words in which these sounds are prominent and practice them, both in speaking and in reading. Keep at it until the resonance back of the nose and on the roof of your mouth can be felt. "When you have this feeling in both places at once, you are vocalizing correctly and your voice will have sufficient carrying power for all the demands you can make upon it." [7]

WORD PRODUCTION

Producing sounds is not speaking. One speaks when sounds are incorporated in words. Words are composed of vowels and consonants. Altogether there are fifty separate sounds produced by the use of the twenty-six letters of the alphabet. Twenty-five of these are vowel sounds and twenty-five consonant sounds. If words are to be understood and communication to take place, the syllables of words must be enunciated properly so sounds will convey words to the minds of the hearers. If any of the sounds is indistinct a blank occurs in the word and this makes an incomplete sentence.

If the listener hears a wrong sound he gets a mistaken idea. One child repeating the Lord's Prayer said, "Harold be thy name." Another prayed, "Give us this day our jelly bread." A New York

[7] Prochnow, op. cit., p. 178.

lad prayed, "Lead us not into Penn Station." Prochnow tells of three women overhearing Mrs. Smith make a remark to her husband. One woman said, "They must have been to the zoo, because I heard her mention 'a trained deer.'" Another said, "No, no. They were talking about going away and she said to him. 'Find out about the train, dear.'" The third woman interrupted, "I think you are both wrong. It seemed to me they were discussing music, for she said 'a trained ear' very distinctly." When Mrs. Smith appeared her friends told her of their disagreement. She laughed saying, "Well, that's certainly funny. You are poor guessers, all of you. The fact is, I'd been out to the country overnight, and I was asking my husband if it rained here last night." [8] Poor enunciation of words makes it necessary for hearers to guess what the speaker is saying and guessing is often fatal for accurate communication.

Hence, speech is not satisfactory unless words are articulated. Reference was made above to the fact that sounds are shaped or formed, and sometimes created by the different positions of the tongue, lips, and jaw and their relation to one another. Until we put our minds consciously on it we do not realize what an important part in speech is played by the tongue moving quickly here and there with precise adjustments, contacts, and shapes to help make the proper sounds. The position of the lips also modifies and shapes sounds. Some tones are made with the lips relaxed and close together, some with the lips slightly apart and the tongue against the upper teeth, and others by puckering the lips as in whistling.

For proper production of words one must learn to do three things.

1. Learn to sound the individual letters distinctly. Consonants are sounded properly by stopping the tone momentarily with the tongue or lips and then releasing it suddenly with a slight explosive action. Consonants may be divided into *lip* consonants and *tongue* consonants. The lip consonants, *p, b, m, f, v, w,* and and the combination *wh,* are made by pressing the lips tightly together. Sound them as an exercise several times, being careful to speak them distinctly, and you will discover this.

[8] *Ibid.,* p. 200.

If you take pains to localize the sensation in the center of the lips just in front of the upper teeth, you will be sure of getting those sounds correct. . . . In connection with the lip sounds, remember that the words should seem to be formed by the upper lip and come out through it. Then it will be easy to pronounce distinctly. In this way the words will be formed outside the mouth and will be readily heard. Give this method a trial and you will agree with this statement.[9]

Tongue consonants may be divided into three groups: (a) those made with the tip of the tongue—*t, d, n, I,* and the combination *th;* (b) those made with the middle of the tongue—*k, g,* and the combination *ng;* and (c) those made with the sides or edge of the tongue—*s, z, j,* or soft sound *g,* and the combination *ch.*

If you will take care always to press the tongue tip tightly against the upper front teeth, you will make these sounds correctly and distinctly. If you learn to produce these tongue-tip sounds accurately, you will go far toward solving the problem of indistinctness, for your muscles will automatically adjust themselves to the requirements for other sounds.[10]

As previously stated, vowel sounds are produced properly by the way they are shaped or molded by the changed positions of tongue and lips. McCall explains this process clearly as follows:

A study of the anatomical adjustments for pronunciation of the various sounds will reveal that the true vowels are characterized by a relatively open mouth cavity, each vowel achieving its character by the position of the tongue in the floor of the mouth, and by the degree and type of the lip opening. The soft palate is lowered to some degree for each normal vowel, so that the nasal cavity may contribute its resonance potentialities. . . . Note that in forming vowels the tongue never makes contact with the hard or soft palate or upper teeth, and only incidentally with the lower teeth.[11]

The best way to understand this is to pronounce the vowels one at a time and make mental note of the positions of the lips and tongue as they shift in producing the several sounds. Con-

[9] *Ibid.,* p. 203.
[10] *Ibid.,* p. 204.
[11] *Op. cit.,* p. 154.

tinue this as an exercise regularly for a while and you will find yourself making the sounds perfectly. Practicing this exercise "will help you in two ways. First, it will make your articulation apparatus, tongue and lips, more flexible and sensitive. Second, it will train your ear, so that you will notice more closely the sounds you produce and thereby produce them more accurately." [12]

2. Learn to articulate all syllables and keep them distinct. Some letters are left completely out of spoken words. For example: *singin* for singing, *comin* for coming, *insiss* for insists, *fif's* for fifths, *tol* for told, *wite* for white, *wich* for which. Sometimes a syllable is left out. For example: *particuly* for particularly, *hosbil* for hospital, *goverment* for government, *pome* for poem, *prator* for operator. A common fault is to add an extra sound—*a, ah, er,* or *uh*—at the end of a word. This is often done rhythmically, at regular intervals, at the end of phrases, clauses, and sentences where ordinarily a pause would be made. When done habitually the result is somewhat similar to stuttering or stammering. The cure for this is to think about it, consciously pause instead of making a sound, and practice until the habit is broken.

3. Learn to articulate words and keep them distinct. Prochnow calls the practice of running words together "clipping and telescoping words." Hoffman calls it "lazy articulation," "cutting corners jargon" and says it is due to "mental slovenliness." For example: "he hadduh win" for "he had to win," or "he hajuh there" for "he had you there." The only way to avoid this is to practice speaking clauses and sentences with the conscious intention of articulating every word distinctly and keeping each word in the sentence separate.

Good speech habits, like all other good habits, are formed by practice, practice, practice—continuous repetition of the correct sounds and articulation until they become second nature. In the early stages of the process one will be more or less self-conscious. The way to overcome this is to practice as much as possible before Sunday, using for this some of the words and phrases in the sermon that give the most difficulty. This will put the subconscious mind at attention concerning these particular difficulties. When one actually starts preaching, however, he should forget pronunciation and articulation and throw himself into his message. The chances are that the subconscious mind, acting as a monitor, will remind one to pronounce and enunciate distinctly. When the habit of speaking one set of words and phrases is well formed, select another group to work on. Ultimately, correct speaking will become almost automatic.

SOME MISCELLANEOUS DO'S AND DON'T'S

1. Watch the rhythmic singsong or "holy whine." "A speech," said Phillips Brooks, "should be like the leaping of a fountain, not the pumping of a pump." Luccock indicates a great difference between rhythm and singsong. The former ought to be provided for, the latter "in the pulpit, is an offense against both God and man." [18]

2. Do not bawl or bellow. Lyman Beecher said, "I always holler when I have nothing to say." "If you have the facts on your side," a law professor said to his class, "hammer them into the jury; and if you have the law on your side, hammer it into the judge." "But if you have neither the facts nor the law?" asked a student. "Then hammer on the table," replied the professor.

3. Do not drop the voice in the last words of a sentence: sustain it to the end. When Sir Christopher Wren planned St. Paul's Cathedral of London he estimated that a preacher with an "average voice might be heard fifty feet in front, twenty behind, and thirty on either side, *provided he did not drop his voice at the end of sentences.*"

4. Project the voice instead of elevating it. Keep muscles relaxed. Don't shriek or shout. Use the middle tones. Open your mouth and aim the sound at the person on the back seat.

5. Use natural tones as in conversation. Don't be a "two-voiced"—Dr. Jekyll and Mr. Hyde—speaker: one voice for talking naturally in conversation and one voice for talking unnaturally in the pulpit.

6. Avoid monotony. Aim at variety of pitch and force.

7. Study timing by use of pauses. Speech can often be greatly improved by better grouping and phrasing of words. Watch the

---

[18] *In the Minister's Workshop,* p. 199.

duration of sound. Consonants require more time than vowels and some consonants require more time than others.

8. Learn to be your own critic. During his first few years in London, Spurgeon received a weekly letter from an anonymous critic listing the young preacher's faults. In later years Spurgeon thanked God for his self-appointed censor and regretted he could not express appreciation to him in person. His criticisms were invaluable and made a distinct contribution to Spurgeon's speaking effectiveness. If one's wife or friend can call attention to his speaking faults, without irritating him, it will be a distinct service. But the correction of most faults will depend upon whether he can make himself aware of them. Learn to be your own critic and do not be too soft and lenient with yourself.

9. Learn what words to emphasize and how to pause to do it.

10. Exercise self-discipline. Practice regularly. Work hard. Stay on the job until it is finished.

11. When you start your sermon forget your voice and give exclusive attention to your message and to the people you want to believe it.

VISIBLE COMMUNICATION

Thus far attention has been given to *audible* communication: what the preacher can do to make sure the listeners *hear* his message. Listeners are also spectators and need to *see* the preacher in order to understand his message. They actually listen with their eyes. They hear better, can concentrate better on what is being said, if they can see the speaker. If their view is obstructed, or if they must sit in a strained, uncomfortable position in order to see him, their ability to hear is diminished.

But there is much more to it than that. If they cannot see the preacher they lose a large part of the effect, meaning, and worth of what he says. He expresses the emotional quality of the truth, the intensity of his feelings and thoughts, by bodily actions. These actions are his *visible* means of communication. For the full, complete understanding of his message the people need not only to hear what he says but to see how he says it. Thoreau was right: "A man has not seen a thing until he has felt it." The preacher helps his congregation feel the truth by communicating his feelings to them through their eyes. Feelings are expressed partly through vocal tones, and partly through actions.

People express themselves as naturally through bodily movements as through words. In fact, these movements may have been a primitive form of communication, a "sign language." We say of someone, "He literally radiates happiness." By that we mean he reveals his inner joy by the brightness of his eyes, his beaming countenance, the animation of his conversation, the spring in his step, and the quality of every other movement of his body. Any person under a strong emotion, completely free from all self-consciousness, uninhibited by timidity or fear, will express himself through every part of his body.

Eyes twinkle, snap, blaze, or cloud with tears. Facial muscles pull the eyebrows, forehead, lips and cheeks into clear patterns. Indeed, scientific tests have shown that a great range of emotions may be communicated by facial expressions alone. After the eyes and face, the hands are next in impressiveness. . . . Shoulders, trunk and head also gesture. It is natural to cower in fear, bow in humility, look up in hope, strut in pride and crouch in belligerent anger. . . . Even the feet rush into the speech situation when other movements are inhibited.[14]

When people are expressing themselves naturally their actions nearly always suit their words. They make movements that express their feelings appropriately, fit their moods nicely, reveal their thoughts clearly. The principles of bodily action are not arbitrarily laid down by professors of speech. They are discovered by watching people's movements when they are expressing themselves without inhibitions. While complete uniformity is not found in these movements, the same actions for expressing the same emotions are so consistently made by most people that they may be regarded as natural. Hence the secret of effective action in public speech: *speak as naturally to a large group as you would converse with a few friends.*

A young clergyman once asked David Garrick, the famous actor, to make some suggestions about his pulpit manners. Garrick said:

You know how you would speak in the parlor to a dear friend who was in immediate danger of his life. . . . You would not think of play-

[14] Garrison, *The Preacher and His Audience*, pp. 237-38.

ing the orator. You would be yourself; and the interesting nature of your subject, impressing your heart, would furnish you with the most natural tone of voice, the most proper language, the most engaging pictures, and the most suitable and graceful gestures. What you would be in the parlor, be in the pulpit; and you will not fail to please, to effect, to profit.[15]

Many others have observed that when people converse natural-ly they almost invariably use the appropriate actions, tones, and words. For this reason it has become customary to refer to public speaking as "animated conversation," or "glorified think-ing out loud." If one expresses his thoughts and feelings to a group just as he would to one person, it is said, his actions will take care of themselves.

This is valuable insight. But it is an oversimplification of the problem of action. To begin with, it assumes everybody ex-presses himself easily and naturally in conversation when he feels deeply about something. This is an unwarranted assump-tion. First and last a great many people find it difficult to express themselves freely in personal conversation. Again, this position assumes that carrying on a personal conversation and speaking in public are parallel situations. That also is a gratuitous assump-tion. The two situations are similar but different.

Hoffman says it is easy to *call* public speaking "heightened conversation." One should speak in public as simply and as naturally as he converses. He should not try to put on an exhibi-tion or use fancy "stage tricks," or "assume a manner that is foreign to him." So far, so good. But the word "heightened"

warns us that while spirited, friendly informal talk may be the model for public speaking, something has been added. And that some-thing requires thought and training. *Heightened* refers to the con-tent as well as to the delivery of the speech: it means having pur-pose, ideas, plan, organization, detail, illustration, proof or propositions worth listening to and delivery that is clear, distinct, varied enough to hold attention and in the language and articulation acceptable to the audience.[16]

Few people can carefully prepare in all these details and be as informal and relaxed in delivering a speech as when they run

[15] McComb, *Preaching in Theory and Practice*, p. 174.
[16] Hoffman, *op. cit.*, p. 4.

over to tell a neighbor a bit of good news. The psychology of the two situations is not the same. They must therefore be treated somewhat differently.

If one only would, or could, be as natural in public speaking as in ordinary conversation he would make expressive bodily movements gracefully. But that cannot be done merely by deciding to do it. What one should do is one thing, learning how to do it is quite another. Learning how is a process requiring conscious effort, over a period of time, on three closely related but separate problems.

1. *The problem of avoiding bad habits.* That is the negative aspect of the situation, but it usually arises first; and is due largely to the difference between a conversation-situation and a speaking-situation. Simply because there is something unnatural about one person standing on a raised platform before the eyes of a large number of people and delivering a prepared speech, relatively few people can do it without self-consciousness. Before he has time to overcome his self-consciousness the average person unconsciously falls into nervous mannerisms of one sort or another.

"You have as few mannerisms as any preacher we ever had," is a compliment that warms most ministers' hearts. Only those who have made a study of these mannerisms are aware of how many and how varied they are and of how unnecessary, unnatural, ineffective, diverting, and, sometimes, offensive they can be. Rare indeed is the preacher who does not acquire a few of them within the first months of his ministry. These nervous actions become compulsive, a Sunday ritual, to be gone through again and again without the average person's being aware of it. But count on this: the people are aware of it. There are always some members of the congregation who will count the number of times the preacher repeats his mannerisms and will compare their figures with one another after the close of the service.

Because most preachers are unconscious of these habits the first thing one needs to do is to become aware of them. Everyone should take someone into his confidence and get him to give an honest report on his unconscious compulsive actions. Then he should assign himself the task of breaking any bad habits found in the report. As everyone knows, habits are easy

217

to form and difficult to break. One must *want* to break them, *determine* to break them, and *be willing* to give continuous attention to the task until it is accomplished. Here as elsewhere, one of the most important steps one can take is to make his subconscious mind his ally: give it the job of reminding him when he is about to do what he is striving to avoid.

2. The problem of forming desirable habits. This, too, requires continuous conscious effort. The first important step here is to make a study of what constitutes natural action in speaking. Some consider this of doubtful value. First, because the actions used in speaking vary with different individuals, what is natural with one person is not necessarily natural with another. Second, trying to work out action in theory is more or less mechanical. While both of these points are true, it is also true that there are some principles of action common to all people.

Since all human bodies are built alike, there are certain movements and postures which are more expressive and more graceful than others. . . . In the course of ages, certain principles with respect to postures and movements that are effective before an audience have been discovered. It will be well . . . to consider them. These are not matters of theory. When you are dominated by your feelings so that you forget yourself, your muscles will automatically move in the ways suggested. . . . If you continue your study of effective speaking so that addressing audiences becomes a matter of course with you, your gestures will eventually come to follow the lines . . . indicated. It will save time, however, to have these principles in mind from the start.[17]

Practically all phases of learning how to preach are more or less mechanical to begin with. But getting basic principles clearly established in the mind is one sure way to assure freedom in later performance.

These desirable habits have to do with three things.

a) *Posture.* Before entering the sanctuary take a few deep breaths. Throw your shoulders back. Assume a bearing of vigor, of alertness. Stimulate your mental alertness at the same time. Physical bearing and mental moods mutually influence each other. Do not permit yourself to slump or slouch in your seat. When you arise stand erect and to your full height. Stand

[17] Prochnow, op. cit., pp. 236-37.

squarely on your feet. Look your audience in the face. Let your posture give you a feeling of assurance and courage. The people will immediately catch your mood.

b) *Expression of the face.* The expressiveness of the eyes has already been mentioned in other connections. In conversation the person who wishes to say something to you usually looks you in the eyes. A shifty-eyed person gives the impression he is afraid he will reveal his real thoughts and feelings, or indicate in his eyes something he wishes to conceal. By looking at them, give the people the feeling you have something important to say to each of them directly. This does not mean fastening your gaze long—or necessarily at all—upon one individual, but keeping the entire congregation within the range of your eyes so it appears to each person you are looking at him.

While preaching do not inhibit feelings. Give them a chance to beam through your facial expressions.

Good eye-contact cannot be achieved by merely acquiring the habit of looking at the listeners; something much deeper is involved. It grows out of a strong sense of communication—an urgent desire, not only to perform one's duty by filling twenty minutes with pious sounds, but to communicate, to convey a message. In its finest form, this is an aspect of sense of mission—a conviction that one has no choice; he must speak because he is unable to remain silent.[18]

c) *Gestures with arms and hands.*[19] Make a brief study of how to gesture gracefully and naturally. The arms and hands are used more often than any other part of the body, and, next to the eyes and face, are the most expressive and the most impressive. Gestures should be made from the shoulder, with the free movement of the whole arm, not from the elbow. Try making gestures from the elbow and you will realize how awkward— almost ludicrous—it appears. Hands should be open with all fingers relaxed and extended normally. One of the most expressive parts of the hand is the thumb. The hand should never be closed with the thumb clasped inside the fingers. Try making a gesture of anger with the thumb inside the fingers, instead of on the outside, or opening the hand with the thumb in the palm,

---

[18] Garrison, *op. cit.*, p. 236.

[19] At this point the term "gesture" has been restricted arbitrarily to movements of the arms and hands.

and you will see what is meant by the expressiveness of the thumb.

One should not gesticulate with the hands higher than the head or lower than the heart. Most gestures should be made with the palm up and fingers outspread. But if one wishes to disapprove of something he pushes it away, so to speak, with the palm down. And if he wishes to emphasize something or assert it positively, he closes the hand except for the forefinger. Try "laying down the law" to the congregation with hand outspread and palm up. Instantly and instinctively you will see its inappropriateness. "When the gesture reaches the climax, the hand flicks open or the fist clinches. A gesture in which the hand assumes position first and then is pushed out by the arm tends to be unnatural." [20] One need only try this a few times to realize it is so. When a gesture is made the arm should be thrown out in a short arc with hands completely relaxed.

One can wisely practice graceful movements during the week, as he speaks various sections of the sermon aloud, until he sees for himself why they are the natural ways of expressing the ideas that go with them. Once this formal exercise is finished, however, let him bury those principles deep in this subconscious mind and assign it the task of reminding him, when preaching, to make gestures only when they mean something, and not to make motions merely to express nervous energy.

Once one starts to preach he should not inhibit an impulse to make a gesture. That is a weakness characteristic of many preachers. Sydney Smith asked:

Why are we natural everywhere but in the pulpit? No man expresses warm and animated feelings anywhere else with his mouth alone, but with his whole body; he articulates with every limb, and talks from head to foot with a thousand voices. Why this holoplexia on sacred occasions only? Why call in the aid of paralysis to piety? Is it a rule of oratory to balance the style against the subject, and to handle the most sublime truths in the dullest language and the driest manner? [21]

But beware of simulating feelings you do not possess. Like facial expressions, gestures must come from genuine inner im-

[20] Prochnow, *op. cit.*, p. 237.
[21] Hesketh Pearson, *The Smith of Smiths* (London: Hamish Hamilton, 1945), p. 36.

pulses. Spurgeon remarked that some men "mistake perspiration for inspiration." Real feelings will produce bodily movements, but bodily movements cannot generate real feelings. When gestures are made for their own sake they are nearly always artificial and mechanical.

3. The problem of centering attention upon the message. This is the crux of the matter. Once you get on your feet, center your attention upon what you want to say instead of upon the way you wish to say it. A preacher should do all the work on how he wants to speak before he goes into the pulpit. Once there he should concentrate on the *what*, the *to whom*, and the *what for* of his preaching, instead of the *how*, as John A. Kern once put it. Moods and methods as such, all desire to impress, all fear of making a mistake should be forgotten. Avoid listening to yourself while speaking. That is a dangerous form of vanity. All forms of self-consciousness are fatal to delivery and stimulate undesirable nervous habits.

Senator George F. Hoar of Massachusetts, an outstanding speaker in his day, said: "I believe that the most successful speakers whom I know would find it hard to tell you whether they themselves make gestures or not. They are so absolutely unconscious of the matter." No man can be eloquent, just as he cannot be happy, by merely trying to be. Happiness is a by-product of a way of living. Pulpit eloquence is a by-product of a way of throwing one's self with abandon into his sermon. "The abandonment of oneself is for the sake of self-concentration upon three things: upon your subject, upon your audience, and upon your object." [22] If one concentrates upon these things he will not be conscious of gestures.

After Spurgeon had spent two lectures on criticizing and caricaturing all the bad habits of posture, action, and gesture characteristic of some preachers, he said to his students:

Be natural in your action. . . . Do not allow my criticism upon various grotesque positions and movements to haunt you in the pulpit; better perpetrate them all than to be in fear, for this would make you cramped and awkward. Dash at it whether you blunder or no. A few mistakes in this matter will not be half so bad as being nervous.[23]

[22] Kern, *The Ministry to the Congregation*, pp. 495 ff.
[23] David Otis Fuller, *Spurgeon's Lectures to His Students*, Lectures XVIII and XIX (Grand Rapids: Zondervan Publishing House, 1945).

Spurgeon was trying to get his students to take the steps suggested in this section. First, get a clear picture of how unnatural gestures look to others. Second, get in mind a few fundamental principles of how natural gestures are made. Work on these during the week. Then push them into the background of the mind. Third, forget them all when preaching. Concentrate on delivering the sermon with genuine earnestness and feeling. If one does these things week after week he will find that, in due time, right actions will come with the right feeling at the right time, as a matter of course—habitually—almost automatically.

The Soul Behind the Mechanism

After all this has been said, it must also be said with some emphasis that one cannot become an effective speaker merely by giving himself speech lessons. The voice and actions do not speak: the man speaks through them. "Delivery has its residence not in the mouth, but in the *sentiment* and the *thought*," said Adolphe Monod. . . . "It is at bottom, the soul of the speaker which addresses the soul of the hearer." [24]

The most important thing in delivery is the man: what he is, what he thinks, how he feels, his motives, purposes, and yearnings. These constitute what someone calls the "imperative plus" in preaching. Hoffman, himself a teacher of public speech, says, "A few voice exercises cannot take the place of spiritual rebirth." [25] Above and beyond the speech mechanism is the person using it. Spurgeon considered eloquence as "logic set on fire." William Jennings Bryan called it "thought on fire." One must be absorbed to the "point of glowing fervor" in his message. He must come to a point of "spontaneous combustion" in his preaching. His soul must be aflame.

These inner feelings must be genuine. One cannot screen his real feelings out of his delivery. What he is will show in his eyes, his face, his gesture, the tones of his voice. What one says must come from the heart if it goes to the heart.

Yourself must feel it first, your end to capture.

* * * * * * * * * *

[24] McComb, *op. cit.*, p. 152.
[25] *Op. cit.*, p. 184.

... heart to heart ye will not sway and fashion,
Save in your heart ye feel it first.

. . . .
All unrefreshed the soul still sickens,
Till from the soul itself the fountain burst! [26]

What are your genuine convictions? What is your passion? Do you "tingle and vibrate" with the truths of the gospel? What do you most want to impart to the souls of your listeners? What do you most want them to do and to become? In short, what is your "soul's sincere desire"? The answers to these questions will reveal what gives force or communicative power to your preaching. Your speaking mechanism is the instrument of your soul.

SUGGESTED READING

Fuller, David Otis. *Spurgeon's Lectures to His Students*. Grand Rapids: Zondervan Publishing House, 1945. Chapters XVIII-XIX. (Every preacher should give himself the pleasure of reading these two chapters.)

Hoffman, W. G. *How to Make Better Speeches*. New York: Funk & Wagnalls Co., 1948. Chapters XVIII-XXII.

Kern, John A. *The Ministry to the Congregation*. Nashville: Publishing House, M. E. Church, South, 1897. Pp. 485 ff. (An amazing account of faults of preachers of a former generation.)

Lantz, John Edward. *Speaking in the Church*. New York: The Macmillan Co., 1954.

McCall, Roy C. *Fundamentals of Speech*. New York: The Macmillan Co., 1949. Chapter IX.

Prochnow, Herbert V. *The Successful Speaker's Handbook*. New York: Prentice-Hall, Inc., 1951. Part III.

Weatherspoon, J. B. Revision of Broadus *On the Preparation and Delivery of Sermons*. New York: Harper & Brothers, 1944. Part V, Chapters IV and V.

---

[26] Goethe's *Faust*, tr. Albert G. Latham. Used by permission of J. M. Dent & Sons, Ltd.

BUILDING UP A RESERVOIR FOR PREACHING

---

13. Accumulating Sermon Ideas

Early in his first parish, Ralph Waldo Emerson wrote in his journal, "I fear nothing now except the preparation of sermons. The prospect of one each week, for an indefinite time to come, is almost terrifick." [1] That same prospect strikes fear into the hearts of most beginners, and continues to strike fear into the hearts of some ministers throughout life. Such ministers find it difficult to believe a time can ever come when for every subject they choose to discuss they will lay aside several others they wish they had opportunity to discuss. But that time comes to all ministers who work at their jobs assiduously and systematically.

CUMULATIVE BIBLE STUDY

In Chapter IV reasons were given for the custom of using passages of scripture as texts for sermons. There it was explained that the Bible is the authoritative source of the gospel and therefore of all Christian instruction and preaching designed to proclaim and explain it. Also, it was stated that the Bible contains a wide range of moral, religious, and social truth valid for people of every new generation. Hence, the first, and in some ways the most important, study habit a minister needs to form is regular, systematic Bible study.

A certain period of every morning spent in his study should be allotted to this task. Throughout one's ministry he should have some form of serious Bible study under way all the time. This study is a major source for the continuous supply of sermon ideas. Within the first few years of his ministry one should begin to accumulate from this source alone several lists of possible

[1] Quoted by Ralph L. Rusk, *The Life of Ralph Waldo Emerson* (New York: Charles Scribner's Sons, 1949), p. 138.

sermon subjects with biblical settings for a variety of occasions and purposes. These should be kept going for the remainder of his preaching ministry.

1. One of these lists might be **Sermons on Books of the Bible.** When one finishes a careful study of a book of the Bible he may find himself gripped by its message as a whole and by a desire to put that message in a single sermon. Take the book of Ruth for example. This tells of a foreigner who exhibited nobility of soul, married a Jew, and became the grandmother of David, to whom the loyal Jews delighted to point as their common progenitor. This story was written to counteract the antiforeign sentiment then existing among the Jews. During brotherhood week, one could use this for a sermon on the race problem, using 2:10b as a text.

Or, suppose one is concluding a study of the brief letter of Paul to Philemon, in which he appeals to a Christian master to receive back his runaway slave, Onesimus, as a "beloved brother" in Christ. One is impressed by the fact that Paul was in reality attacking the ancient system of slavery indirectly through the heart of a slaveholder (vs. 16). That stimulates a sermon in which the social wrongs of our generation are attacked indirectly through the hearts of individuals who are in a position to treat groups of human beings as brothers.

A list of sermon ideas on biblical books will grow slowly because it takes time to make a careful, detailed study of a book of the Bible. Moreover, some books of the Bible do not lend themselves to this method of sermonizing. But, in time, this list might include the following books, with subjects and texts for sermons as indicated.

a) *Old Testament. Judges* (21:24-25): "Allegiance to Common Ideals, the Foundation of National Unity." *Job* (42:5): "An Eternal Setting for Our Little Lives." *Ecclesiastes* (2:17): "The Anatomy of Pessimism." *Daniel* (3:17-18): "Wanted: A New Puritanism." *Hosea* (11:8): "The Mystery of Love." *Amos* (5:24): "Putting Religion to Work in Social Relations." *Jonah* (4:10-11): "Modern Jonahs," who find it difficult to believe God loves other people as well as them. *Habakkuk* (1:13): "The Problem of Triumphant Wrong." *Haggai* (1:4): "Keeping the Church at the Center of Community Life."

b) *New Testament.* A course of evangelistic sermons on "The Five Gospels": *Mark* (2:12b), "The Challenging Fact of Christ"; *Matthew* (16:16b), "The World's Messiah"; *Luke* (7:34), "The Divine Friend of Man"; *John* (20:31), "The Eternal Christ"; *Acts* (1:8), "The Fifth Gospel: The Spiritual Acts of Christ." *I Corinthians* (3:1): "The Problem of Making Christians Out of Pagans." *Galatians* (5:1): "The Price of Liberty." *Ephesians* (6:12-13): "The Fight Within a Man." *Philippians* (4:12-13): "Christian Contentment." *Colossians* (1:17b): "The Cosmic Christ." *I Timothy* (4:6): "A Good Minister of Jesus Christ." *II Timothy* (1:14): "Guardians of the Faith." *James* (1:27): "Unadulterated Religion." *I Peter* (4:12-13): "The Fellowship of Suffering." *II John* (vs. 1): "The Place of Women in the Church." *III John* (vs. 2): "A Healthy Soul." *Revelation* (21:3): "God Our Great Contemporary Companion."

2. Another list of possible sermon ideas might be **Sermons on Biblical Characters.** Characters of the Bible are a perennial source of sermons. There are so many mentioned in the Bible that sermons of this kind are limited only by the imagination and ingenuity of the preacher. Repeatedly one will see in the men and women of the Bible the virtues and vices, the personality problems, the emotional difficulties, and the possibilities for good and for evil characteristic of men and women in his own community. To illustrate the possibilities in this area, a few of these characters will be mentioned, with a possible text and subject for a sermon on each.

a) *Major Characters in the Old Testament.* Abraham (Gen. 12:1-3; Heb. 11:8): "Modern Pioneers." Isaac (Gen. 27:34): "Living on the Bread Line." Jacob (Gen. 25:26): "Bargaining One's Way Through Life." Joseph (Gen. 45:4-5): "The Man Too Big to Hold a Grudge." Moses (Exod. 3:11-12): "What One Man Can Do with the Help of God." Deborah (Judg. 5:7): "An Ancient Joan of Arc." Gideon (Judg. 6:12 ff.): "Man's Greatest Enemy: Himself." Sampson (Judg. 15:11): "Living by the Leaden Rule." Saul (I Sam. 15:35): "A Near-Great Man." David (I Sam. 16:7b): "A Man with a Magnanimous Heart." Solomon (I Kings 4:29-31): "A Foolish Wise Man." Elijah (I Kings 19:4): "When Our Spirits Are Low."

b) *Major Characters in the New Testament.* Judas (Matt. 27:3-5): "The Easy Way Out." Peter (Matt. 26:74-75): "The

Difference Between Remorse and Repentance." *Pilate* (Matt. 27:24): "That's Your Business, Not Mine." *Paul* (Phil. 4:11-13): "The Man Who Knew No Defeat." *Stephen* (Acts 7:59–8:1): "The Immortality of Influence." *John* (John 19:26): "What Love Can Do for a Man." *John Mark* (Acts 15:37-40; II Tim. 4:11): "The Man Who Came Back."

c) *Minor Characters in the Old Testament. Lot's Wife* (Gen. 19:26): "Double-mindedness." *Jehu* (II Kings 9:20): "Living at a Mad Pace." *Haman* (Esth. 7:10): "The Victim of Our Own Hatred." *Caleb* (Num. 13:30): "Tackling the Impossible." *Hannah* (I Sam. 1:11): "Godly Mothers." *Jonathan* (I Sam. 18:1): "Friendship, the Master Passion." *Shadrach, Meshach and Abednego* (Dan. 3:17-18): "Convictions More Precious than Life."

d) *Minor Characters in the New Testament. The Wealthy Women* (Luke 8:1-3): "Putting Money to Work for the Kingdom." *Mary and Martha* (Luke 10:38-42): "A Study in Values." *Matthias* (Acts 1:26): "The Man Who Never Got into the Limelight." *Dorcas* (Acts 9:39): "Where the Sewing Societies Originated." A course of sermons on "Christian Vocations": *Lydia* (Acts 16:11-15), "Christian Business Women"; *Luke* (Col. 4:14), "Christian Physicians"; *Tertius* (Rom. 16:22), "Christian Stenographers"; *Erastus* (Rom. 16:23), "Christian Treasurers"; *Zenas* (Tit. 3:13), "Christian Lawyers." *Priscilla and Aquila* (Rom. 16:3): "The First 'Mr. and Mrs.' Team." *Lois and Eunice* (II Tim. 1:5): "Transmitting the Christian Faith from Generation to Generation." *Eutychus* (Acts 20:9): "Asleep in Church." *Epaphras* (Col. 4:12): "Putting Our Prayers to Work." *Quartus* (Rom. 16:23): "The Brotherhood of All Believers." *Demas* (II Tim. 4:10): "The Man Who Couldn't Stand Group Pressure." *Phoebe* (Rom. 16:1-2): "The First Woman Officer in the Church."

3. Still another list of possible sermon ideas might be **Sermons on Important Chapters and Incidents of the Bible.** A few of these are listed to illustrate further the amount and variety of sermonic material in the Bible. But no attempt will be made to indicate how they may be used for specific sermons.

a) *Old Testament.* The Creation stories (Gen. 1–2). The story of the Fall (Gen. 3). Abraham's magnanimous proposal to Lot that they live as brothers (Gen. 13). The love story of

Isaac and Rebekah (Gen. 24). The Ten Commandments (Exod. 20), which sooner or later every preacher wants to use for a series of sermons. How Moses had to beg the people to quit giving to the church (Exod. 35-36). David's magnificent behavior when he bought the threshing floor for the site of an altar (II Sam. 24). Solomon's prayer at the dedication of the Temple (I Kings 8). Nehemiah's courageous and wise leadership in rebuilding the walls of Jerusalem (ch. 4). Isaiah's call (ch. 6), his comforting promises (ch. 40), his contrast of the Lord and the idols (ch. 44), his description of the suffering servant of the Lord (ch. 53), and his offer of mercy (ch. 55). Jeremiah's doctrine of the new covenant (ch. 31). Ezekiel's doctrine of individual responsibility (chs. 14, 18).

To these should be added the Psalms, which, taken together, deal with practically every mood of the soul. Athanasius called the Psalms a "mirror" for those who use them. Basil described them as "a general hospital for the soul." Luther labeled them "a Bible in miniature." Calvin spoke of them as "an anatomy of all parts of the soul." They have been the hymnbook, prayer book, and book of personal and group devotions for numerous people over the centuries. There is a Psalm suitable for every worship occasion and for every mood of the soul: hatred, wonder, awe, doubt concerning the immunity and prosperity of the wicked, questions about the vanity of life and of riches and whether it pays to be good, joy, thanksgiving, grief, sorrow, fear, hope, sin and guilt, repentance and confession, private and public prayer, personal and corporate worship, patriotism and national aspirations and hopes. More than half the one hundred fifty poems constituting the book are suitable for single sermons. Every preacher will want to use these for a variety of preaching purposes throughout his ministry.

Also, mention should be made of the parables of the Old Testament, the most important of which are the following: the trees choosing a king (Judg. 9:7-15); Nathan's parable of the ewe lamb (II Sam. 12:1-14); Isaiah's parable of the unfruitful vineyard (5:1-7), which may have suggested Christ's allegory of the vine and branches; Jeremiah's parable of the potter (18:1-4); Ezekiel's parables of the two sisters (23:1-4) and of the valley of dry bones (37:1-14); and Amos' parable of the plumb line (7:7-9).

b) The New Testament. The nativity stories of Matthew (1:18–2:12). The temptation of Jesus (Matt. 4:1-11). The Sermon on the Mount (Matt. 5–7), almost every verse of which is a suitable text for a sermon and which will be used for several groups of sermons, especially on the Beatitudes and the Lord's Prayer. Jesus' commission to the Twelve (Matt. 10). The eight parables of the Kingdom (Matt. 13). The Transfiguration (Matt. 17:1 ff.). Christ's teaching on the importance of childhood (Matt. 18:1-14); his teaching on marriage and divorce (Matt. 19:1-12); his denunciation of the Pharisees (Matt. 23), the Magna Charta of Christian liberty; his parables of the virgins, of the talents, and of the last judgment (Matt. 25); his teaching on the perils of riches (Mark 10:17-31).

Luke's nativity story (2:1 ff.). The parable of the Good Samaritan (Luke 10:25-37). The parables given at mealtime (Luke 14). The parables of the lost sheep, the lost coin, and the lost boy (Luke 15). Christ's teaching on prayer (Luke 18:1-14); his doctrine of the second birth (John 3). The parable of the Good Shepherd (John 10). The raising of Lazarus (John 11). Jesus' teaching about the Counselor (John 14); his allegory of the vine and the branches (John 15); his farewell prayer (John 17). To these should be added the parables of Jesus not already mentioned. There are some fifty parables in the first three Gospels alone, each of which conveys a distinct and important truth.

Still other preachable passages in the New Testament include the following: the story of Peter and Cornelius (Acts 10), one of the turning points in Christian history; the story of how Paul, a prisoner, took command of the ship in a storm (Acts 27); the mystery of human personality (Rom. 7); God's stake in the human drama and his providential oversight of his world (Rom. 8); the functions of a Christian in his world (Rom. 12); the Christian's supreme right to give up his rights (I Cor. 9); there's a place for everybody in the church (I Cor. 12); Paul's ode to love (I Cor. 13); Paul's doctrine of the Resurrection (I Cor. 15); his Christian doctrine of stewardship (II Cor. 8–9); his allegory of the armor of God (Eph. 6:12 ff.); his discussion of the mind of Christ (Phil. 2:5 ff.); his advice about how to handle ugly, destructive emotions (Col. 3:8 ff.); Christians ought to outlive their contemporaries (I Thess. 5); the heroes of the faith (Heb. 11); professions and deeds (Jas. 2:14-26); taming the tongue (Jas. 3); the Christian's dream and hope of a new heaven and a new earth (Rev. 21:1–22:5).

4. The final list of possible sermon ideas might be **Sermons on Texts of the Bible.** No texts will be offered by way of illustration because innumerable books, new and old, containing texts for sermons, are available. Suffice it for our present purposes to state, if one will spend some time each day in Bible study, sermon ideas will "jump out at him" so often he will wish he could preach every day of the year so as to make use of them. One preacher recently wrote a book containing 2,200 texts and subjects covering the entire Bible.[2] This book is valuable, not only for its wealth of sermon ideas, but because it illustrates the inexhaustible resources for preaching found in the Bible. This it does both by what it includes and by what it omits. No other preacher would see the same possibilities in the same texts as he does. But given time, every preacher can find many more than 2,200 texts that suggest seed thoughts for sermons relevant to modern life.

KEEPING EYES AND EARS OPEN TO HUMAN NEED

As a minister goes about the regular activities of his pastorate, sermon ideas will literally shout for attention, if he keeps his eyes and ears open to human need. One way of doing this is to keep in general touch with the world about him. A well-known radio news reporter begins his daily broadcast with the question, "What's going on in the world?" A preacher learns what is going on in the world partly by reading newspapers, magazines, and books, as will be shown in the next section of this chapter.

He learns this also by using other modern mediums of communication, such as radio and television programs, movies, public meetings, small social gatherings, conversations, pastoral visits and personal conferences. These mediums are his spiritual X-ray machine for finding hidden diseases eating at men's souls, his spiritual thermometer for discovering rising emotional temperatures, his spiritual stethoscope for listening to human heartbeats, his spiritual devices for testing hardening of the arteries of the mind and metabolic disturbances in personality.

[2] See George Brown Thomas, *What Shall I Preach?* (New York and Nashville: Abingdon Press, 1948).

Another obvious way to discover people's needs is to live with them. In 1897 John Jay Chapman, the American author and critic, heard that Josiah Royce, professor of philosophy at Harvard, was going abroad. He said: "I am awfully glad. Let him have no money. Let him come in grinding contact with life. Let him go to Greece and get into a revolution, somewhere where he can't think. Let his mind get full of images, pains, hungers, contrasts—life, life, life. He's drawing on an empty well." [3]

We understand what he meant. But participating in the sordid experiences of people can corrode the soul to no good purpose. "Come now," says the preacher to himself, "I must go out and get a taste of real life and learn how people are living." So he goes on a private slumming expedition for a few days. He observes the goings on in the crowded tenement sections of his city. He moves in and out of the dens of vice. He takes in the night life of the worldly pleasure seekers. Then he goes back into his study feeling he has been living with people. He has been doing nothing of the kind. He has been engaging in a bit of superficial and artificial observation of questionable value to himself or to others.

If a minister is to practice his own vocation with a degree of thoroughness, it is impossible for him to spend any appreciable amount of time going here and there to share the living experiences of various groups in his parish. Furthermore, by going into certain situations he is inviting temptation unnecessarily. Ministers as well as other people need to be reminded that:

> Vice is a monster of so frightful mien,
> As to be hated, needs but to be seen.
> But seen too oft, familiar with his face
> We first endure, then pity, then embrace. [4]

There are wiser and healthier ways of discovering the needs of people than living their lives with them.

The minister can live his own life in the community without losing the common touch. He can have friendly fraternal relations with all sorts of people without participating in their sins,

[3] M. A. DeWolfe Howe, *John Jay Chapman and His Letters* (Boston: Houghton Mifflin Co., 1937), p. 163.
[4] Alexander Pope, "Essay on Man."

or being tinged with their drab surroundings. Let him keep in circulation among the people, making normal contacts all the while: shopping, paying bills; engaging in ordinary business transactions; attending public meetings, showing up where people gather for group activities; carrying on conversations casually on the streets; visiting the sick, the shut-ins, the bereaved, the troubled, the needy; counseling those who have personal and marital difficulties; and ministering wherever his services are needed. If he is thoroughly democratic in his attitudes as he moves among the people and convinces them he is genuinely interested in them as human beings, he will be surprised how much he comes to know about how they live.

They will unveil their minds, expose their emotions, unburden their hearts to him, until he wonders how God himself can stand to look upon the troubles of his world. If he is a good listener, not too easily shocked, a trustworthy confidant, and knows how to interpret what he sees and hears, these normal contacts will provide him with opportunities to see as far as it is possible for one person to see, and as far as any preacher needs to see, into the minds and hearts of others. Farmer is right: "Preaching is essentially a pastoral activity." [5]

As a matter of fact every minister has stored up in his mind, waiting to be tapped, a vast reservoir of information about the needs and problems of people. Within the first twenty-five years of his life, he was successively a child, a youth, and a grownup. During that time he had firsthand experiences in the problems of childhood and of youth and of living together in families, neighborhoods, crafts, and interest groups. He came to know a good deal about schools, churches, governments, business, hospitals, and other social institutions and the people associated with them. In general he touched the life of the community and of its people at nearly every point. If he will call those experiences from the storeroom of his memory, relive them, reflect upon them with his mature insights, he will be able to understand much about the concerns and problems of the various groups in his community.

We are to suppose Jesus came to know the needs of people by living among them normally during the twenty-five or thirty

[5] *Servant of the Word,* p. 93.

years preceding his public ministry. One can hardly conceive of Jesus saying, "I must go out now and live among people to get material for preaching." He participated naturally in the life of his community from year to year, while all kinds of information were storing themselves in his mind. This became one main source of his intimate knowledge of people that amazes every careful reader of the Gospels. If every preacher will draw upon his own experiences as far back as memory goes, he will discover a wealth of insights to use in helping people.

We may be sure Jesus was doing something else also that every preacher needs to do: He was entering sympathetically into the experiences of people. John said Jesus "knew all men and needed no one to bear witness of man; for he himself knew what was in man." (John 2:25.) We make a great mistake to suppose John was referring solely to a superhuman ability to read the minds of people which is denied to us. He possessed empathy, a stronger feeling than sympathy. He could project his own consciousness into the consciousness of others and enter into their feelings, emotions, motives, and thoughts. To a larger degree than others, to be sure! But every man who shares the compassion of Jesus for people has that ability to some extent. In fact, Jesus implied his followers should possess it when he exhorted them to live by the Golden Rule. Most of us know how we want to be treated, how we react under ordinary conditions. Very well, put yourself in the other fellow's place, said Jesus, project yourself into his consciousness, turn your imagination loose on what he is thinking about and how he is feeling, and then treat him as you would like to be treated under similar conditions.

Someone said of Donald Hankey, that noble young Christian who lost his life in the first World War, that he had "a sensitive soul like a photographic plate that registered the most delicate reflections of the soldier's nature." Walt Whitman possessed empathic imagination: "I do not ask the wounded man how he feels," he said; "I myself become the wounded man." Eugene Debs, the noted labor leader, had it: said he, "While there is a lower class I am of it, while there is a criminal class, I am of it, while there is a soul in prison I am not free." A preacher needs and can have a measure of that same ability to project himself into the experiences of others.

But beware of having too much of it! Too much empathic imagination can make one morbid and miserable to no good purpose. That is what someone had in mind when he prayed, "O God, give me imagination, but do not give me too much." There is such a thing as one's wearing his nerves thin and making himself wretched by imaginatively putting himself in others' places, and thus increasing instead of decreasing the sum total of human sufferings. But, nevertheless, the preacher should learn to enter into the inner experiences of others in imitation of his Master. That will keep him sensitive to human need.

Moreover, if he enters vicariously into the lives of others, he will perpetuate the redemptive work of Christ. In George Bernard Shaw's play *Saint Joan*, one of the men who sent her to the stake said afterward he did not know what cruelty really was until he saw her burning to death. "It was dreadful," he said. "But it saved me. I have been a different man ever since." Whereupon the Bishop asked, "Must then a Christ perish in torment in every age to save those who have no imagination?" Must Christ be crucified again and again because his chosen preachers have insufficient ability to enter with Christlike imagination into the sufferings of others?

From all these ways of discovering the moral and spiritual problems of people will come more ideas for sermons dealing with those problems than a person can possibly preach in the time at his disposal. As these ideas come, however, they should be kept. As they increase, it will become necessary to divide them into groups, file them under proper headings, and add them in some suitable manner to the groups growing out of Bible study.

SYSTEMATIC READING

The importance of reading for the preacher cannot be over-emphasized. Now and then one hears of a minister who believes reading is a means of escape into a world of unreality. He prides himself on being concerned about the world of people rather than the world of books. That is a false distinction. The world of books is produced by the world of people. What people write reflects what they are thinking and how they are living. For the most part, books deal with a world beyond the range of our immediate experiences, but it is a sector of real life, not an imaginary world.

A preacher should read for the sheer thrill of discovering that larger world. This diversifies his interests, widens the span of his knowledge, adds to his cultural attainment. Reading builds up a reservoir upon which to draw for the enrichment, broadening, and deepening of one's preaching. The people of one's congregation expect him to keep in touch with the world outside his community. Just as they expect their friends who travel to distant lands to tell them upon their return not only what they saw but how they interpret what they saw, so they expect their pastor to make journeys afar into the world of books and, in his weekly sermons, to give them the boiled-down results of his journeys. So important are these journeys for preaching that James Black said, somewhat seriously, the only way to preach well is to begin ten years ago. Much of the preacher's reading should not be with a view of preparing next Sunday's sermon, but with a view to self-culture and with a desire to make himself a wiser man.

But one should also read to discover the needs of people and what they are thinking. He can then direct sermons to those needs in terms familiar to them. In his book *Contemporary American Literature and Religion*,[6] Halford E. Luccock makes a study of "some of the creative literature of America" following the first World War. His study, he explains, is not "an exercise in literary criticism" but a look "at literature as the expression of life, the symptoms of the moods of the time, its health and its sickness, its despairs and its hopes; the wrist of the common body of life, as it were, where we can count its heart beats." He says: "The literature of a period is significant, also, because it is often the most sensitive barometer, indicating what shall be some dominating trends of the immediate future." He rightly insists, "Organized religion can neglect the literature of its time only at its peril." (Pp. 2, 4.) He could just as truly have said also that organized religion can neglect the best literature of other times only at its peril, for the present is the child of the past. All great literature—the literature that lives—reflects not only the life of its own time but the problems and needs common to people of all times.

⁶ Chicago: Willett, Clark and Co., 1934.

For these reasons a preacher should map out a course of reading and follow it as religiously as he performs any other important function of his ministry. But he should not think of this so much as an obligation as an opportunity. While it is one of the duties of his vocation it should also be his avocation. Garrison advises a preacher to "fall in love with a functional hobby," to find "play values in some activity closely related to his major ends." [7] That is exactly what most ministers do with reading. Hosts of preachers would confess there are a thousand books they wish they could read tomorrow. As they approach the end of their active ministry they feel as did Friedrich Humboldt, the noted German naturalist, who, dying at the age of ninety, exclaimed, "Oh, for another one hundred years."

One's course of reading should include newspapers, magazines, and books. Newspapers nowadays are more than mere newssheets presenting current happenings. They offer interpretative comments on the news by some of the keenest minds in our society, informative articles by experts about almost every phase of life, reviews of books, criticisms of drama, music, and art, and series of articles analyzing community and national problems. A preacher cannot afford to ignore this source of information. Ideas for sermons are likely to come any time from any department of a daily paper: from the news columns, the editorial page, the sports section, the financial page, the magazine sections, the advertisements, and even the comic strips.

Never before have there been quite as many magazines—weeklies, monthlies, and quarterlies—of such high caliber containing material of human worth and interest, designed to appeal to the average reader. Some deal with general scientific, medical, and other semitechnical subjects prepared for popular consumption. Some deal with subjects of literary interest. Some are planned for women, some for children, some for the family and home. Others are of a general theological and religious nature, and still others are put out by denominational, nondenominational and interdenominational groups for the religious public. A few are professional magazines intended to serve the specific needs of preachers and pastors. As his income permits, a minister should subscribe for magazines that afford a "balanced diet" for himself and his family. From the reading of these magazines

[7] *Op. cit.*, pp. 141-42.

will flow a steady stream of ideas for sermons covering the same general fields as those that come to him in his pastoral work.

But a major portion of the preacher's reading will be devoted to *books*. Books are the principal tools in the practice of his vocation. Throughout his ministry every person should have a list of books he intends to read and to purchase for his library. As books on the list are secured they should be checked off. As new books are heard of they should be added to the list.

I know of one minister who bought the best textbooks available on American and English literature and from them made a list of classics—novels, dramas, poems, essays, etc.—with which he ought to be familiar. He checked the advertisements and book reviews in secular and religious journals and in the alumni publication of his seminary for important new books, and made notations of the books recommended by his fellow ministers in conversations and in denominational and interdenominational gatherings. These he added to his list from time to time. He arranged the titles under headings representing the various fields of knowledge, with special emphasis on the several phases of religion. From time to time he purchased a few books, one from each of several areas, checking them off as they arrived. Thus he always had before him, inviting his interest and clamoring to be read, four or five books on as many subjects. By following this procedure for many years he became widely read in both the classics and in current literature and kept in touch with general trends in all major fields of knowledge. Other ministers have followed other methods with equally good results. The important thing is to have a method and to use it consistently.

While the preacher should keep abreast of the currents of thought in all fields, there are a few fields of more practical value to his preaching than others. *Biography* and historical sketches that deal with people, their family backgrounds, their personalities, their lives and letters and diaries, and their relations with their fellow men are probably the most prolific source of sermon ideas. This is because they deal with interests and problems common to all men. Books on *psychology*, especially those that study the emotional or personality problems of various age groups, likewise are most suggestive for sermon ideas. *Fiction*—novels, dramas, short stories—and *poetry* reflect the

237

moral and religious problems and aspirations of the writers and the groups in which they live. Such books are laden with ideas of daily concern to ministers.

A variety of *religious books* of high quality come off the press annually. One can read almost any religious book, listed in the offerings of reputable publishers of our time, with confidence that it will provide a few stimulating ideas for sermons. Ministers are sometimes advised not to read the *printed sermons* of other preachers. That unnecessarily closes the door to a source of homiletical ideas of considerable worth. Unless a man is essentially too lazy to do his own thinking, or too weak to resist the temptation to plagiarize another's outlines, there is every reason why he should read the sermons preached by both his contemporaries and his predecessors. From printed sermons a preacher can discover to his profit not only how others preach— their actual techniques of sermonizing—but helpful insights into truths and interpretations of scripture. Insights and interpretations may be taken as legitimately from this source as from any other—as, for example, from Bible commentaries, theological treatises, and devotional books.

A preacher's wide range of reading enables him to preach the gospel in its largest setting. George Santayana makes one of the characters in *The Last Puritan* say, "People wouldn't become ministers unless they had rather second-hand minds." Apparently he did not mean this as a compliment. But the world owes a great debt to its secondhand minds. They put to practical uses what original minds discover. Society cannot do without a group of men who feel obligated to take what the creative minds in every field of human interest are thinking and weave it into a philosophy of life, or way of living, and utilize it to increase the sum of human happiness.

Preachers are privileged to belong to that group. They relate the gospel to the whole of life, to all knowledge, all experience, all truth. Every Christian preacher should know how to put Christ at the center of the universe and of history, at the heart of the divine-human struggle we call the contemporary scene. In order to do this he needs what his reading gives him: a general working knowledge of what is going on in all realms of human thought. "All things are yours, whether Paul or Apollos or Cephas or the world or life or death or the present or the future" [whether science or philosophy or literature or sociology or history or psychology or government or politics or art or religion], "all are yours; and you are Christ's; and Christ is God's." (I Cor. 3:21-23.)

A few suggestions, representing the consensus of opinion of a considerable number of ministers about building up a library, may be helpful. Buy a few selected books every year. Buy according to areas and check every now and then to be sure you are not neglecting an important area or buying too many books in your own interest or hobby area. Aside from certain reference books, buy only such books as you expect to read. Be cautious about purchasing sets of books. Too many books on one subject or by one author are more forbidding than inviting, and some of them are likely to go unread. Secure a wide variety of books by buying moderately priced books. A large number of low-priced reprints of classics and of current popular books are being put out now by several publishing houses.

Spend little time on a system of cataloguing books. As they are purchased, stamp your name and its number (in numerical order) in each book and make note of title, author, publisher, copyright date, and price in a book provided for the purpose. In order to keep track of books, make notations, on a slip of some kind, when and by whom they are borrowed and when they are returned. Arrange the books in groups on shelves according to general subjects. If you read practically all the books purchased, you will be so familiar with them as to be able at a glance to locate any book wanted.

A few suggestions about reading habits may also be useful. Read systematically and, in general, by reading schedules. Learn to read rapidly. Many books and pamphlets are now available as helps toward this end and can be secured from any good library. Keep two or three types of books in process of being read all the time. Vary from one type to another in the same long reading period. Do some light reading solely for recreation. Read magazines mostly in odds and ends of time. Beware of reading merely to gather homiletical material. Books should be read appreciatively for their own value, not primarily, as someone puts it, for the purpose of extracting from every book, Shylock-like, a pound of homiletical flesh.

239

Capturing and Preserving Ideas

There is no way to tell where, in the reading of a book, ideas for sermons are likely to come. They may come from the book as a whole, from its title, from a character, from an incident described, from a bit of dialogue, from a striking sentence, or from an illuminating insight into truth. But once they come, they should be written down and added to the groups of sermon ideas that come from other sources.

Each person should devise a method of preserving ideas that come from all these sources. Many of them come in a flash and, if not preserved, go in a flash. Some ministers carry a notebook with them for jotting these ideas down. Some keep a pencil and pad on a table beside their beds for recording ideas that come after they have retired for the night. Many of the most fruitful ideas for sermons come when one gets thoroughly relaxed just before going to sleep. The poet Wordsworth used to say that so many of his inspirations came to him in the night he had to teach himself to write in the dark to keep from losing them.

Many of these ideas will never be used. But enough of them will develop into sermons to make it wise to devise some method of trapping all of them. Lewis Carroll, in *Through the Looking-Glass*, makes the King say, "The horror of that moment I shall never, never forget." Whereupon the Queen remarked, "You will, though, if you don't make a memorandum of it." Some of the best scholars and writers in all ages have found it necessary to make memorandums of thoughts that darted into their minds at unexpected moments.

When Pascal, the illustrious French philosopher, took his walks he wrote down his thoughts on scraps of paper he happened to have with him. Occasionally, unable to find paper, he returned from his walk with his fingernails covered with characters scratched with a pin, characters representing thoughts he did not wish to lose. Jonathan Edwards used to write down ideas that came to him while riding horseback and pin them to his coat. He is said to have arrived at his destination at times all aflutter with paper slips. Neither of these methods is commended, but some way of accomplishing the same ends needs to be devised.

Each of the initial notes should be made on, or transferred to, separate sheets of paper of uniform size, so they can be filed for future use. A half sheet of ordinary typewriter paper is convenient for this purpose. As these sheets accumulate, they should be added to the appropriate groups of possible sermon ideas arranged under major headings, to be described in more detail in the next chapter.

If a preacher performs his weekly duties diligently, according to a well-planned work schedule, he will never lack for sermon subjects. His problem will not be, "What shall I preach about?" but, "From among all the timely subjects pressing for consideration, which shall I choose?" One of the great satisfactions in preaching grows out of the feeling of having a full instead of an empty sermonic larder. James Black said:

Real joy in preaching depends on our having more ideas and suggestions for preaching than we can ever use: and this fine joy, akin to elation, only comes when our minds, and notebooks, are crammed full. The best preaching is always the *natural overflow* of a ripe mind and the expression of a growing experience. A good sermon is never "worked up" but "worked out." [8]

SUGGESTED READING

Coffin, Henry Sloan. *What to Preach*. New York: Geo. H. Doran Co., 1926.

――――――. *Communion Through Preaching*. New York: Charles Scribner's Sons, 1952.

Craig, A. C. *Preaching in a Scientific Age*. New York: Charles Scribner's Sons, 1954.

Grant, Frederich C. "Preaching Values in the Revised Standard Version," *Religion in Life*, Winter, 1950-51.

Handy, Francis J. *Jesus the Preacher*. New York and Nashville: Abingdon Press, 1949. Chapters V-VIII.

Luccock, Halford E. *Communicating the Gospel*. New York: Harper & Brothers, 1954.

MacLennan, David A. *Pastoral Preaching*. Philadelphia: Westminster Press, 1955.

Rogers, Clement F. *The Parson Preaching*. London: S. P. C. K., 1949.

Stewart, James S. *A Faith to Proclaim*. New York: Charles Scribner's Sons, 1953.

The reader is also referred to the books listed under "The Use of the Bible in Preaching," in the Bibliography.

[8] *The Mystery of Preaching*, pp. 71-72.

14. Planning Ahead

A preacher cannot make the best use of long lists of sermon ideas without devising a satisfactory method of developing them into full-grown sermons and of fitting them systematically into the general purposes of his preaching ministry. To accomplish these purposes it will be necessary regularly to do some long-range planning.

MAKING USE OF A CHURCH YEAR

The first step should be to make a calendar, or schedule of events, for the various seasons, observances, and special days of the church year. This is one of the work schedules, discussed in an earlier chapter, that is necessary if one expects to perform his numerous duties with efficiency and with a minimum of mental and emotional strain. Speaking of the person who has no work schedule to which he habitually adheres, William James said: "There is no more miserable human being than one in whom nothing is habitual but indecision and for whom the lighting of every cigar, the drinking of every cup, the time of rising and going to bed every day, and the beginning of every bit of work, are subjects of express volitional deliberation." [1] Many ministers keep themselves in an emotional stew a large share of the time because next Sunday's sermon is the subject of "express volitional deliberation" early each week. In effect, they start out afresh every Monday morning on a search for another sermon.

Just as one plans a work schedule for the duties he knows ahead of time must be performed every week, and performed on time, he should plan a work schedule in advance for the sermons he knows a year ahead must be ready for certain specified days. This schedule conserves nervous energy, makes for maximum productivity, enables one to perform all the duties in a crowded schedule, and makes for systematic, well-rounded preaching. Fortunately the general outline of what an annual schedule should include is provided by the customs of many Christian churches.

In one form or another, most denominations have a calendar of events for local churches consisting of a combination of the

[1] *Op. cit.*, p. 145.

major seasons of the traditional Christian year, the important national holidays and festivals sometimes spoken of as the civil year, and the special days, causes, and observances in its own program and in the program of interdenominational agencies.

In its traditional form the Christian year was the result of an effort of the Church to divide the calendar year into periods that conformed to the events in the life of Christ and to incorporate therein some of the main seasonal festivals common to the peoples the Church was trying to Christianize. Strictly speaking, it was outlined in detail for only half of the calendar year—the six months extending roughly from the end of November to the end of May. The year included the following seasons in succession: Advent, Christmas, Epiphany, Pre-Lenten, Lenten, Eastertide, Ascension Tide, Whitsuntide (or Pentecost), and Trinity Season. Once Trinity Sunday was reached, the Sundays thereafter were labeled "1st Sunday after Trinity," "2nd Sunday after Trinity," and so on, until a possible "25th (or 26th) Sunday after Trinity" (according to the early or late date for Easter Sunday) had been reached just before "Sunday next before Advent." That is, the Trinity Season in some years may have as many as twenty-eight Sundays—more than one-half the calendar year.

Since there are no events in the life of Christ left to include in the last six months of the calendar year, this period, by a number of modern churches, has been labeled "Kingdomtide." Into the calendar of those months—June, July, August, September, October, and November—have been inserted various festivals and observances that for one reason or another have become the special interest of the church in modern times. Since, aside from its major seasons, the Christian year has been more or less flexible, many of the special days of the modern churches also have been interspersed among those seasons. Consequently, whatever his denomination may be, a preacher is likely to be provided with a church calendar suggesting special days and seasons from September of one year through August of the next year. If his church does not provide him with a calendar he can wisely make one for himself.

Conceivably such a calendar might include, and in approximately this sequence, the following: Labor Sunday, Rally Day, World Communion Sunday, Christian Education Sunday, Layman's Sunday, Reformation Sunday, World Peace (or Armistice) Sunday, Men and Missions Sunday, Thanksgiving Sunday, Universal Bible Sunday, Christmas Sunday, New Year Sunday, Theological Education Sunday, Young People's Sunday, Race Relations Sunday, Brotherhood Sunday, Palm Sunday, Easter Sunday, Christian Family Sunday, Pentecost Sunday, Vocation (or Baccalaureate or Graduation) Sunday, Memorial Sunday, Children's Day, Independence Day Sunday, and Sundays emphasizing the special interest of Rural Life. Somewhere in between the other Sundays, perhaps coinciding with some of them, will come the following: Communion Sundays (as often as custom determines), Budget (or Every Member Canvass or Stewardship) Sunday, Evangelism Sunday, Social Education and Education Sunday, or other Sundays for whatever may be the special interests of a particular denomination.

The actual calendar of the preacher's denomination may have, in some instances, more special days and seasons and, in other instances, fewer. But this calendar as roughly outlined will suffice for the consideration of the problem at hand, namely, planning a preaching schedule well in advance.

Sometime before the beginning of the fall activities—preferably during his summer vacation—one should make out a tentative calendar for the church year, using the exact dates for special days provided by his denominational publications. If he accedes to all the requests for special days that come to his desk, he may find there are relatively few Sundays left to use as he sees fit for his pastoral preaching. If his denomination is wise it will not make the mistake of imposing a close-knit, inflexible church calendar upon him. But rather it will allow him some freedom to decide whether he is obligated, or whether it is wise, to make every Sunday a special day, or to celebrate the complete church calendar in the year ahead.

On the other hand, if he is wise he will not jump to the conclusion that he must cease to be a preacher of the gospel and become a pleader and promoter for special causes, merely because he has a calendar for the year. Nor will he conclude that following a calendar as a guide necessarily crowds out all spontaneous, pastoral preaching to known human needs. To begin with, unless his denomination adheres rather rigidly to the church calendar and lectionary, there will be, first and last, a goodly number of Sundays, especially at certain periods of the year, when he will be free to choose what to preach about. In the next place, observing special days and preaching sermons that grow out of his pastoral experience are by no means mutually exclusive. A special occasion may be an opportunity to meet a basic need. The values of following the calendar and of preaching sermons that speak to the conditions of the people may be merged to the enrichment of his total ministry, if he will use a generous amount of sanctified imagination in his annual planning.

At the outset of his first pastorate every preacher should form the habit of making a general outline of the church year. He will then know well ahead of time that each year he will need so many Communion sermons, so many sermons for special occasions, so many sermons for young people, so many for laymen, a Christmas sermon, so many sermons during the Lenten season that deal with self-examination, penitence, and the cultivation of the inner life, a Palm Sunday sermon, an Easter sermon, a Reformation Sunday sermon, and so on through the whole list of special seasons and occasions.

He should keep these in mind as he makes notes on sermon ideas that grow out of his Bible study, out of his reading, and out of his pastoral observations and contacts. As suggested in the last chapter, when one is making initial notes about sermon ideas he should indicate the persons who need that particular truth and the human situation to which it applies. At the same time he should state that the particular sermon under consideration at the moment would be suitable for Layman's Sunday or Young People's Day or Easter or New Year's Day or Christian Education Sunday or Family Day, as the case may be. Once this habit is formed he will be surprised how consistently he will think of special days and seasons as these initial sermon notes are made.

As the number of sermon ideas increases he will find it advisable to arrange them under a series of headings such as these. (1) Sermons for special seasons and days: Labor Sunday, Communion Sundays, Reformation Sunday, Family Sunday, Christmas, Easter, etc. (2) Sermons for national holidays: Thanksgiving, Armistice, Independence Day, Memorial Day, etc. (3) Sermons for Church-designated days: Budget Sunday, Missions,

245

Layman's days, Young People's days, Christian Education Day, Rally Day, Children's Day, etc. (4) Sermons dealing with the psychological problems of people: worry, fear, guilt, anger, anxiety, antipathy and hostility, inferiority, self-pity, self-condemnation, aggressiveness, boredom, melancholy, etc. (5) Sermons dealing with social problems: marriage and divorce, political corruption, race relations, war and peace, gambling, alcoholism, economic injustice, etc. (6) Sermons on Christian doctrines: God, Christ, the Holy Spirit, the Bible, the Church, the Atonement, the Incarnation, the Resurrection, death and the afterlife, suffering, forgiveness, prayer, faith, repentance, justification, providence, etc. (7) Sermons for various age groups and classes of people: the sick, the bereaved, young couples, parents, old people, church officers and leaders, teachers, businessmen, professional men, laboring men, craftsmen, etc.

When one is filling in the calendar for the year, these groups of sermon notes should be drawn on for subjects for special days. Sermon subjects that promise to meet human needs and at the same time are appropriate for particular days should be allocated tentatively to those days. For example, one need not always preach on one of the nativity stories at Christmastime. There may be a book, a chapter, a long passage, a character of the Bible, or a doctrine that would be suitable for that day also. One need not—indeed should not—preach a sermon every Easter in which he attempts to prove that the soul is immortal. There are many other subjects, many passages of many kinds, that would be more suitable for meeting the actual needs of people on that day than texts dealing with life after death.

There is nothing but one's own choice that prevents any special-day sermon from being the type the preacher wants it to be—even as thoroughly evangelical or evangelistic as he desires. In short, the sermon ideas that come out of one's prayerful study and pastoral experiences can be made the basis of special-day sermons. They can be used as the content of those messages. If this is done carefully and systematically, annual seasonal sermons may serve pastoral purposes, and church-designated days need not become mere occasions for promoting causes.

Once procedures of this nature are established as work schedules, courses of possible sermons on which to draw for weekly sermons begin to appear. A "course" of sermons is to be distinguished from a "series" of sermons. All the sermons in a "series" are announced before the first one is preached. The sermons in a course are used at the option of the preacher without previous announcement. Some preachers plan courses of sermons as far ahead, in some instances, as five years. Instead of planning for one Thanksgiving sermon, one Christmas sermon, and one Easter sermon, for example, they plan for five of each, one for each of the next five years. This prevents them from falling into the bad habit of using the same approach to these special occasions each year, and at the same time makes for broader, more balanced, more comprehensive preaching.

The general lists of possible sermons suggested in this and the last chapter—sermons on the books of the Bible, on characters of the Bible, on chapters and long passages of the Bible, on texts, on the Psalms, on the parables, on the Sermon on the Mount, on personal and group and social problems, on doctrines —might be thought of as *master* courses and kept going throughout one's ministry. From these a number of secondary courses of the kind suggested immediately above can be made and kept active. These can be drawn upon from time to time for sermons for the days listed on the church calendar. A plan of this general nature keeps preaching from being desultory or hit and miss, hand-to-mouth, "hop, skip, and jump" preaching that has characterized too much of the preaching of Protestantism.

KEEPING SERMONS "COOKING"

Work on future sermons has just begun, however, when items such as "Young People's Sermon," "Layman's Sermon," "suitable for Christmas," have been entered upon a calendar at the proper date. These notations are little more than *occasions* on which one *intends* to preach certain sermons. The sermons have yet to take shape, grow, and mature. A process must still be initiated by which the subjects, themes, purposes, and outlines take shape, and the materials begin to accummulate.

This necessitates periods of intensive work on small groups of sermons. As many as twelve to sixteen sermons can be carried along together quite satisfactorily. Once one starts his mind to thinking of that many sermons at once, he is always surprised how much material for each sermon flows into his hands from his reading, observation, and thinking. Charles E. Jefferson said:

One never knows what is going to happen when he puts a truth to soak in the juices of the mind. The mind is a capacious receptacle and one can put twenty themes into it as well as one, and all the twenty will have room in which to develop. Put twenty subjects into the mind at the beginning of the year, and no matter what book you open, sentences will fly out of the book and light on one or another member of this group of themes, just as bees when let loose in a field light on the flower which contains the nectar which they most relish.[2]

William L. Stidger speaks of the ideas gathering material "like a snowball." Rabbi Stephen S. Wise used to keep from twenty to thirty envelopes on his desk containing material on subjects about which he was planning to preach. These gathered material to themselves by a process he called "sermon ripening." When a sermon is allowed to develop thus for a period of time, it is likely to have a fullness it cannot possess if prepared entirely between Sundays.

This period of "cooking" or "ripening" is not one of passiveness on the preacher's part. All the while he should be engaged in his usual weekly program of reading, Bible study, pastoral work, recording of ideas, etc., with accustomed vigor. Then, and only then, will materials for these sermons flow into his hands. From time to time he should reshape and rethink his notes on this group of sermons. Little by little, the sermons will take definite form. As has already been said, this whole process should be regarded as giving the Spirit of God opportunity to work through one's conscious efforts and through his unconscious mind. Giving God time to shape and mold one's thoughts is time well spent.

METHODS OF FILING SERMONIC MATERIALS

As minimum equipment a preacher will need two types of files for materials that go into his sermons.

1. A card index for biblical texts dealt with helpfully in books read. Standard 3 x 5 cards are suitable for this purpose. The books of the Bible can be arranged in alphabetical order.

[2] *The Building of the Church* (New York: The Macmillan Co., 1910), pp. 256-57.

248

The cards, as they accumulate, can be arranged under each book according to chapters and verses. On these cards may be cited the texts of printed sermons in one's library and illuminating explanations, expositions, and exegeses of passages of scripture found in other books. When one is preparing a sermon on a particular passage of scripture he can use the index to run down any ideas on that passage heretofore discovered in his reading. This will prove to be an important source for sermonic material.

2. *A general file for material for sermon illustrations.* Luccock insists "the only index worth having is that in a man's own head." [3] No one would deny that is the best possible index. But unless a person is endowed with a photographic memory or is otherwise a genius at remembering, and few men are, he needs some method of filing material to supplement his memory and to make that material accessible for ready use. All filing systems have their limitations and, perhaps, their perils. Jefferson warned that a man "may form the habit of using his scissors when he ought to be using his head." [4] Similarly, Luccock says, "Many a minister's mind has been buried in a filing cabinet, the promising capacity of original thinking imprisoned behind the stout bars of a card index." [5] Both of these men are right, of course. But their warnings mainly serve to emphasize the necessity of making a filing system an aid to, not a substitute for, the use of one's own mental powers.

Different methods have been used satisfactorily by different types of minds. Some ministers have kept notebooks in which they laboriously copied material they wished to preserve. In time the number of these increases until they in turn become books requiring an index. Other ministers have used extensive card indexes, scrapbooks, envelopes for clippings, and drawers for storing sermonic material. From the experiences of many ministers, a few simple rules have emerged, although not a great deal of wisdom has accumulated on what type of filing system best fits the rules. The rules most often suggested are three: (1) keep the system as simple as possible; (2) make things as easy to find as possible; (3) spend as little time on filing as possible. Much valuable time and energy can be wasted on operating filing

[3] *In the Minister's Workshop*, p. 180.
[4] *Op. cit.*, p. 289.
[5] *In the Minister's Workshop*, p. 173.

systems. In fact, they sometimes become a fascinating but distracting ministerial hobby.

Bishop George Craig Stewart, of the Episcopal Church, explained his index system as follows:

> Every book as it is read, and this means several books a week, bears upon its last page or two a topical index created as I go along. When the book is read my secretary indexes these topics on cards which now number a great many thousand. All magazines are read and marked for clipping and filing. When, therefore, I come to the elaboration of my outline, such books and clippings as may be involved in the subjects which develop in the outline are carefully searched for allusive and illustrative material.[6]

This was of special interest to me because I used a similar method for many years. That is, I had two files. One was a card index of topics arranged alphabetically on which were placed items from the index in the back of books read. The other was a set of envelopes containing a portion of the same topics alphabetically arranged in a large filing cabinet of several drawers. In these the clippings were placed.

I made the mistake of entering on the small cards only the general topic, with the proper citation to the book. After a period of time these notations became so "cold" I wasted considerable time running down references that were of no particular value to me in the preparation of the sermon on which I was working at the time. If, in each instance, I had indicated on the card something about the type of material to which reference was made, I could have discovered almost at a glance whether it would serve my immediate purpose. But notations of this length would have increased the system beyond reasonable limits.

So in recent years I have used only one file—the envelope file —for everything. Into the envelopes go clippings, items I have copied from books I do not own, and notations, formerly placed in the card index, concerning the topics indexed in the back of the books I read. Sheets of paper of proper size for the file (not cards, because their thickness makes the files expand too quickly) are used for making references to the material in the books. Enough is put on the sheet about each item to indicate clearly

[6] See Newton, *If I Had Only One Sermon to Prepare*, p. 158.

the general nature and contents of what is cited. Often a brief quotation, with a further explanation of its nature, is sufficient for the purpose. The amount of copying is limited rigidly, partly to save time and partly to limit the dimensions of the file. But I can usually tell by a rapid examination of all the citations on the sheets which items are appropriate for the sermon under consideration.

Several items on the same topic are put on the same sheet in numerical order. Both sides of the sheet are used in order to limit the expansion. When one sheet is filled others are added as necessary, the numerical order being continued. All sheets in the same envelope are kept carefully attached to one another. Pamphlets are not put in the envelopes because they fill up the files too rapidly. They are placed on the shelves with books on the same subject, although notations of their whereabouts are sometimes placed in the proper envelope. Envelopes are better than folders, unless folders are closed at the ends to prevent material from dropping out when being handled. Hence, in the process of perparing a sermon I now look in only one file for all the material on a particular subject I have gathered or indexed in the course of my regular studying. For me this system reduces to a minimum the amount of time required to look up or trace down material and to discover the nature of its contents.

Once one is sure he has devised the filing system best for him, he should purchase a durable filing cabinet with average capacity and make up his mind never to expand it. This forces him to reduce the number of items to be filed, to copy only significant portions of the items, and to clean out the files from time to time, discarding material that likely will never be used or that has become outdated. At this point every preacher can take a lesson from Emmet Leahy who "has made a career of showing people how to save money by not saving papers." His methods were briefly described in an article entitled "Don't File It—Throw It Away!" in the *Reader's Digest*, September, 1954. One of the basic principles he instills into his clients is this: Use a file with very few drawers, and as soon as it fills up, clear it out.

A little practice and experience in these matters will soon enable each person to maintain as satisfactory a filing system as can be devised. There is no such thing as a perfect system. Most items can be filed under several headings and often should be.

But even then one is likely to search in vain for something he knows was filed carefully but cannot recall where. A filing cabinet has been defined facetiously as "a place where you can lose things systematically."

POSTLUDE

Here at the close the reader is reminded of what was said in the preface: this book is written primarily for the minister who is eager to learn how to preach well and is willing, in a normal preaching situation, to pay the price of the learning. We considered together the experiences and the equipment that constitute the background out of which effective preaching springs. Then we made a study, step by step, of the principles and procedures, the disciplines and the drills involved in developing preaching skills. Others would deal differently with the same topics, no doubt, but I hope they have proved stimulating and suggestive.

Assuming that a person has a modest endowment of the native abilities requisite for the preaching ministry, that he has been called and is committed to this vocation, and that he will be "zealous to confirm [his] call" (II Pet. 1:10) by investing and applying his gifts to the limit of his opportunities, there is no doubt he can develop and keep on improving the skills necessary to preach the gospel effectively to his generation.

SUGGESTED READING

Blackwood, A. W. *Planning a Year's Pulpit Work.* New York and Nashville: Abingdon Press, 1942.

————. *The Preparation of Sermons.* New York and Nashville: Abingdon Press, 1948. Chapter XXIV.

Bowie, Walter Russell. *Preaching.* New York and Nashville: Abingdon Press, 1954. Chapters IV-VII.

Bryan, Dawson C. *The Art of Illustrating Sermons.* New York and Nashville: Abingdon Press, 1938. Chapter VI.

Gibson, George Miles. *Planned Preaching.* Philadelphia: Westminster Press, 1954.

Jefferson, Charles E. *The Building of the Church.* New York: The Macmillan Co., 1910. Lectures VII-VIII.

Luccock, Halford E. *In the Minister's Workshop.* New York and Nashville: Abingdon Press, 1944. Chapter XVI.

Robbins, Howard Chandler. *Preaching the Gospel.* New York: Harper & Brothers, 1939.

SELECTED BIBLIOGRAPHY

On the Preacher and Preaching

The Preacher and His Calling

Brown, Charles R. *The Making of a Minister*. New York: The Century Co., 1927.

Davison, F. E. *I Would Do It Again*. St. Louis: The Bethany Press, 1948.

Guffin, Gilbert L. *Called of God*. New York: Fleming H. Revell Co., 1951.

Harmon, Nolan B. *Ministerial Ethics and Etiquette* (Rev. and Enl.). New York and Nashville: Abingdon Press, 1950.

Hoyt, A. S. *The Preacher*. New York: The Macmillan Co., 1909.

―――――. *Vital Elements of Preaching*. New York: The Macmillan Co., 1914.

Hutton, John A. *That the Ministry Be Not Blamed*. London: Hodder and Stoughton (n.d.).

Jefferson, Charles E. *Quiet Hints to Growing Preachers*. New York: Thomas Y. Crowell Co., 1901.

Lewis, Thomas H. *The Minister and His Own Soul*. New York: Geo. H. Doran Co., 1926.

Mursell, James L. *How to Make and Break Habits*. Philadelphia: J. B. Lippincott Co., 1953.

Neill, Stephen C. *Fulfill Thy Ministry*. New York: Harper & Brothers, 1952.

Robinson, A. W. *The Personal Life of the Clergy*. New York: Longmans, Green & Co., Inc., 1902.

Sangster, W. E. *The Approach to Preaching*. Philadelphia: Westminster Press, 1952.

Spann, J. Richard, ed. *The Ministry*. New York and Nashville: Abingdon Press, 1949.

Turnbull, Ralph G. *A Minister's Obstacles*. New York: Fleming H. Revell, 1946.

Watson, John, *et al*. *The Clerical Life*. New York: Dodd, Mead & Co., 1898.

Webb, Robert L. *The Ministry as a Life's Work*. New York: The Macmillan Co., 1922.

Wilson, Woodrow. *The Minister and the Community*. New York: Association Press, 1912.

X., R. E. *Morals for Ministers*. New York: The Macmillan Co., 1928.

Textbooks on Homiletics

A. Older

Blaikie, W. G. *For the Work of the Ministry*. London: Strachan and Co., 1873.

Broadus, John A. *Preparation and Delivery of Sermons*. New York: A. C. Armstrong and Son, 1901.

Fisk, W. F. *Manual of Preaching*. New York: A. C. Armstrong and Son, 1884.

Hoppin, James. *Homiletics*. New York: Funk & Wagnalls Co., 1883.

Hoyt, A. S. *The Work of Preaching*. New York: The Macmillan Co., 1905.

Kern, John A. *The Ministry to the Congregation*. Nashville: Publishing House of the M. E. Church, South, 1897.

Pattison, T. H. *The Making of a Sermon* (Rev.). Philadelphia: Judson Press, 1946.

Phelps, Austin. *The Theory of Preaching*. New York: Charles Scribner's Sons, 1881.

Vinet, A. *Homiletics*. Translated by Thomas H. Skinner. New York: Ivison and Phinney, 1866.

B. More Recent

Blackwood, A. W. *The Preparation of Sermons*. New York and Nashville: Abingdon Press, 1948.

Booth, John N. *The Quest for Preaching Power*. New York: The Macmillan Co., 1943.

Bowie, Walter Russell. *Preaching*. New York and Nashville: Abingdon Press, 1954.

Breed, David R. *Preparing to Preach*. New York: Geo. H. Doran Co., 1911.

Bull, Paul B. *Preaching and Sermon Construction*. New York: The Macmillan Co., 1922.

Burrell, David J. *The Sermon, Its Construction and Delivery*. New York: Fleming H. Revell Co., 1913.

Davis, Ozora S. *Principles of Preaching*. Chicago: University of Chicago Press, 1924.

Evans, William. *How to Prepare Sermons*. Chicago: Moody Press, 1913.

Johnson, Herrick. *The Ideal Ministry*. New York: Fleming H. Revell Co., 1908.

Jordon, G. Ray. *You Can Preach*. New York: Fleming H. Revell Co., 1951.

Liske, Thomas V. *Effective Preaching* (Roman Catholic). New York: The Macmillan Co., 1951.

Luccock, Halford E. *In the Minister's Workshop*. New York and Nashville: Abingdon Press, 1944.

Montgomery, R. Ames. *Preparing Preachers to Preach*. Grand Rapids: Zondervan Publishing House, 1939.

Oman, John. *Concerning the Ministry.* New York: Harper & Brothers, 1937.

Patton, Carl S. *Preparation and Delivery of Sermons.* Chicago: Willett, Clark and Co., 1938.

Reu, J. Michael. *Homiletics.* Chicago: Wartburg Publishing House, 1924.

Rhoades, Ezra. *Case Work in Preaching.* New York: Fleming H. Revell Co., 1942.

Sangster, W. E. *The Craft of Sermon Construction.* London: The Epworth Press, 1949.

Stevenson, Dwight E. *A Road-Map for Sermons* (Pamphlet). Lexington: The College of the Bible, 1950.

_____. *A Guide to Expository Preaching* (Pamphlet). Lexington: The College of the Bible, 1952.

Weatherspoon, J. B. Revision of Broadus, *On the Preparation and Delivery of Sermons.* New York: Harper & Brothers, 1944.

LECTURES ON PREACHING

A. The Lyman Beecher Lectures on Preaching (Yale)

"The most outstanding contribution in the field of homiletics yet produced in America." These lectures have been delivered at the Divinity School of Yale University each year since 1871, with three or four exceptions. At present there are approximately seventy-five volumes in the series. Two summaries of the series have been published in recent years:

Baxter, B. B. *The Heart of the Yale Lectures.* New York: The Macmillan Co., 1947. (Summarizes the principles of preaching found in the lectures.)

Jones, Edgar De Witt. *The Royalty of the Pulpit.* New York: Harper & Brothers, 1951. (Primarily a study of the persons who gave the lectures.)

Selected group of the volumes in the series:

Beecher, Henry Ward. *Yale Lectures on Preaching* (Ser. 1, 2, 3). Boston: Pilgrim Press, 1872.

Brooks, Phillips. *Lectures on Preaching.* New York: E. P. Dutton & Co., Inc., 1877.

Brown, Charles R. *The Art of Preaching.* New York: The Macmillan Co., 1922.

Buttrick, George A. *Jesus Came Preaching.* New York: Charles Scribner's Sons, 1931.

Dale, R. W. *Nine Lectures on Preaching.* London: Hodder and Stoughton, 1890.

Faunce, W. H. P. *The Educational Ideal in the Ministry.* New York: The Macmillan Co., 1908.

Forsyth, P. T. *Positive Preaching and the Modern Mind.* A. C. Armstrong and Son, 1907.

Horne, Charles Sylvester. *The Romance of Preaching.* New York: Fleming H. Revell Co., 1914.

Jefferson, Charles E. *The Building of the Church.* New York: The Macmillan Co., 1910.

Jowett, J. H. *The Preacher: His Life and His Work.* New York: Geo. H. Doran Co., 1912.

Kennedy, Gerald. *God's Good News.* New York: Harper & Brothers, 1955.

Luccock, Halford E. *Communicating the Gospel.* New York: Harper & Brothers, 1954.

Noyes, Morgan P. *Preaching the Word of God.* New York: Charles Scribner's Sons, 1943.

Oxnam, G. Bromley. *Preaching in a Revolutionary Age.* New York and Nashville: Abingdon Press, 1944.

Park, J. Edgar. *The Miracle of Preaching.* New York: The Macmillan Co., 1936.

Pepper, George Wharton. *A Voice from the Crowd.* New Haven: Yale University Press, 1915.

Phillips, H. C. *Bearing Witness to the Truth.* New York and Nashville: Abingdon Press, 1949.

Scherer, Paul. *For We Have This Treasure.* New York: Harper & Brothers, 1944.

Simpson, Matthew. *Lectures on Preaching.* New York: Nelson and Phillips, 1879.

Sockman, Ralph W. *The Highway of God.* New York: The Macmillan Co., 1942.

Sperry, Willard L. *We Prophesy in Part.* New York: Harper & Brothers, 1938.

Stewart, James S. *A Faith to Proclaim.* New York: Charles Scribner's Sons, 1953.

Tittle, Ernest Fremont. *Jesus After Nineteen Centuries.* New York: The Abingdon Press, 1932.

Van Dyke, Henry. *The Gospel for an Age of Doubt.* New York: The Macmillan Co., 1896.

Watson, John. *The Cure of Souls.* New York: Dodd, Mead & Co., 1896.

B. Other Lectures (and Books) on Preaching

Atkins, G. G. *Preaching and the Mind of Today.* New York: The Round Table Press, 1934.

Black, James. *The Mystery of Preaching.* New York: Fleming H. Revell Co., 1924.

Blackwood, A. W. *Planning a Year's Pulpit Work.* New York and Nashville: Abingdon Press, 1942.

―――――. *The Fine Art of Preaching.* New York: The Macmillan Co., 1937.

Cadman, S. Parkes. *Ambassadors of God.* New York: The Macmillan Co., 1920.

Caldwell, Frank H. *Preaching Angles.* New York and Nashville: Abingdon Press, 1954.

Carpenter, W. Boyd. *Lectures on Preaching*. London: The Macmillan Co., 1895.

Chappell, Clovis G. *Anointed to Preach*. New York and Nashville: Abingdon Press, 1951.

Cleland, James T. *The True and Lively Word*. New York: Charles Scribner's Sons, 1954.

Coffin, Henry Sloane. *What to Preach*. New York: George H. Doran, 1926.

_____. *Communion Through Preaching*. New York: Charles Scribner's Sons, 1952.

Craig, A. C. *Preaching in a Scientific Age*. New York: Charles Scribner's Sons, 1954.

English, John M. *For Pulpit and Platform*. New York: The Macmillan Co., 1919.

Farmer, H. H. *The Servant of the Word*. New York: Charles Scribner's Sons, 1942.

Ferris, Theodore P. *Go Tell the People*. New York: Charles Scribner's Sons, 1951.

Fuller, David Otis. *Spurgeon's Lectures to His Students* (Condensed). Grand Rapids: Zondervan Publishing House, 1945.

Garvie, Alfred E. *A Guide to Preachers* (Lay Preachers). New York: Hodder and Stoughton, 1906.

_____. *The Christian Preacher*. New York: Charles Scribner's Sons, 1921.

Gibson, George M. *Planned Preaching*. Philadelphia: Westminster Press, 1954.

Gossip, Arthur John. *In Christ's Stead*. New York: Geo. H. Doran Co., 1925.

Gresham, Perry Epler. *Disciplines of the High Calling*. St. Louis: Bethany Press, 1954.

Handy, Francis J. *Jesus the Preacher*. New York and Nashville: Abingdon Press, 1949.

Jeffrey, George J. *This Grace Wherein We Stand*. London: Hodder and Stoughton, 1949.

Kennedy, Gerald. *His Word Through Preaching*. New York: Harper & Brothers, 1947.

_____. *With Singleness of Heart*. New York: Harper & Brothers, 1951.

Macartney, C. E. *Preaching Without Notes*. New York and Nashville: Abingdon Press, 1946.

Macgregor, W. M. *The Making of a Preacher*. Philadelphia: Westminster Press, 1946.

MacLennan, David A. *A Preacher's Primer*. New York: Oxford University Press, 1950.

_____. *Pastoral Preaching*. Philadelphia: Westminster Press, 1955.

Macleod, Donald, ed. *Here Is My Method* (Symposium). New York: Fleming H. Revell Co., 1952.

McComb, Samuel L. *Preaching in Theory and Practice*. New York: Oxford University Press, 1926.

Morris, Frederick M. *Preach the Word of God.* New York: Morehouse-Gorham Co., 1954.

Newton, Joseph Fort. *The New Preaching.* Nashville: The Cokesbury Press, 1930.

_____. *If I Had Only One Sermon to Prepare* (Symposium). New York: Harper & Brothers, 1932.

Oxnam, G. Bromley, ed. *Effective Preaching.* New York: Abingdon Press, 1929.

_____. *Contemporary Preaching.* New York: Abingdon Press, 1931.

_____. *Varieties of Present-Day Preaching.* New York: Abingdon Press, 1932.

_____. *Preaching and the Social Crisis.* New York: Abingdon Press, 1933.

Poteat, Edwin McNeill. *Rev. John Doe, D.D.* New York: Harper & Brothers, 1935.

Prichard, H. A. *The Minister, the Method and the Message.* New York: Charles Scribner's Sons, 1932.

Reed, David C. *The Communication of the Gospel.* London: S. C. M. Press, Ltd., 1952.

Reid, James. *In Quest of Reality.* New York: Geo. H. Doran Co., 1925.

Robbins, Howard Chandler. *Preaching the Gospel.* New York: Harper & Brothers, 1939.

Rogers, C. F. *The Parson Preaching.* London: S.P.C.K., 1949.

Schloerb, Rolland W. *The Preaching Ministry.* New York: Harper & Brothers, 1946.

Schroeder, Frederick W. *Preaching the Word with Authority.* Philadelphia: Westminster Press, 1954.

Scott, A. Boyd. *Preaching Week by Week.* New York: Richard R. Smith, Inc., 1909.

Sizoo, J. R. *Preaching Unashamed.* New York and Nashville: Abingdon Press, 1949.

Slattery, Charles L. *Present Day Preaching.* New York: Longmans, Green & Co., 1909.

Smith, David. *The Art of Preaching.* London: Geo. H. Doran Co., 1924.

Smyth, Patterson. *The Preacher and His Sermon.* New York: Geo. H. Doran Co., 1922.

Spurgeon, Charles. *Lectures to My Students.* New York: Sheldon and Co., 1875.

Stewart, James S. *Heralds of God.* New York: Charles Scribner's Sons, 1946.

Stidger, William. *Preaching Out of the Overflow.* Nashville: Cokesbury Press, 1929.

Vance, James I. *Being a Preacher.* New York: Fleming H. Revell Co., 1923.

Weatherspoon, J. B. *Sent Forth to Preach.* New York: Harper & Brothers, 1954.

STYLE

Ball, Alice Morton. *The Compounding and Hyphenating of English Words*. New York: Funk & Wagnalls Co., 1951.

Chrisman, Lewis H. *The English of the Pulpit*. New York: Geo. H. Doran Co., 1926.

Fernald, James C. *English Grammar Simplified* (Rev). New York: Funk & Wagnalls Co., 1946.

_____. *Standard Handbook of Synonyms, Antonyms and Prepositions* (Rev.). New York: Funk & Wagnalls Co., 1947.

Flesch, Rudolph. *The Art of Plain Talk*. New York: Harper & Brothers, 1946.

_____. *The Art of Readable Writing*. New York: Harper & Brothers, 1949.

_____. *How to Make Sense*. New York: Harper & Brothers, 1954.

_____ and Lass, A. H. *The Way to Write*. New York: Harper & Brothers, 1947.

Fowler, H. W. *Dictionary of Modern English Usage*. London: Oxford University Press, 1950.

Funk and Wagnalls Standard Handbook of Prepositions, Conjunctions, Relative Pronouns and Adverbs. New York: Funk & Wagnalls Co., 1953.

Garrison, Webb B. *The Preacher and His Audience*. New York: Fleming H. Revell Co., 1954.

Hollingsworth, H. L. *The Psychology of the Audience*. New York: American Book Co., 1935.

Jones, E. W. *Preaching and the Dramatic Arts*. New York: The Macmillan Co., 1948.

Opdyck, John Baker. *Harper's English Grammar*. New York: Harper & Brothers, 1941.

_____. *Get It Right* (Rev.). New York: Funk & Wagnalls Co., 1941.

_____. *Say What You Mean*. New York: Funk & Wagnalls Co., 1944.

_____. *The Opdyck Lexicon of Word Selection*. New York: Funk & Wagnalls Co., 1950.

Phelps, Austin. *English Style in Public Discourse*. New York: Charles Scribner's Sons, 1883.

Quiller-Couch, Arthur. *On the Art of Writing*. New York: G. P. Putnam's Sons, 1916.

Shipley, Joseph T. *Dictionary of Word Origin* (2nd ed.). New York: Philosophical Library, 1945.

Skeat, W. W. *An Etymological Dictionary of the English Language* (Rev.). Oxford: The Clarendon Press, 1910.

Webster's Dictionary of Synonyms. Springfield: G. & G. Merriam Co., 1951.

ILLUSTRATING SERMONS

Bryan, Dawson C. *The Art of Illustrating Sermons*. New York and Nashville: Abingdon Press, 1938.

Opdyck, John Baker. *The Opdyck Lexicon of Word Selection*. New York: Funk & Wagnalls Co., 1950.

Sangster, W. E. *The Craft of Sermon Illustration*. Philadelphia: Westminster Press, 1950.

Shipley, Joseph T. *Dictionary of Word Origins*. New York: Philosophical Library, 1945.

Skeat, W. W. *An Etymological Dictionary of the English Language* (Rev.). Oxford: The Clarendon Press, 1910.

Spurgeon, Charles. *The Art of Illustration*. New York: Wilbur B. Ketcham, 1894.

THE DELIVERY OF SERMONS

Crocker, Lionel. *Henry Ward Beecher's Art of Preaching*. Chicago: University of Chicago Press, 1934.

————. *Henry Ward Beecher's Speaking Art*. New York: Fleming H. Revell Co., 1937.

Kirkpatrick, R. W. *The Creative Delivery of Sermons*. New York: The Macmillan Co., 1944.

Lantz, John Edward. *Speaking in the Church*. New York: The Macmillan Co., 1954.

Macartney, Clarence E. *Preaching Without Notes*. New York and Nashville: Abingdon Press, 1946.

Storrs, Richard S. *Conditions of Success in Preaching Without Notes*. New York: Dodd, Mead & Co., 1875.

Zincke, F. Barham. *Extempore Preaching*. New York: Charles Scribner's Sons, 1867.

PUBLIC SPEAKING

Bautain, M. *The Art of Extempore Speaking*. New York: McDevitt-Wilson, Inc., 1921.

Curry, S. S. *Foundations of Expression*. Boston: The Expression Co., 1907.

Dolman, John. *A Handbook of Public Speaking*. New York: Harcourt, Brace & Co., 1922.

Grace, William J. and Grace, J. C. *The Art of Communicating Ideas*. New York: The Devin-Adair Co., 1952.

Hoffman, Wm. G. *Public Speaking Today*. New York: McGraw-Hill Book Co., 1940.

————. *How to Make Better Speeches*. New York: Funk & Wagnalls Co., 1948.

Mears, A. G. *The Right Way to Speak in Public*. New York: Emerson Books, Inc., 1953.

McCall, Roy C. *Fundamentals of Speech*. New York: The Macmillan Co., 1949.

Phelps, Arthur Stevens. *Speaking in Public*. New York: Richard R. Smith, 1930.

Phillips, Arthur Edward. *Effective Speaking*. Chicago: The Newton Co., 1924.

Prochnow, Herbert V. *The Successful Speaker's Handbook.* New York: Prentice-Hall, Inc., 1951.

Sarett, Lew and Foster, W. T. *Basic Principles of Speech.* Boston: Houghton Mifflin Co., 1936.

Vizetelly, Frank H. *How to Speak English Effectively.* New York: Funk & Wagnalls Co., 1933.

Watkins, Dwight Everett. *An Introduction to the Art of Speech.* New York: W. W. Norton & Company, Inc., 1934.

Weaver, A. T., *et al. The New Better Speech.* New York: Harcourt, Brace & Co., 1938.

Winans, James A. *Public Speaking.* New York: The Century Co., 1923.

———. *Speech-making.* New York: D. Appleton-Century Co., Inc., 1938.

THE USE OF THE BIBLE IN PREACHING

Blackwood, A. W. *Preaching from the Bible.* New York and Nashville: Abingdon Press, 1941.

———. *Preaching from Samuel.* New York and Nashville: Abingdon Press, 1946.

———. *Preaching from the Prophetic Books.* New York and Nashville: Abingdon Press, 1951.

———. *Expository Preaching for Today.* New York and Nashville: Abingdon Press, 1953.

———. *Biographical Preaching for Today.* New York and Nashville: Abingdon Press, 1954.

Jeffs, H. *The Art of Exposition.* Boston: Pilgrim Press, 1910.

Littorin, Frank T. *How to Preach the Word with Variety.* Grand Rapids: Baker Book House, 1953.

Luccock, Halford E. *Preaching Values in New Translations of the New Testament.* New York and Nashville: Abingdon Press, 1928.

———. *Preaching Values in the Old Testament in the Modern Translations.* New York and Nashville: Abingdon Press, 1933.

———. *The Acts of the Apostles.* (1 vol.) Chicago: Willet, Clark and Co., 1942.

Mack, Edward. *The Preacher's Old Testament.* New York: Fleming H. Revell Co., 1923.

Meyer, F. B. *Expository Preaching.* New York: Hodder and Stoughton, 1910.

Miller, Donald G. *Fire in Thy Mouth.* New York and Nashville: Abingdon Press, 1954.

Patton, Carl S. *The Use of the Bible in Preaching.* Chicago: Willett, Clark and Co., 1936.

Roach, Corwin C. *Preaching Values in the Bible.* Louisville: The Cloister Press, 1946.

Thomas, George Brown. *What Shall I Preach?* New York and Nashville: Abingdon Press, 1948.

Waugh, R. M. L. *The Preacher and His Greek Testament.* London: The Epworth Press, 1953.

Whitsell, Faris D. *The Art of Biblical Preaching*. Grand Rapids: Zondervan Publishing House, 1950.

THE USE OF LITERATURE IN PREACHING

Adler, M. J. *How to Read a Book*. New York: Simon and Schuster, Inc., 1950.

Bailey, Elmer James. *Religious Thought in Greater American Poets*. Boston: Pilgrim Press, 1922.

Chapman, Edward Mortimer. *English Literature in Account with Religion*. Boston: Houghton Mifflin Co., 1910.

Davies, Trevor H. *Spiritual Voices in Modern Literature*. New York: Geo. H. Doran Co., 1919.

Flewelling, Ralph Tyler. *Christ and the Dramas of Doubt*. New York: Abingdon, 1913.

Gobrecht, Walter R. *The Gospel Message in Great Poems*. New York: Funk & Wagnalls Co., 1928.

Guild, L. T. *The Cosmic Ray in Literature*. Nashville: Cokesbury Press, 1929.

Hovis, W. F. *Poetic Sermons*. New York: Fleming H. Revell Co., 1932.

Howse, Ernest Marshall. *Spiritual Values in Shakespeare*. New York and Nashville: Abingdon Press, 1955.

Kerr, Hugh T. *The Gospel in Modern Poetry*. New York: Fleming H. Revell Co., 1926.

Luccock, Halford E. *Contemporary American Literature and Religion*. Chicago: Willett, Clark and Co., 1934.

Luccock, Robert E. *The Lost Gospel*. New York: Harper & Brothers, 1948.

McCall, Oswald W. S. *The Uses of Literature in the Pulpit*. New York: Harper and Bros., 1932.

Mims, Edwin. *Great Writers as Interpreters of Religion*. New York and Nashville: Abingdon-Cokesbury Press, 1945.

_____. *The Christ of the Poets*. New York & Nashville: Abingdon Press, 1948.

Moldenhawer, J. V. *The Voice of Books*. New York and Nashville: Abingdon-Cokesbury Press, 1940.

Roberts, Richard. *The Preacher as a Man of Letters*. New York: Abingdon Press, 1931.

Schauffler, Robert Haven. *The Poetry Cure*. New York: Dodd, Mead & Co., 1925.

Slack, E. *Christ in the Poetry of Today*. New York: Woman's Press, 1928.

Steferud, Alfred, ed. *The Wonderful World of Books*. Boston: Houghton Mifflin Co., 1953.

Stidger, William L. *Great Hours with Poet Preachers*. New York: Abingdon Press, 1918.

_____. *Flames of Faith*. New York: Abingdon Press, 1922.

_____. *Finding God in Books*. New York: Geo. H. Doran Co., 1925.

_____. *The High Faith of Fiction and Drama*. New York: Harper & Brothers, 1928.

_____. *Personal Power*. New York: Ray Long and Richard R. Smith, 1929.

_____. *Preaching Out of the Overflow*. Nashville: Cokesbury Press, 1929.

_____. *Planning Your Preaching*. New York: Harper & Brothers, 1937.

_____. *There are Sermons in Stories*. New York and Nashville: Abingdon Press, 1942.

_____. *More Sermons in Stories*. New York and Nashville: Abingdon Press, 1944.

_____. *Sermon Nuggets in Stories*. New York and Nashville: Abingdon Press, 1946.

_____. *Sermon Stories of Faith and Hope*. New York and Nashville: Abingdon Press, 1948.

Strong, Augustus H. *The Great Poets and Their Theology*. Philadelphia: The Griffith and Rowland Press, 1897.

_____. *American Poets and Their Theology*. Philadelphia: The Griffith and Rowland Press, 1916.

Townsend, Atwood H., ed. *A Guide to Good Reading*. New York: Hendricks House-Farrar, Straus, 1948.

The Use of Art in Preaching

Bailey, Albert Edward. *The Gospel in Art*. Boston: Pilgrim Press, 1931.

_____. *Christ in Recent Art*. New York: Charles Scribner's Sons, 1935.

_____. *Christ and His Gospel in Recent Art*. New York: Charles Scribner's Sons, 1948.

Branch, Harold Francis. *Christ's Ministry and Passion in Art*. Philadelphia: H. M. Shelley, 1929.

_____. *Sermons on Great Paintings*. Philadelphia: H. M. Shelley, 1930.

_____. *Religious Picture Sermons*. Philadelphia: H. M. Shelley, 1934.

Carter, James. *The Gospel Message in Great Pictures*. New York: Funk & Wagnalls Co., 1929.

Cavert, W. D. *Story Sermons from Literature and Art*. New York: Harper & Brothers, 1939.

Harby, Clifton, ed. *The Bible in Art*. New York: Covici-Freede, 1936.

Maus, Cynthia Pearl. *Christ and the Fine Arts*. New York: Harper & Brothers, 1938.

_____. *The Old Testament and the Fine Arts*. New York: Harper & Brothers, 1954.

Pace, C. N. *Pictures that Preach*. New York: Abingdon Press, 1924.

Sollitt, Kenneth W. *Preaching from Pictures*. Boston: W. A. Wilde Co., 1938.

The Use of Hymns in Preaching

Bailey, Albert Edward. *The Gospel in Hymns*. New York: Charles Scribner's Sons, 1950.

Benson, Louis F. *Studies in Familiar Hymns*. Philadelphia: Westminster Press, 1903.

Boyd, Charles, A. *Stories of Hymns for Creative Living*. Philadelphia: Judson Press, 1938.

Brown, Theron and Butterworth, Hezekiah. *The Story of Hymns and Tunes*. New York: The American Tract Society, 1906.

Covert, William Chalmers and Laufer, C. W. eds. *Handbook to the Hymnal*. Philadelphia: Presbyterian Board of Christian Education, 1936.

Duncan, Joseph. *Popular Hymns*. London: Sheffington and Son, 1910.

Hart, William J. *Hymn Stories of the 20th Century*. Boston: W. A. Wilde Co., 1948.

Laufer, Calvin W. *Hymn Lore*. Philadelphia: Westminster Press, 1932.

McCutchan, R. G. *Hymns in the Lives of Men*. New York and Nashville: Abingdon Press, 1945.

Price, Carl F. *One Hundred and One Hymn Stories*. New York and Nashville: Abingdon Press, 1923.

Robinson, Charles Seymour. *Annotations upon Popular Hymns*. Cleveland: F. M. Barton, 1893.

Sankey, Ira D. *My Life and the Story of the Gospel Hymns*. Philadelphia: The Sunday School Times Co., 1906.

Sanville, George W. *Forty Gospel Hymn Stories*. Winona Lake, Ind.: Rodeheaver-Hall-Mack Co., 1943.

Wells, Amos R. *A Treasury of Hymns*. Boston: United Society of Christian Endeavor, 1914.

The History of Preaching

Brastow, Lewis O. *Representative Modern Preachers*. New York: The Macmillan Co., 1904.

Byington, E. H. *Pulpit Mirrors*. New York: Geo. H. Doran Co., 1927.

Dargan, E. C. *A History of Preaching*. Grand Rapids: Baker Book House, 1954.

Garvie, Alfred E. *The Christian Preacher*. Part I. New York: Charles Scribner's Sons, 1921.

Howard, Harry C. *Princes of the Christian Pulpit*, Ser. 1. Nashville: Cokesbury Press, 1927.

————. *Princes of the Christian Pulpit*, Ser. 2. Nashville: Cokesbury Press, 1928.

Kerr, Hugh T. *Preaching in the Early Church*. New York: Fleming H. Revell, 1942.

Petry, Ray C. *No Uncertain Sound*. Philadelphia: Westminster Press, 1948.

————. *Preaching in the Great Tradition*. Philadelphia: Westminster Press, 1950.

Thompson, Ernest Trice. *Changing Emphases in American Preaching*. Philadelphia: Westminster Press, 1943.

INDEX